A flexible financial solution can help them make a business of their hobby.

Insurance, banking or investment: no matter which it is, every Fortis company believes in flexible solutions. Not just for the short term, but also for the distant future.

Because no two people want the same thing, because everyone in business has his own way of doing things and because we all like to take our own life-style decisions.

If you would like to know more about Fortis, please call us on 31 (0)30 257 65 49.

FORTIS

Solid partners, flexible solutions

Operate your supply chain in real time.
Not behind the times.

PeopleSoft Manufacturing. Respond to changes in supply and demand in real time.

Only PeopleSoft Manufacturing with Pure Internet Architecture™ synchronises your entire supply chain. Collaborate online with customers and suppliers. Manufacture products anywhere, anytime. Bring products to market faster. Deliver customer orders on time. Reduce obsolete inventory. It's your supply chain running at its leanest and most responsive. Learn more by visiting us at www.peoplesoft.co.uk/ad or call +44 (0) 118 9522011.

PeopleSoft. ® | **Manufacturing**

THE WORLD IN 2004

EDITOR:
Daniel Franklin
MANAGING EDITOR:
Harriet Ziegler
DEPUTY EDITOR:
Steve King
EDITORIAL ASSISTANT:
Sophie Hargreaves
DESIGN:
Bailey and Kenny
DESIGN ASSISTANT:
Anita Wright
CHARTS:
Michael Robinson,
Phil Kenny, Peter Winfield
ILLUSTRATIONS:
Derek Cousins
PICTURE RESEARCH:
Juliet Brightmore
RESEARCHER:
Kristina Cooke
EDITORIAL ASSISTANCE:
Ingrid Esling, Sheila Allen
ADVERTISING DIRECTOR:
John Dunn
CIRCULATION DIRECTOR:
Alastair Cotton
PRODUCTION:
Andrew Rollings,
Katy Wilson, Sophie Hawe
FOREIGN RIGHTS:
Hutton-Williams Agency
ASSOCIATE PUBLISHER:
David Gill
PUBLISHER:
David Hanger
ENTERPRISES DIRECTOR:
Martin Giles

The
Economist

25 St James's Street,
London SW1A 1HG
Telephone:
020 7830 7084
E-mail: worldineditor
@economist.com
Internet : http://
www.theworldin.com

The

"PREVENT LEGAL EXPOSURE"

storage software company.

Middle East and Africa

International

The world in figures

Business

Finance

Science and technology

PHOTOGRAPHIC SOURCES:
AFP/Getty News & Sport: Torsten Blackwood, Frederic J. Brown, Gustavo Cuevas, Larry Downing, Toshifumi Kitamura, Oliver Laban-Mattei, Inacio Rosa. Alamy Images. Associated Press: Adam Butler, Ng Han Guan, Themba Hadebe, Vahid Salemi, Murad Sezer, US Navy, Richard Vogal, Andy Wong. BBC Photo Library. Bettmann/Corbis. Corbis: Robert Essel NYC, Owen Franken, Kaveh Kazemi, Brooks Kraft. Mary Evans Picture Library. Getty Images: Walter Bibikow, DTF Productions, Ed Honowitz, Keith Wood. Globe Newspaper Company Inc, Boston. Holt Studios UK. Hotel du Vin Limited/Georgia Glynnsmith. Hulton Archive/Getty Images. Kobal Collection. Niall McDiarmid. Magnum Photos: Patrick Zachmann, Francesco Zizola. NASA. National Museum of the American Indian, Washington, DC. PA Photos. Reuters: Christian Charisius, Wilson Chu, Claro Cortes IV, Sherwin Crasto, Erik de Castro, Ali Jarekji, Daniel Joubert, Faleh Kheiber, Kevin Lamarque, Paul McErlane, Kimimasa Mayama, James Morgan, Jamal Saidi, Jim Young, Shamil Zhumatov. Science Photo Library: Andrew Syred.

Printed by TPL Printers (UK) Ltd, Kidderminster, England Reprographics by Mullis Morgan Group Ltd Printed on UPM-Kymmene Star 80gsm

In business

Disruptive technology promises to bring huge benefits. **Larry Ellison** expects great things from Linux, grid computing and software as a service, *page 115*. But the internet, for all its wonders, might also be turned into a weapon of mass disruption. **Craig Mundie** outlines the ways to counter cyber-terrorism, *page 91*.

Upheavals in the boardroom have followed the corporate scandals of recent years. Rules alone cannot restore confidence in corporate America, says **William Donaldson**. A new mindset is needed, *page 134*.

As business prepares for the next growth cycle, **Ian Davis** poses three key questions for top management, *page 120*. **Frances Cairncross** predicts a humble recovery, *page 21*. But cheer up, says **Lucy Kellaway**, the business lunch will be back, *page 126*.

Health and happiness

Times have been hard for the luxury-goods industry. In 2004, predicts **Giorgio Armani**, there will be a return to glamour as well as a quest for quality. And fashion companies will invade China, *page 125*; meanwhile, Chinese companies will start to invade the world, *page 122*.

A glitzier world—and a healthier one? **Claude Bébéar** thinks the time is ripe for health insurance to go global, *page 140*.

At home, time to rearrange the furniture: it's back to the medieval great hall, says **James Dyson**, *page 144*.

Small world

Can't see the next IT revolution? You're not meant to. **Alun Anderson** glimpses the tiny silicon sensors, known as smart dust, that will change the way information is gathered and transmitted, *page 141*.

Oliver Morton strains his eyes in the other direction, as he contemplates the various rovers on their way to Mars, *page 143*.

Back on earth, it's a bug's life. **Geoffrey Carr** sets biotech bugs to work in industry, *page 142*. **Shereen El Feki** rounds up the killer bugs that will stalk the globe in 2004, from SARS to West Nile virus, *page 146*. And essay prizewinner **Diane Pleninger** puts a friendlier face on the microworld: nothing is more fun than fungi, *page 94*.

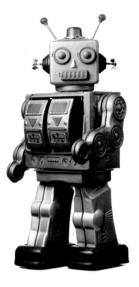

JAPAN
Robot

SOUTH AFRICA
Robot

Never underestimate the importance of local knowledge.

Play with a robot or stop at a robot? It's just something you know when you're a local.

At HSBC, we have banks in more countries than anyone else. And each one is staffed by local people.

We have offices in 79 countries and territories; Europe, Asia-Pacific, the Americas, the Middle East, and Africa. Being local enables them to offer insights into financial opportunities and create service initiatives that would never occur to an outsider.

It means our customers get the kind of local knowledge and personal service that you'd expect of a local bank.

And a level of global knowledge and widely sourced expertise that you wouldn't.

HSBC

The world's local bank

Issued by HSBC Holdings plc.

2004 will be a year for voters. During the year, countries that account for nearly half the world's population (the most ever) will hold nationwide elections. In November Americans will judge George Bush less by the wars he has waged than by the state of the national economy. They will weigh America's return to growth against the loss of more than 2.5m jobs in the Bush years. The contest will be close—and nasty—with Mr Bush the likely winner. But even if he loses, the world should not expect America's foreign policy (as outlined in these pages by Colin Powell, the secretary of state) to change fundamentally.

Among other polls expected in 2004, two stand out as especially important: those in the world's biggest and newest democracies. India, the biggest, will go to the polls by October; with luck, the country will keep its communal cool so that it can get on with the business of joining China as an emerging economic giant. Iraq, with even more luck, will be on its way to becoming the newest democracy (and the first in the Arab world). In 2004 its economy will at last be on the mend, growing by perhaps 20%; a referendum on a new constitution should come before the end of the year, in preparation for elections for a new government. Iraq's progress, or otherwise, towards democracy will send a powerful message to Muslims everywhere.

In Europe, a moment of triumph for democratic transition will come in May, when ten mostly ex-communist countries join the European Union. This will be a stunning symbol of the Union's success in spreading stability across the continent. But Europeans will hardly pause to celebrate between arguments over a new EU constitution and campaigning for European elections and referendums, in which voters will express misgivings about the pace and direction of change. Britain will again grow fastest among the big European economies, which is why (heartbeat permitting) Tony Blair's job is safe. A healthy competition for reform of bloated welfare systems will start to develop in France and Germany. And the EU newcomers, to the surprise of many, will

prove a breath of fresh air. People will start to take note of the Baltic tigers, the Slovak flat tax and suddenly trendy cities like Ljubljana.

For business, the squeeze on costs will go on, spurred by low-cost competition from places such as China and India. But there will be a renewed focus on growth, and how to manage it. Some signs of the changing emphasis: the business lunch will be back; dotcoms will be making money; and even Europe's 3G (third-generation) mobile telephony will at last show signs of life. New technologies, such as silicon dust and industrial biotechnology, will show that the tech revolution still has the power to excite. Any exuberance will remain rational, though. Corporate leaders will talk a lot about integrity and transparency, and keep a low profile.

What of the clouds that could spoil this low-key recovery? The risks are plenty: another terrorist outrage, a return of the SARS epidemic, currency shocks, security crises in the Middle East or North Korea. But the most glaring threat is the one politicians could inflict on themselves, if they allow the collapse of the global system of trade negotiations that has fostered growth and prosperity for half a century. In an American election year, the temptation of playing with protectionism—dividing the world for the sake of short-term gain at home—is particularly great.

In August, however, the world will come together when all eyes turn to Athens, as the Olympic games go back to where they began. After all the doubts about whether the Greeks would be ready on time, Athens will sparkle. The games should be a feast.

And so, I hope, is *The World in 2004*. Like top athletes, its contributors have stretched to be ahead of the rest as they contemplate the year ahead. Not all their predictions will prove winners. But across a rich range of subjects (from foreign policy to fashion) and around the world and even beyond it (from Malaysia to Mars), they provide both entertainment and insight. One thing's for sure about 2004: it will not be dull.

Daniel Franklin
Editor, *The World in 2004*

Online access.
No wires attached.

With Vodafone Mobile Connect Card™ in your laptop you've got direct access to your company network. So you're connected to everything you need…email, files, company intranet, even the internet – no matter where you are.

Fast? Absolutely. It works on GPRS. Cost effective? Of course, you only pay for the information you send and receive. Our clear tariffs mean cost control is simple and you can call our support line whenever you need it. No strings attached.

For more information on being connected wherever you are go to www.vodafone.com/office – or contact your local Vodafone representative.

Find out why more business people prefer Vodafone.

How are you?

Roseg Glacier, Engadine, Switzerland

Thomas Streiff, Sustainability Expert, Swiss Re

Thomas Streiff and his team identify environmental and man-made risks and develop sustainable strategies to cope with them. For example, Swiss Re was among the first to recognise the potential impact of climate change on the financial services industry and to study effective ways of managing associated risks. Offering a combination of expertise and financial strength, Swiss Re is ideally positioned to provide your company with tailored solutions to mitigate your exposure and protect your balance sheet – ensuring, in a climate of uncertainty, that you feel secure. www.swissre.com

Expertise you can build on. **Swiss Re**

Right on in America

George Bush looks the narrow favourite to win the presidential election. Even if he loses,
don't expect America to change much, argues **John Micklethwait**

All American presidential elections are deemed to be crucial ones, and rightly so. They choose the most powerful person in the world. However, George Bush's attempt to win a second term in 2004 seems particularly vital—especially for those who disagree with the Bush administration's determinedly conservative course. At home, it represents something of a last chance for the Democrats to stop the Republicans refashioning the country. Meanwhile, many of America's allies abroad imagine that a Democratic president would be a more collegial, less unilateral partner.

The only thing that seems certain about the presidential election is that it will be close. Mr Bush won the 2000 election by a whisker—and plenty of Democrats dispute the idea that he won at all. In 2002 he pulled off a magnificent victory in the mid-term elections, helping the Republicans recapture the Senate. But that was back in the days when his approval ratings were sky-high. This time will be different.

Mr Bush will have to prove that his Iraq policy is making progress. That is not quite as tough an assignment as many Europeans think (or in some cases hope). The polls indicate that most Americans are willing to accept casualties in far-off Mesopotamia, as long as they can see some form of victory at the end of it. The much bigger challenge for the president, electorally, is likely to be the economy. Here Mr Bush—who will go into the election probably having overseen the loss of more than 2.5m jobs—has some reason to feel unjustly persecuted. The economy will still be recovering from the imbalances built up during what the Republicans call "the Clinton bubble". Moreover, one reason why next year's recovery is likely to remain a fairly jobless one augurs well for the longer term: productivity has improved, so firms can make do with fewer workers. Still, that is a hard line for any politician to sell. And Mr Bush will have an even harder time explaining away the ballooning budget deficit.

So the Democrats plainly have a chance, especially if the recall of California's Democratic governor reflects an anti-incumbent (rather than anti-Democrat) mood. But their position is weaker than it looks at first. In 2004 Mr Bush will have far more money than his opponent, and a clearer mandate from his party. Thanks to his staunch conservatism, Mr Bush's approval ratings among Republicans have remained extremely high throughout his presidency. By contrast, the Democratic primary is likely to be a hellish fight. Whichever candidate emerges will be quickly set upon by Mr Bush's political rottweilers and portrayed as a north-eastern liberal (Howard Dean, John Kerry), a political ingénue (Wes-

John Micklethwait: United States editor, *The Economist*, and co-author of "The Right Nation", to be published in May (Penguin Press)

ley Clark, John Edwards), an old-fashioned leftie (Richard Gephardt) or a hopeless moderate (Joe Lieberman).

The worse news for the Democrats is that the presidency is probably the only battle they stand a chance of winning in 2004. The Republicans may well increase their majority in the Senate, and in the House of Representatives a recent disgraceful bout of redistricting means there are precious few disputed seats to fight over. Meanwhile, the Republicans control the governorships of America's four biggest states (Texas, New York, Florida and the newly Schwarzeneggered California) and a majority of the state legislatures. Thus the worry for the Democrats will be that a second term for Mr Bush will allow his party to "conservatise" the judiciary and start dismantling New Deal programmes (for instance, by partly privatising Social Security).

The politics of personality

For many Europeans, a second Bush term may seem even more dismal. This is the "toxic Texan" who, from their perspective, pulled America out of the Kyoto protocols, called Ariel Sharon "a man of peace", refused to join the world criminal court and invaded Iraq without the United Nations' permission. Disregard the accuracy of this caricature; these Europeans should ask themselves whether a Democratic president would really represent a dramatic change.

In most cases, a Democratic alternative to Mr Bush would offer a change of tone, not of substance. The Kyoto protocols were voted down in the Senate by a margin of 95-0 in 1997; even Mr Dean, the most leftish of the current Democratic front-runners, has dithered over signing the environmental treaty. Mr Dean is the only likely candidate unambiguously to oppose the Iraq war, which most of the American public backed. All the Democratic candidates support Israel just as fervently as Mr Bush and some of them have already chastised him for being too soft on Arab allies, notably the Saudis. As for the United Nations, a Democratic president might show more enthusiasm for that body than Mr Bush (not hard); but he would be unlikely to let it have the sort of central role in American foreign policy many Europeans want. Mr Dean's argument with Mr Bush was over the single example of Iraq, not the principle of pre-emption.

For the immediate future, presidents of both parties will be strongly tempted by unilateralism for two reasons. First, America can afford to think like this: its military clout is equal to that of the next two dozen nations combined. Second, America, understandably, still takes the war against terror far more personally than Europe.

Which introduces the final ghastly variable for 2004: another attack by al-Qaeda on American soil. Were it to happen, the chances are that the country would again rally around Mr Bush. Even the threat of such a horror may be enough to help him get re-elected. But it will be close. □

The trade trap

Some risks are hard to avoid. Some you volunteer for, suggests **Clive Crook**

The year will be hazardous for the world economy—in part, needlessly so. One kind of risk, admittedly, is probably unavoidable, and anyhow not susceptible to ordinary economic policy. This is the danger that America's slow expansion will fade or stall, owing to lack of business and consumer confidence. But the larger hazard is one for which governments can claim all the credit: the risk that the current system of international trade negotiations, and with it the broader trade regime that has supported global prosperity these past 50 years, will collapse.

America's expansion has been hesitant, and growth elsewhere in the rich world tepid at best, because the recession that went before was so remarkably tame. Given the violence of the late-1990s' boom, the subsequent combination of mild slowdown and timid expansion should be regarded as a good result. After the bursting of the stockmarket bubble, businesses cut investment right back, not just in America but in many other industrial countries as well. The slowdown in the United States was nonetheless mild because of what didn't happen next: consumers didn't panic. Financially overstretched, they could have cut their spending abruptly, to control their debts and gird themselves for harder times. Mostly, they kept borrowing and spending, and the fearsome recession that might otherwise have happened never came.

That was fine while it lasted. But the debts of America's imperturbable consumers continue to hang over the world economy. This fact, and its various manifestations—America's burgeoning current-account deficit, instability in currency markets and the country's awesome appetite for foreign capital, to name just three—will sooner or later make themselves felt. With luck, when the inevitable squeeze on spending comes, it will happen gradually; when American business sentiment is firm; with clearer signs of sustained recovery in Japan; and alongside a healthier showing by continental Europe. Then all will be well.

It could happen that way. Stockmarkets have been predicting lately that it will. If they are right, 2004 will be a year of higher global growth and relatively painless adjustment. But if a sudden consumption slump in America turns out to align with bad economic news on one or two other fronts, the result would be grim. It would not be the first time stockmarkets got their forecasts wrong.

Can the odds of success be improved? Consumer confidence, still the crucial factor in all this, is a law unto itself. Governments cannot hope to drive it directly. But they can ▶

Clive Crook: deputy editor, *The Economist*

affect the context in helpful ways. In America the most useful step would be a plan to reduce government borrowing over the medium term—or even some sign, absent thus far, that the Bush administration cares a hoot about its colossal long-term budget deficit. Rapid cuts in spending or increases in taxes are certainly not called for, with the economy still poised between stagnation and growth. But believable plans to do both those things beyond the short term would help to settle currency markets, stabilise interest rates and make a traumatic interruption of the capital flowing to America less likely.

Europe and Japan, meanwhile, must still do more to spur demand, mainly by keeping their monetary policies loose, and more to improve their productivity, mainly through regulatory reform. On the latter, Japan seems to be making some progress; and the signs are that France and Germany are also, at last, taking up the challenge. All quite encouraging. At this rate, the rest of the world could soon see clearer signs of the productivity breakthrough that America has been enjoying since 1995.

Pointing the finger

However, the last thing the world needs at such a delicate juncture is the unforced error of a breakdown in the global trading system. Oddly enough, this is exactly what governments have been conspiring to arrange.

One could argue that the fiasco of the World Trade Organisation's talks in Cancún in September 2003 was no great cause for concern. (Many developing-country governments, of course, and most of the North's development and anti-globalisation activists, found it a cause for celebration.) Trade negotiators are past masters at brinkmanship and phoney crises: none of this bogus drama amounts to very much, one might conclude. Well, the Doha round is not dead yet, that much is true; and it would be surprising if attempts to revive it failed altogether over the coming months. Yet the setback in Cancún was an ominous event nonetheless.

At the very least, a splendid opportunity to advance the welfare of rich and poor countries alike—and to improve the global economic climate when it badly needed improving—was squandered. The deal that should have been done required the United States, the European Union and Japan to roll back their agricultural protection. This is something which all the governments concerned have promised to do at various times; and which, by the way, would make their own citizens better off even if it were done unilaterally, without "concessions" from their trading partners.

In return, the developing countries were not required to do much (far less than would be in their best interests, in fact). Europe insisted that they open negotiations on some of the so-called Singapore issues, which touch on matters such as competition policy and customs procedures. That idea went down badly. In the end, the industrial countries, and enough of the developing countries, preferred to do nothing—some even calling it victory—rather than strike a deal that would have made the world, with poor farmers in the third world to the fore, much better off.

This loss, though bad enough, is insignificant compared with the harm that will follow if the WTO now falls apart. And it might. American negotiators, who watched as their developing-country counterparts walked away punching the air, are inclined to say, "So screw 'em." As for developing countries, their anger at rich-country hypocrisy (call for free trade, then exempt your own farmers) is both genuine and justified. The breach is real.

America is already exploring what it sees as a more productive avenue: bilateral free-trade agreements with "can do" developing countries, selected case by case. That path does not lead to genuinely liberal trade. Adding to the problem, a presidential election is coming, and anti-trade interests are drawing up their demands. Asia, meanwhile, has regional, as opposed to multilateral, trade options of its own to consider. And don't expect much of the European Union, increasingly preoccupied with enlargement. Its determination to revive the WTO process is in doubt in any case, since an end to its mad but tenacious common agricultural policy might be the price.

Post-Cancún, pre-disaster, America needs to make the first move—not because it is the principal wrong-doer (the EU probably deserves that distinction), but because only the United States is powerful enough to break the impasse at its own initiative. America should commit itself to, and demand from Europe, deep, genuine and early cuts in agricultural subsidies. A challenge, in the circumstances—and one that will get harder as the year progresses. But it may take action of this sort to revive the Doha round. As far as economic policy is concerned, nothing in 2004 is more important. □

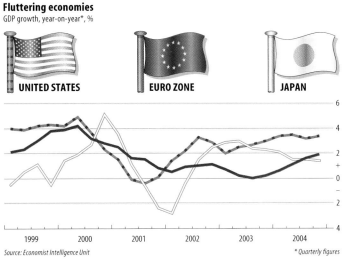

Fluttering economies
GDP growth, year-on-year*, %

UNITED STATES   EURO ZONE   JAPAN

1999 2000 2001 2002 2003 2004

Source: Economist Intelligence Unit   * Quarterly figures

Dell
High-performance supply chain, delivered.

When the world's number one computer company set out to upgrade its already world-class manufacturing infrastructure several years ago, they began with a bold, yet simple premise: "build more systems with less inventory." In about 100 days, Accenture and Dell conceived and implemented an approach that allows Dell to operate on no more than two hours of inventory at a time. Now in place in Dell's plants around the world, the programme paid for itself five times over during the first 12 months of operation. Dell is able to adapt more quickly to rapidly changing technologies and maintain its position as a high-performance business.

New York City 311
High performance delivered for government.

More than 900 non-emergency city services in 170 languages for 8 million residents—services that once took 14 pages of telephone numbers in New York City—are now available 24/7 with a single call to 311. Working closely with the city's Department of Information Technology and Telecommunication, Accenture took the United States' largest 311 project live in just seven months, introducing not just new applications and technologies, but a new way of doing business. Having surpassed the 2 million call milestone in just five months, the system is giving the city of New York the agility required for high performance.

Conditions change. Results shouldn't.

Go on. Be a Tiger.

No matter the climate, high performers find new and innovative ways to prevail. To see how we can help your business become a high-performance business and stay that way, visit accenture.com

• Consulting • Technology • Outsourcing

> accenture

High performance. Delivered.

Slowly does it in the Middle East

Don't hold your breath for a sudden outbreak of peace and democracy, explains **Peter David**

A thousand wise commentators agree that 2004 will be a decisive year in the Middle East. It is easy to see why they think so. America occupies Iraq, which George Bush promises to turn into the Arab world's first proper democracy, thereby setting an inspiring example for the region. Next door in Iran, the theocratic revolution Ayatollah Khomeini launched more than 20 years ago is running out of puff and may soon give way to a secular, democratic counter-revolution. As for Palestine, the international "road map" decrees that the Palestinians are within a year or so of independent statehood. Surely the misery and bloodletting of the latest *intifada* cannot drag on for much longer?

All of the above means that 2004 will be eventful in the region. In an area that always surprises, this could be the year that Israel launches a surprise attack on Iran's nuclear facilities. But, with due respect to the thousand commentators, it is not likely to be a decisive year. The shock waves sent out by America's removal of Saddam Hussein are being absorbed by an edifice of political forces that has endured many shocks before. The violent arrival in the heart of the Arab world of a superpower bent on imposing democracy may very well begin to undermine this system's foundations. But it could take many years before the walls above begin to wobble.

Some optimists in Washington believe that it will not take much more than a year for America to organise democracy in Iraq. Yet three decades of Saddam, three wars and a decade

Not so fast

of sanctions inflicted such harm on Iraq that America will need to build many institutions from the ground up. Think how long it has taken to get the lights back on and you see why building stable, representative political institutions will almost certainly take a good deal more than a year.

Conversely, some pessimists think Iraq may go so badly wrong that America will decide to cut and run. And it may. But within a year? It would require extraordinary mayhem in Iraq for Mr Bush, or a successor, to accept the humiliation of quitting so soon. Of course, the Americans may grow so rattled by the cost and complications that they set up a weak or bogus democracy and rush for the exit. But that would be a dangerous mistake, an admission of weakness damaging to America's standing in places well beyond Iraq.

What about Iraq's impact on the region? The cartoon version is that the Arab world must now choose between the competing values of America and al-Qaeda, between liberal democracy and Islamic fundamentalism. Actually, this is not a real choice at all for most Arabs. Even if an exemplary democracy arises in Iraq, the authoritarian regimes of Egypt, Syria and the rest will not want to copy it and so lose power. Such regimes are so well dug in that there is little immediate prospect of them being toppled either by al-Qaeda (in most countries the Islamists were comprehensively crushed by the end of the 1990s) or by home-grown democrats.

Patience is a virtue, except on Palestine

To say that 2004 will not be decisive is not to say that it will be unimportant. Over time, the changes unleashed by America's invasion of Iraq could indeed have profound consequences for the whole Muslim world. However, most of these beyond-Iraq changes are going to be changes of attitude and philosophy: they will, in other words, be slow-acting. This suggests that the most useful virtue for America's foreign-policymakers to have in 2004 will be patience. Though it is a good idea to rebuild Iraq's electricity grid as soon as possible, it is a bad one to short-circuit the creation of a democracy.

Still, in one part of the Middle East America should be impatient. The impasse between Israel and the Palestinians will grow even more violent if the superpower does not become more deeply engaged in efforts to revive diplomacy. This will be hard in an American election year, but much is at stake. Whatever the positive results of the Iraq war turn out to be, they will be cancelled out in Arab eyes if the Israeli occupation of the West Bank and Gaza drags on without any prospect of implementing the land-for-peace deal. Though neither Ariel Sharon nor Yasser Arafat will be willing in 2004 to yield to the other, the Palestinians and Israelis are exhausted by violence and will be receptive to a compromise. Over the past year Mr Bush said all the right things about creating an independent Palestine alongside a secure Israel. The coming year will show whether talk is all it was. □

Peter David: foreign editor, *The Economist*

Direct Relief
INTERNATIONAL
SINCE 1948
Healthy people. Better world.

Since 1948, Direct Relief International has assisted people in need – both in poor regions of the world and wherever disaster has struck – by providing essential resources to locally run health programs.

In 2002, Direct Relief International provided more than $67 million in material assistance in 57 countries – enough provisions to provide care to millions of people. To learn more, visit www.directrelief.org.

BD

Helping all people live healthy lives

Partners in disaster relief

Natural and man-made disasters take an alarming toll on the victims. Those who survive are often left tragically devastated. Helping them requires compassion and teamwork to ensure that the necessary medical and humanitarian supplies are quickly distributed to all those who desperately need them.

With the aid of BD and other donors, Direct Relief has delivered emergency medical supplies and health services to millions. From refugees displaced by war to victims of hurricanes and earthquakes, these efforts provide the poor, sick and needy with the care they require and the hope they need.

BD donates syringes, surgical instruments, blood collection devices and other medical supplies in support of these efforts.

BD is a medical technology company serving some of the greatest needs of the global community. Healthcare institutions, life sciences researchers, clinical laboratories, industry and the general public all rely on BD products every day.

BD is privileged to partner with Direct Relief and organizations like it to protect life by addressing fundamental healthcare issues in every corner of the world.

BD – Helping all people live healthy lives.

At the beginning of the day, it's all about vision.

At the end of the day, it's all about the courage to execute it.

And everything in between is about
how we'll help you get there.

Mellon Financial Corporation
Asset Management
  Institutional Asset Management
  Mutual Funds
  Private Wealth Management
Corporate and Institutional Services
  Asset Servicing
  Human Resources & Investor Solutions
  Treasury Services

www.mellon.com

 **Mellon**
The difference is measurable.®

Life in the hot seat

A humble recovery is in store for businesses and their bosses, predicts **Frances Cairncross**

Business will start 2004 feeling a lot more cheerful than it did a year earlier. Profits are up, recovery is palpable. But the recovery will still feel hesitant, and companies will go on looking for ways to screw costs down and squeeze up productivity.

Outsourcing will race on. Manufacturing will continue fleeing to China, services to India. In Europe plenty of work will pour eastwards into the new low-wage members of the European Union. The fuss in America about the shift of information-technology and call-centre jobs to India will spread to Europe.

Companies will also push up productivity by getting more out of past investments in IT. Increasingly, firms are learning new ways to apply IT in areas such as supply-chain management and distribution. For instance, one of Dell's computer factories cleared 25% of the floorspace of a plant by redesigning inventory management—only to fill the space within months to meet new demand. In a sense, the company built a virtual new factory, out of nifty new business processes and renegotiated arrangements with suppliers. Such incremental improvements will spread to other, less adventurous firms in 2004, but will hardly show up on corporate balance sheets. The consequent rise in productivity will be largely passed on in lower prices.

As a result, companies will seem to be spending little on new capital investment. Investment in computers and software (about a third of the total) will grow faster than other kinds of capital spending; that slump is now over. But there will not be the sort of splurge in capital spending that leads to expansion and creates jobs.

In America companies will start hiring again, but they will be cautious. Demand is recovering in the job-intensive service sector. But while product prices have been falling since the start of 2002, people are becoming an alarmingly expensive input. This is not because wages and salaries are rising—on the contrary, they will remain flat in 2004. Rather, it is that benefit costs, in the shape of both pensions and health care, continue to shoot upwards. This divergence between labour costs and product prices is strongest in manufacturing, which is under constant price pressure from foreign imports.

As companies hunt for ways to hold costs down, they will pay increasing attention to the location of their head offices. Too much tax (on either the company or its senior executives) or too much regulation of a burdensome sort will both become stronger reasons to consider uprooting. Countries in northern Europe, including Germany, will be especially vulnerable to losing head offices or to becoming just one of several locations among which a company's executive functions are spread.

Businesses will rearrange affairs in the boardroom to comply with new rules on corporate governance. The market for independent directors, and especially for those with financial experience, will boom: chief finance officers will enjoy frequent requests to join some corporate board or other, and retired accountants will prosper. Consultants will flourish by developing a new line of work, evaluating the performance of corporate boards and their members. The burden of work on individual directors will keep growing.

But attention will shift from corporate directors to institutional investors. New plans for corporate governance tend to assume that investors will behave like owners. However, institutions are often merely agents for the true owners, as

No lavish perks visible

when an investment bank handles a pension fund's money. There will be much discussion of ways to improve the transparency of institutions' voting and to give owners more information. But don't expect the owners or the institutions to show as much interest as they would if they were private-equity companies or founder-owners.

Under-promise, over-perform

Chastened by bad publicity in 2003, chief executives will still be cautious about being seen to accept lavish perks or pay. Philanthropy will become more fashionable, as a way to curry favour with a disapproving public and justify bonuses. But CEOs will be wary about appearing to seek publicity. They will talk a lot about execution. The key will be to under-promise and over-perform. In 2004 humility will be in, arrogance out, and a CEO's picture on the cover of *Fortune* will still be a signal to short the stock. □

Frances Cairncross: management editor, *The Economist*

Water, water everywhere

And scarcely a drop of common sense on its pricing, says **John Peet**

For years environmentalists have bleated on about imminent food shortages, spreading pollution, accelerating climate change and the early exhaustion of the world's oil and other minerals. Their forecasts have seldom come true. Yet they have overlooked the most essential substance of all: water. Now, however, there are dire predictions of water shortages in many countries, and even claims that wars of the future will be fought over water, not oil.

In 2004 water will rise further up the world's agenda. There will be more conferences to succeed the Johannesburg earth summit in 2002 and the Kyoto world water forum in 2003. Governments will come to realise how hard it is to meet the goals they set in Johannesburg: to cut by half, by 2015, the number of people without clean water and adequate sanitation. A billion lack the first, and nearly 2.4 billion the second. A panel at the Kyoto forum reckoned that it could cost an extra $100 billion a year to meet the Johannesburg goals.

In fact, it could be done for a lot less: perhaps no more than an extra $25 billion. But far more important, the real problem is neither a lack of money nor even a physical scarcity of water—there is plenty of both. The two main reasons why so many people in poor countries do not have clean water are, first, that most of it is wasted in subsidised irrigation by farmers, who use over 75% of all water in developing

countries; and second, that water utilities tend to be corrupt, inefficient and to charge too little.

The chronic underpricing of water does not help the poor, as one might perhaps hope. Rather, the beneficiaries are the middle classes. Large rural farmers can afford to pump out free groundwater or to lobby for big dams that will yield irrigation benefits. Rich households have access to piped water from municipal utilities. The poorest have to pay door-to-door water vendors.

The solution of raising water prices, politically controversial as it is, does not have to hit the poor either. Chile and South Africa have both raised water prices substantially, but have acted to protect the poorest. In Chile they are given special water stamps to help them pay their utility bills; in South Africa the first 25 litres a day are delivered free, but the rest is charged at full cost. Both countries are entering 2004 well on the way to achieving universal coverage.

As for farmers, proper pricing would create new incentives not just to conserve supplies but also to trade their water rights to those who can make best use of the water. Places as diverse as Australia, Chile, Spain and California have established markets in water, and they are likely to grow fast in 2004. If a farmer growing water-intensive crops is faced with higher prices for his water, he will often find it pays more to stop growing and sell the water instead—either to another farmer who can use it more efficiently, or to a thirsty city. In either case the result is both less water use and more sensible allocation.

Yes to more competition, no to giant dams

The two other controversial issues are how to improve the performance of water utilities, and whether to build more big dams. On the first, the lesson from Europe and America is to harness the private sector. This does not mean full-scale privatisation of water: water can continue to be publicly owned, but a contract to deliver it can be awarded to private companies. Unfortunately, political interference and exchange-rate problems are discouraging the water companies, such as Suez or RWE/Thames, from going into emerging markets. Yet without the spur or at least the threat of private competition, local monopoly utilities will remain immune to reform.

Dams will cause more argument than ever, with China's Three Gorges dam filling up in 2004 and both China and India embarking on huge river-diversion projects. Developing countries, above all in Africa, do need more dams, but not on the scale that China and India are planning. There are usually cheaper and better ways of storing water, delivering irrigation and protecting against floods. The trouble is that expensive capital projects are always alluring to politicians. The backlash against dams will build in 2004, and on this issue at least the environmentalists are largely in the right. If only they would embrace proper pricing as well. □

John Peet: Europe editor, *The Economist*

IN SCOTLAND, YOU'LL FIND THE SAME
NATURAL RESOURCE DEDICATED TO MATURING A FINE WHISKY
IS NOW GOING TOWARD FINDING A CURE FOR CANCER.
IT'S CALLED DOGGED, BULLHEADED DETERMINATION.

Surgery. Penicillin. CAT scans and stem cell research. These are testaments to the Scots' irrepressible curiosity and drive to improve on everything around them. Everything, that is, except our whisky.

From a 400-year-old and painstakingly perfect distillation process to breakthrough after scientific breakthrough, one thing is certain: determination is alive in Scotland.

Our scientists are making history in drug discovery and development, genomics, cardiovascular research, bioelectronics and neuroscience.

Dr. Ian Wilmut cloned the first mammal. Sir Philip Cohen is breaking ground in signal transduction and cancer treatment. And Sir David Lane is also working to cure cancer with the p53 gene. This, coupled with a thriving biomanufacturing centre, makes ours the fastest-growing biotech community in Europe.

We're proud. We admit it. But we judge our success based on its global impact. That's why we established Scottish Development International. So if you're considering collaboration abroad, call us or visit our Web site.

Find out how a resolute firmness of character or stubborn will in its purest form has produced everything from a 25-year-old scotch to impossible medical miracles.

SCOTTISH DEVELOPMENT INTERNATIONAL

www.scotsinnovate.com/biotech
+44 141 228 2828

Ye gods, the modern Greek Olympics

What would the ancients have made of them? wonders **Johnny Grimond**

Back to Greece: on August 13th 2004 the Olympic games return to Athens, the city in which the first modern Olympics were held in 1896. How will the games turn out? *The World in 2004* decided to consult the oracle at Delphi, just across the Gulf of Corinth from Olympia, where the original games were staged some 3,000 years ago. The deity, speaking through a priestess perched on a tripod, made three prophecies. They are characteristically ambiguous.

Finished first, finished last, Willing hands and heads turned fast.

This is particularly difficult to interpret. It may suggest that all those taking part, whether they come first or last, will be regarded as noble contestants who will turn the heads of the millions of people watching. That would be very much in the tradition of the original Greek games, which were part of a religious festival and organised primarily for the competitors, not the public. The first recorded champion, Coroebus of Elis, who won the sprint in 776BC, was a cook.

It has to be said, however, that this amateurism soon began to give way, and the rewards of victory were such that by the 5th century BC the typical champion was likely to be an athlete who had undergone months of intensive training. By the time the Romans were running Greece, in the second century BC, the games had utterly changed in character, with the accent firmly on entertainment. Chariot-racing was particularly popular, as were boxing and wrestling, especially the pancratium—a contest in which only biting, eye-gouging and fingers up the nostrils were forbidden. Entertainment is, of course, the name of the games these days.

More likely, the oracle was saying something quite different. Possibly it was a reference to the problems host cities often have nowadays in completing the arrangements on time. Whereas Los Angeles arguably "finished first" with a highly successful games in 1984, Montreal had notorious difficulties in 1976. Athens was given a grave warning in 2001 that it was behind schedule. One reason, it is said, is the absence of volunteers ("willing hands", to the oracle?)

who had been expected to help. A bungled Olympics could lead to heads rolling—the correct translation of the ancient Greek word *anakylio* in this context? Some critics are already scornful of Gianna Angelopoulos-Daskalaki, who led the bid to bring the games back to Greece and is now head of the organising committee. They fear she will preside over a loss-making exercise that will leave few useful legacies.

No winning without oils, To the victor go the spoils.

This prediction would seem to be straightforward, but for the puzzling reference to oils. Some may be tempted to believe that "oils" means drugs, which were not banned in ancient Greece. More likely, "oils" refers to the olive oil with which the athletes covered their naked bodies before competing. This raises the interesting implication that all the competitors will once again be naked for the games in Athens.

Shorts, singlets and so on have indeed become scantier over the years, but this return to the past may prove controversial. After all, women (along with slaves and foreigners) were not allowed to compete in the original Olympics, though unmarried girls were allowed to watch. The nudity requirement will surely be challenged especially vigorously by contestants in the equestrian events and the pole vault. It will be necessary to reinstate the old practice of accompanying events with flute music, not so much to aid co-ordination of mind and body as to drown cries of pain.

That old banality "to the victor go the spoils" is, of course, a reference to the vast riches that champions can expect (imagine their faces if they were offered just a crown of leaves), but it also has another meaning. The winners at Olympia were believed to have been chosen by the deities, who sent down a winged messenger called Nike, meaning Victory, to deliver rewards. Good news, therefore, for one maker of athletics equipment in 2004. Tough luck, Adidas, Reebok and the rest.

Rome, Georgia, Athens, Texas, and Paris, Tennessee Eight years hence that's where I want to be.

Some people believe these to be the first lines of a country-and-western song, but it is more likely to be a prediction of where future Olympics will be held. After Athens, Rome (1960), Atlanta (Georgia, in 1996), and the Beijing games due in 2008, a host of cities are vying to hold the 2012 Olympics. Evidently they will be held in Paris. But oracles are notoriously casual about punctuation. The world will have to wait to find out whether the capital of France is to be the host, or whether the oracle was speaking of Paris, Tennessee. □

Johnny Grimond: writer at large, *The Economist*

The legend reveals
another dimension

Reverso
Grande Date
The extra-large case
revolves majestically to reveal
its unique dual personality.
On one side, the large date and
8-day power-reserve. The reverse,
in sapphire crystal, displays the
complicated mechanical movement,
Jaeger-LeCoultre calibre 875 that
makes this a major event in the
Reverso's history.

JAEGER-LECOULTRE

DIARY FOR 2004

Our selection of events around the world

JANUARY

Ireland takes over the presidency of the EU

Top government, industry and NGO figures meet at the World Social Forum and the World Economic Forum, in India and Switzerland respectively

The Special Summit of the Americas, bringing together presidents and prime ministers of 34 member-countries of the Organisation of American States, is held in Mexico

China celebrates the Year of the Monkey

The American election season heats up with the New Hampshire primary

President George Bush delivers the state-of-the-union address

The African Cup of Nations soccer tournament kicks off in Tunisia

FEBRUARY

Jean Chrétien steps down after more than ten years as Canada's prime minister

The Delhi Sustainable Development Summit is held in India

Samba beats shake Rio de Janeiro during the flamboyant annual carnival

Parliamentary election in Iran

The Academy Awards are held in Los Angeles, a month earlier than usual

The Superbowl touches down in Houston

MARCH

The 50th anniversary of America's biggest ever H-bomb test at Bikini Atoll in the central Pacific

Parliamentary election in Spain, presidential elections in Russia, Indonesia and Taiwan

Super Tuesday sees primaries in 12 states across America, including California

The World Indoor Athletics Championships, the biggest meeting of its kind, springs into action in Budapest

APRIL

South Africans celebrate the tenth anniversary of the end of apartheid; a general election is likely around the same time

Iraqis hold their new national day, which marks the first anniversary of the fall of Saddam Hussein's regime in Baghdad

With the help of contributions from

foresightnews
www.foresightnews.co.uk

Ministers from the 30 OECD member-states meet in Paris to discuss environmental policy; their previous meeting was in 2001

More than 20,000 runners compete in the Boston marathon

MAY

Ten more countries join the EU

The 9/11 Commission is due to publish its report on the 2001 terrorist attacks on New York and Washington, DC

Presidential elections in Germany, Slovakia, the Philippines and the Dominican Republic

A tidal wave of Hollywood glitz hits the shores of Cannes for the annual film festival

JUNE

G8 leaders meet in America, on Sea Island, off the coast of Georgia

European Parliament elections

The EU takes over NATO's role of policing Bosnia-Hercegovina in the second half of the year

Deadline for WHO members to sign a strict tobacco-control treaty in New York

A possible general election in Afghanistan

Cinemas prepare to be swamped as "Harry Potter and the Prisoner of Azkaban" opens

The Euro 2004 football championship gets under way in Lisbon

JULY

The Netherlands takes on the presidency of the EU

Some 15,000 delegates attend the biennial International AIDS Conference in Bangkok

America's Democrats convene in Boston

Twenty-odd teams of nine riders begin the gruelling Tour de France cycle race

The Scottish Parliament building, modelled on an upturned boat, is scheduled to open in Edinburgh, a mere £300m ($500m) or so over budget

AUGUST

After 12 months of deliberation, Iraq's constitution should be ready. It can then be put to a public vote before the end of the year

Mauritius hosts the summit of the Southern African Development Community, where delegates from 14 African nations discuss regional issues

The Republican National Convention is held in New York

The Olympic games commence in Athens

SEPTEMBER

The UN General Assembly meets in New York

Some 350 religious leaders of all faiths congregate in Milan

The World Bank and the IMF compare notes at their annual meeting in Washington, DC

America's first ground-based missile interceptors are due to be in place, in Alaska and California, with more to follow in the year ahead

OCTOBER

Contestants light up at the European pipe-smoking championship in Copenhagen

The Arctic Council, comprising representatives from eight circumpolar countries and six indigenous groups, meets in Iceland

The world's largest democratic elections are expected to be held in India around now

Paris Fashion Week takes to its heels

Winners of the Nobel prizes for peace and literature are announced in Oslo and Stockholm

NOVEMBER

Americans go to the polls

The current EU commissioners are replaced by a fresh batch of 25

Representatives of the Association of South-East Asian Nations (ASEAN) meet in Laos to discuss regional integration

A general election in Australia is expected around now

Members of the Asia-Pacific Economic Co-operation Forum meet in Santiago, Chile

Miss World contestants outline their proposals for achieving global peace

DECEMBER

Target deadline for the eradication of polio, which would represent a saving of some $1.5 billion a year in health-care costs worldwide

The European Council decides whether Turkey is ready to start EU-membership negotiations

Supposed conclusion of talks about a Free-Trade Area of the Americas pact

The annual rat games, in which rodents trained by teams of student psychologists compete in track, weight-lifting, long-jump, tightrope and climbing events, are held at Nebraska Wesleyan University

The UN-designated World AIDS Day is marked by events across the globe

Sofitel hotels
everywhere in europe

SOFITEL
ACCOR HOTELS & RESORTS

émotions every time

Paris . London . Rome . Madrid . Brussels . Copenhagen .
Lisbon . Athens... and over 100 other destinations to émotions .

www.sofitel.com or www.accorhotels.com

When trust is going, the going gets tough

Matthew Symonds

Can things get any worse for Tony Blair?

In 2003 Tony Blair gambled his reputation on leading his country into a war with Iraq. He did so in opposition to public opinion and despite the deep discomfort of most of his own MPs. Although the war itself went as well as even the most fervent optimist could have hoped, nearly everything associated with it has since gone pretty badly. The long failure to unearth weapons of mass destruction, the fragile security situation in Iraq and the bitterly slow progress in healing the war's diplomatic wounds have combined to make the successful military campaign look increasingly like a strategic blunder. The fallout will cast its shadow over 2004.

The prime minister's collapsing ratings for "trust" are an indication that almost everyone, even supporters of the war, suspects him of having exaggerated the case for military action. Not in the sense, as his more extreme critics claim, of having cynically deceived both Parliament and people. The more substantive charge against Mr Blair is that, having made up his mind about what was the right thing to do, he became blind to any evidence or arguments that might have forced him to think twice.

Winning back the electorate's trust is the most vital task facing Mr Blair in 2004. Even in such a torrid mid-term, in most opinion polls Labour retains a slight lead over the opposition Conservatives, who have been busy ejecting their own leader. Most people would still rather have Mr Blair as prime minister than any of the alternatives. The strength of the economy certainly helps. But the trust issue threatens to be corrosive of everything the government is trying to do. As an election draws closer—mid-2005 has been pencilled in—so the domestic agenda of improving public services will come to the fore.

Unfortunately for Mr Blair, things seem to be going only marginally better in that sphere. When he tells people that schools and hospitals are getting better, even if they are, few are disposed to believe him. His "reform and invest" mantra about the public services is treated with growing scepticism. People know that the "invest-

ment" bit has gone on apace: their own tax returns are proof enough. But the spending splurge began before the government had secured much in the way of changed working practices, let alone reforms designed to put consumers first by stimulating competition and choice. Instead, union hostility to reforms has become more entrenched. Mr Blair can expect bloody-minded opposition, encouraged from the sidelines by an embarrassingly large number of his own MPs. Many Labour MPs have acquired both the habit and the taste for rebellion. A coalition of the sullen has formed, consisting of a well-established left-wing awkward squad, discarded former

More than a passing shower

ministers (quite a numerous category) and resentful backbenchers whose hopes of office have finally vanished after six years of well-merited obscurity.

Mr Blair insists that he has no choice other than to press ahead with reforms. The alternative, he maintains, would ensure the failure of the government's bid to show that well-funded, modernised public services can meet the needs of citizens whose expectations are much higher than those of earlier generations. But while the government will talk tough, it will make concessions in ex- ▶

2004

Foreign nationals wishing to gain full British citizenship will have to pass a special new exam. Among other things, it will test their proficiency in English, Welsh or Scots Gaelic.

Matthew Symonds:
political editor,
The Economist

change for the grumbling acquiescence of its critics. Mr Blair has established a "forum" for the unions to discuss how change in the public sector should be implemented. It may help clear up some misunderstandings, but the unions are hoping to use it to slow down reform.

Another example of how the trust issue is sapping the prime minister's power is the euro. The chancellor, Gordon Brown, is due to report in April 2004 on the progress that has been made in getting Britain ready to join the single currency. Not much, is likely to be the answer, although Mr Brown will no doubt point to the Herculean efforts he has made.

It was always highly improbable that the stars would be sufficiently in alignment to allow a euro referendum in this Parliament, however much store Mr Blair still attaches to leaving the option open. But now the chances are zero. To win a referendum, Mr Blair will need to persuade voters to put their faith in his judgment. Once upon a time, he might have done it. But even before the Swedes had rejected the euro, the hopes of holding a referendum had vanished into the same pit concealing Saddam Hussein's weapons of mass destruction. In the circumstances, the government's determination to resist the clamour for a referendum on the new European constitution is understandable if not creditable. It fears, probably rightly, that soothing reassurances to the effect that the whole exercise is just a much-needed "tidying up" of existing treaties would simply not be believed.

Down but not out

Mr Blair's isolation and loss of popularity over Iraq have emboldened those in his own party—perhaps a majority—who never bought into the idea of New Labour with much enthusiasm in the first place. But what will give them the confidence to continue undermining Mr Blair is their growing belief that they no longer need him to win elections. They may be wrong about that, but it is a remarkable fact that, weakened though Mr Blair may be, the Tories have yet to benefit.

The Conservatives talk about a coming "tipping point" when all the discontent with the government will come together to tilt people back into the arms of the Tories. It is a comforting idea, but not yet a convincing one. For all its mistakes, the government still presides over a relatively strong economy, which in 2004 should strengthen further (see next story). And no matter how flawed the electorate may now judge Mr Blair, they do not seem to think the Tories offer a better alternative. Unless the Conservatives under new leadership quickly mount a much more effective challenge, nothing in 2004 is likely to shatter Mr Blair's conviction that a third term is there for the taking.

That is ignoring one potentially important consideration. If 2004 is even half as bad as 2003, will Mr Blair's appetite for power remain as strong as before? There are days when he looks strained, and he has had a brief scare with a racing heart, but his energy is impressive and his job is probably secure for as long as he wants it. Thoughts about his place in history are never far from Mr Blair's mind and he is deeply conscious of how much remains to be done. The other thing which will drive him on is the certain knowledge of how much his next-door neighbour, Mr Brown, still yearns to succeed him. □

Working shifts
UK employment, '000

Source: EcoWin

Advantage, server

Anatole Kaletsky

Why Britain's economy will stay ahead

Britain has been one of the best-performing economies in the advanced capitalist world since the early 1990s. More good news is in store for 2004. It will be a better year than 2003—certainly in absolute terms and probably in relation to the rest of the world.

The British have worried about the global recession, but they were in fact largely insulated from its nasty effects. This stability was all the more impressive given the country's exposure to some of the worst-affected sectors, such as financial services and telecoms. The reasons why Britain, once derided as the boom-bust capital of the world, managed to avoid both the long-term stagnation of its European neighbours and the cyclical giddiness of America offer some reliable pointers for 2004.

Britain's main advantages relative to continental Europe are obvious. Unlike the euro zone, it has benefited from consciously anti-cyclical monetary management. The Bank of England will continue to set interest rates very flexibly, aiming not just to achieve the government's inflation target but also to keep economic growth as close as possible to its long-term trend. The inflation target, incidentally, will switch in 2004 from a 2.5% increase in Britain's traditional retail-prices index to a 2% increase in the index measured by pan-European definitions. Paradoxically, this will actually allow somewhat higher inflation in Britain (because of differences in definition between the two figures), giving the Bank the scope to keep interest rates a little lower than it otherwise would. Since the economy starts 2004 with an output gap of 1-1.5%, the Bank should be quite tolerant of above-trend growth for most of the year.

Thus British interest rates will rise only slightly in 2004—say, by one percentage point or so. Given that European interest rates are unlikely to rise at all and could well be cut even further, the interest-rate differential in ▶

2004

Burger-flippers across the United Kingdom will contemplate a spending spree as the national minimum wage is increased from £4.50 to £4.85 ($7.50 to $8.10).

Anatole Kaletsky: columnist, *The Times*, and director of GaveKal Research

favour of sterling will widen. Business will once again be surprised by the "unexpected" strength of the pound.

The Bank's proactive monetary policy would not be nearly so effective if it were not for the other great contrast with the euro zone: the flexibility of the British economy created by 18 years of deregulation under the Tories. Britain would not be able to maintain anything like its present low rate of unemployment without the labour-market flexibility, the cuts in welfare payments and the competitive disciplines introduced into previously nationalised utilities and cartelised service industries. To understand why Britain grew right through the global recession while much of the rest of Europe stagnated, contrast the rapid collapse of Marconi and Rover with the endless agonies of Vivendi, Fiat or Alstom.

In 2004 (as in 2003) the government will also be making a big contribution to Britain's growth and employment—and this is where an important contrast with America can be drawn. Britain has shifted from a tight to a fairly expansionary fiscal policy since 2001. This fiscal stimulus, equivalent to roughly 2.5% of GDP, has been much more effective in boosting both growth and employment than the even bigger fiscal stimulus (over 4% of GDP) applied to the United States by President Bush.

America's stimulus consisted largely of cutting taxes on top income brackets, while the cash-strapped states sacked hundreds of thousands of low-paid public-sector workers. In Britain the fiscal stimulus worked exactly the other way round: the government hired thousands of new nurses and teachers and greatly increased their wages. The bills went mainly to the higher-paid through an increase in stealth taxes. Whatever one may think about the long-term effects of higher government spending and taxes, the immediate impact on demand was very much as predicted by Keynesian economics. The workers in the public sector rapidly spent their income gains, giving the economy a significant boost and helping to ensure that the much-dreaded recession never happened.

But what about the longer term? Surely, despite the good cyclical performance, Britain is facing fiscal, pensions and productivity nightmares in the next decade? Problems, yes; nightmares, no.

Now, about that productivity blot

Britain's public finances have moved into deficit and will remain in the red as far as the eye can see. But the sort of deficits in prospect—between 1% and 4% of GDP—will still leave Britain with by far the lowest ratio of debt to GDP among the G7 countries. This prediction is subject to just two provisos. First, the economy must continue to grow at around its trend rate of 2.5%, which seems almost certain. Second, the government must stick to its promise to slow down the growth of public spending from 5% a year in real terms to roughly 3% after 2005. This moderate tightening of the purse-strings will almost certainly be confirmed in the triennial spending review for 2005-08, which the chancellor will finalise in July.

Pensions? Many pension funds will remain under water, but reforms (such as higher retirement ages) will be healthy developments in their own right. And Britain's situation is again much better than that of others in Europe, thanks to its less worrying demography. Britain's population will not start to shrink until 2030.

Productivity growth, the poorest among the G7 countries, has remained the perennial blot on Britain's economic record. But even this cloud has several silver linings. First, the very fact that productivity is low means Britain has more scope to catch up. Second, because employment in Britain is high, future growth will be less labour-intensive and more productivity-enhancing. Third, electronic technology should narrow the productivity gap between manufacturing and services, in which Britain has a comparative advantage. Indeed, Britain's true productivity is higher than it appears, because conventional statistics give great weight to quality improvements in manufactured goods such as computers, but fail to make similar adjustments for high-value services such as finance, law and advertising. The rapid rise in the prices of these services suggests their quality has increased in relation to commodities and manufactures.

Put another way, Britain has enjoyed a huge terms-of-trade gain relative to countries such as Germany and Japan, which specialise in manufactured goods, not to mention Latin America and Africa, which produce commodities. The benefit for Britain of specialising in high-end services may even increase in the years ahead, as China and other developing countries force down the prices of manufactures. Britain is one of the few countries which can face with relative equanimity a future where all manufactured goods are stamped "Made in China". □

Ship-shape

Full steam ahead for the cruise industry

If big is beautiful, then the *Queen Mary 2*—to be launched at Southampton in January 2004—is Mama Cass and Helen of Troy rolled into one. The £540m ($900m) transatlantic liner is three-and-a-half times as long as the tower of Big Ben is high. Her attractions include five swimming pools, six restaurants, 14 bars, a ballroom and a planetarium. She is, boasts Cunard, her owner, the biggest and most luxurious cruise ship ever built.

She reflects the confidence of the industry. In the summer of 2004 Stelios Haji-Ioannou plans to launch easyCruise, a maritime equivalent of his low-cost airline, easyJet. His no-frills approach will include spartan interiors and pay-as-you-go restaurants. A trip on the QM2's maiden voyage will set you back anything from £2,145 (for an interior cabin with no view) to £28,500 (for a "duplex" with all the trimmings). But, at £39 a night, easyCruise's fibre-glass cabins will no doubt have a charm of their own. □

www.emirates.com

Remember the first time you took top prize?
Even after our 250th, we haven't forgotten.
We're just as excited to have been awarded Passenger
Service Airline of the Year, as we were the first time.
It means we haven't stopped finding new ways
to make your flying experience more memorable.

Keep discovering.

Emirates
Passenger Service
Airline of the Year 2003

2004

British potheads can roll a celebratory spliff as cannabis is reclassified from class B to class C. Those found in possession of the drug are unlikely to be arrested.

A question of class

Edward Lucas

Tony tries hard but his results are disappointing

Education will be one of the hottest topics for Tony Blair in 2004. The biggest row will be about allowing universities to charge higher fees—a centrepiece of the government's legislative programme. There will also be much sniping about falling standards in school exams, and continued frustration, in government and outside, about the huge amounts spent on education and the often unsatisfactory results that the system delivers. As will be painfully clear in 2004, the government has two conflicting aims: to have both a world-class education system and one that leads to effective social engineering (which most Labour activists call social justice).

The problem that most vexes the government is that the worst-off people in society fare most poorly in Britain's schools (particularly in England and Wales; the Scottish system is different and a bit better). Around a

CAN'T YOU LOOK A BIT MORE DEPRIVED DARLING?

UNIVERSITY ADMISSIONS INTERVIEWS →

quarter of the school population will leave at 16, barely able to read and write. About half fail to gain the minimum of five decent passes in the GCSE exams taken at 16 necessary for further study to 18, which leads to university entrance thereafter. Overwhelmingly from poor families, they are let down by bad teachers, bad discipline, badly designed lessons, but most of all by bad parents. For taxpayers, it is also a stunningly bad return for the money spent over 11 years for this education, at a cost of roughly £5,000 ($8,340) per child each year.

The failure to help the bottom chunk of the country's school-age children is by far the worst bit of Britain's education record, but dealing with it is tricky. The state will spend another £460m in 2004 on Connexions, a snazzily branded scheme to encourage mentoring and advice for children aged 13 and upwards, in the hope that more of them will take exams and stay on until 18. But the real problems start earlier: research into pre-school children

Edward Lucas: education correspondent, *The Economist*

shows that the brightest infants from poor and bad homes are already losing out to dimmer children with better parents by the age of five.

Standards have gone up in primary schools, largely thanks to increased concentration on simple literacy and numeracy. But even the government's defenders admit there is a long way to go. The big news in 2004 will be in secondary education, with the introduction of more specialist schools (the government wants the majority of children to go to these by 2006); and also the launch of more high-flying City Academies. These have a strong hint of the old grammar schools, abolished by the Labour Party nearly 40 years ago. Unlike those, the new outfits are not allowed to select children (that is still anathema to the Labour left), but they do have a lot of freedom in their management. They also work in tandem with private-sector sponsors—including, from 2004, some of the country's best-known independent schools.

For all the government's efforts, the numbers of parents choosing to go to those independent schools—where fees are between £5,000 and £20,000 a year—will rise in 2004, as they have in previous years. It is a good investment. Around half the places at the country's best universities go to candidates from these schools, although they make up only around 6% of the school-age population. Canny capitalists will be opening more low-cost schools in 2004, tapping the unmet demand from parents for no-frills schools with good teaching and high standards of behaviour. The competition between efficient private schools and the improved City Academies will be a telling pointer to the future of education in England.

Not that everything is happy in the independent sector. An investigation into the fees of top schools, which appear to have been set by informal collusion, will give the poshest head teachers in the country a big headache in 2004. The government may turn the knife by questioning the schools' charitable status. That may force them to think about charging rich parents more in order to find money for bursaries for the bright but poor.

Such tweaking will have little effect overall, though. Much more damaging will be the government's attempt to crowbar open (in the words of Alan Johnson, minister for higher education) the university admissions process. In theory, that sounds like a blow for justice (as well as against the English language). In fact, it will mean admissions tutors being bullied into turning away good students with the wrong—that is, rich—background and accepting underqualified and undermotivated students.

The biggest losers in this will be the best universities, many of which are already falling behind their international competitors. The great hope for these places in 2004 is that the government sticks to its plans of allowing them to charge higher fees—up to £3,000 for a student per year instead of the current £1,100. But to be really effective, they would like the top fee to be much higher or, best of all, set by the market. The government's opponents inside the Labour Party want a flat rate, helping the weaker universities, but shackling the top ones.

That will accelerate one more trend in 2004: the number of students opting for American universities. Those British parents who can afford it will increasingly choose to pay for excellence and meritocracy there, rather than mediocrity and politicisation at home. □

Philip Lader, chairman of WPP Group and former American ambassador to Britain, sees a risk lurking in the impressive pace of change

Not cricket

"Those from other lands who love this country genuinely fear the loss of Britain's essence"

"It is the business of the future to be dangerous," said Alfred North Whitehead. Car-bombers, plutonium merchants, anthrax production and invisible threats to infrastructure are no longer fantasy. Britain's intelligence capability, military preparedness, role in NATO and the European Union, and seat at the UN Security Council will therefore be instrumental in deflecting a thousand potential grenades intended for western culture.

Given Europe's fragmented defence-industrial base, consolidation is probable; military interoperability, imperative. The Ministry of Defence and the Pentagon will arm-wrestle fiercely over technology transfer. Europe and America may finally have resolved their disputes over bananas and Open Skies, but steel, GMOs and other trade and commercial controversies, absent adroit negotiations, threaten to rattle the government's transatlantic bridge.

Corporate misdeeds and misjudgments, fewer than in recent years, will inevitably surface. But as markets rebound, the City's vast, global financial system will play an even greater role in the national economy. London will, more than ever, belong to the world. Canary Wharf, with a revival of residents and restaurants, will finally get a soul.

British-based companies will build greater stakes "across the pond". CEO compensation will become more Americanised. The "magic circle" will find American law firms taking market share.

In his 80s, Winston Churchill cautioned that, "The empires of the future are the empires of the mind." Yet British universities, even the most venerable, will be further marginalised because intellectual muscle is not an absolute substitute for money.

In 2004 a record number of commercial spin-offs from universities—in materials sciences, nanotechnology, genomics, robotics and other emerging technologies—will be announced. But government-sponsored programmes, including the Cambridge-MIT Institute, will be challenged to prove their worth. With the contraction of government funding and philanthropic endowments, arts and education institutions, as well as NGOs, will press benefactors and alumni, in a most non-British way, for support.

Much of what will characterise 2004 will come not from Members of Parliament and captains of industry, but from the sort of ordinary people I met during my time as ambassador when walking from Land's End to John O'Groats and from coast to coast. The Countryside Movement—which is about much more than hunting—will flourish. "Smart growth" policies will be championed to preserve idyllic hamlets, country churches and farms.

Traditional civility and norms will be tested as never before. Can a Church schism over the ordination of gays and same-sex unions be avoided? Will Alpha and other spiritual movements arrest the spread of secularism? For all the talk about multiculturalism, what, in Bradford and around the country, lies in store for hyphenated-Brits? Tim Henman will again be cheered at Wimbledon, but will the 2004 Olympics prove that Britain, inventor of many of the world's greatest games, now celebrates its chefs more than its athletes? These social changes have had a revolutionary impact on Britain, on a scale not seen since tea was dumped in Boston's harbour.

Losing it?

No prognostications about Britain can neglect, of course, the weather, the monarchy, or Tony Blair.

Nobody who spent the summer of 2003 in England would dispute climate change. There will be "weather" in 2004, it can safely be predicted, plenty of it.

Republicanism may rage Down Under and at some neighbourhood pubs, but the Windsors will not be out of jobs anytime soon. As always, the queen will be exemplary, dutiful and more popular in the United States than in her own realm, since Americans love a monarch so long as she is not their own. The Prince of Wales, barring personal controversy, will get well-deserved credit for his many public-service initiatives, especially the Prince's Trust. To the surprise of many, his grandmother's trademark optimism and common touch will emerge.

A battered, irrepressible Tony Blair will show he learned from the Hutton inquiry into the death of a government scientist who committed suicide while caught in a row between Downing Street and the BBC, and from the embarrassment over the hasty plan to abolish the venerable office of Lord Chancellor. On the international stage, Mr Blair's moral leadership will be no less vigorous. However great their talents, Alastair Campbell and other departed architects of New Labour will be proved not to have been indispensable.

A robust, substantive opposition will gather strength. But its time is not yet in sight. If George Bush is somehow not re-elected in November, "Tony" will have a new best friend the next day.

Those from other lands who love this country genuinely fear the loss of Britain's essence: something far deeper than village cricket, Ascot or fish and chips. With his enthusiasm for modernity, the big picture and the little guy, the prime minister must not risk the demise of the nation's identity.

He might re-read Lewis Carroll's "Through the Looking Glass". Remember Alice wondering why the Red Queen is constantly running, but getting nowhere? Then it becomes apparent: the landscape is moving with her. Committed to change, this prime minister, and Britain itself, must move faster than the events of 2004—but not compromise who they truly are. □

More info: contact@laser.fr

Lucy had a fantastic time
with her Galeries Lafayette card today.

She'll never know it,
but it's largely thanks to LaSer.

Contact centres
Customer and after-sales services

Subscription services

Telemarketing campaigns

Operational consultancy

Cards
Loyalty cards

Credit cards

Banking cards

Co-branded cards

Gift cards

We launched our range of LaSer services based on the idea that your objective of satisfying your customers should also be ours - creating an offer designed, first and foremost, to deliver results. One that is both global and modular, providing support from the initial concept through to operational implementation. So, if you are aiming to serve your customers in Europe, our 5,000 strong team is ready and waiting to deliver your CRM strategy.

www.laser.fr

POS Services
Payment systems

Electronic banking equipment

Interactive kiosks

Connectivity

Loyalty enhancement
Relationship marketing

Loyalty programmes

Customer enhancement solutions

Financial services
Personal loans

In store credit

Mortgages

Car finance

Savings

Non-financial services
Insurance

Subscriptions

Holidays and travel

LaSer
LAFAYETTE SERVICES

Give peace a chance

Peter Mandelson

"**Y**ou can never 'solve' the problem of Northern Ireland," I was told when appointed secretary of state, "but you can manage it well or badly." This remains apposite advice at a time when the peace process is in a fragile condition but strong in its fundamentals. In the coming year I believe it will remain intact, and may even move forward, although the politics will be as fraught as ever.

In a sense, this is to be welcomed. The very fact that party and electoral politics—as opposed to sectarian warfare—exist at all is a major step forward and it marks a return to some sort of normality. For three decades, until 1998 when the Good Friday Agreement was signed, terrorism and civil disorder displaced mainstream politics, with Northern Ireland governed from London and security receiving top priority. Since 1998 the agreement has endured in its essentials and Northern Ireland has become a very different—largely peaceful—place in which to live.

But completing its implementation eludes the parties. Perhaps this is inevitable given the competing goals of Irish nationalism and unionism with Britain—goals which are being peaceably managed through the process inaugurated by the Good Friday Agreement. This does not mean that Northern Ireland will slide backwards to the unremitting violence of the past. It will not.

The challenge by republicans to end British governance in the North will continue but the means of pursuing it, by and large, will be democratic, not military. I say by and large because there are always likely to be splinter republican groups using terrorist means for their ends. The Real IRA is at present the main active splinter organisation, heavily dented by successful prosecutions and the imprisonment of its leadership in the Irish Republic. The reason why a reasonable security presence will be maintained is that, although the bulk of paramilitary violence has ended, there are those, like the Real IRA, who will continue violently to disrupt the peace process.

The fact that violence is continuing on this comparatively limited scale is the reason why the politics of the province remains fraught. The mainstream republican movement is segmented between Sinn Fein, its political wing, and the Provisional IRA, its military wing that has been on ceasefire since the agreement. Both wings say they are wholly committed to the peace process and the statement made in October 2003 confirming this was a significant step forward. Both state that there will not be a resumption of terrorist violence. They also say there will be an end to paramilitary activity of any kind. Yet although actual Provisional IRA terrorism has ended, they still practise a military-style discipline among their own population: shootings, knee-cappings, exiling continue.

Peter Mandelson: MP for Hartlepool and secretary of state for Northern Ireland 1999-2001

The tip of the iceberg

This is an important sticking-point for unionists. Until republicans become a completely normal political force, those unionists who support the agreement will remain ambivalent about sitting down in government with people who retain a private army. This will be the dominant political issue in 2004, with a question-mark over the devolved government in Northern Ireland while this equivocation persists.

The divisive impact of this is strongest on the Ulster Unionists, the largest party, led by David Trimble, the first minister of the devolved administration. The majority of Mr Trimble's party believes the Good Friday Agreement continues to be the way forward for Northern Ireland, but rejectionists in the party wage a constant fight against his position. They claim their objection to sharing power with republicans is founded on the failure to disarm and the continuation of violence. Another interpretation is that they have never reconciled themselves to the peace process for fear that it is a slow, slippery slope to ending the British link altogether.

This fissure among unionists, with the more extreme Democratic Unionist Party (DUP), led by Ian Paisley, picking up further grassroots support, is likely to worsen in 2004. While there is a fierce but broadly healthy electoral contest between Sinn Fein and the more moderate nationalist Social Democratic and Labour Party, the battle among unionists could lead to a realignment among the unionist parties. The so-far successful move by Mr Trimble to expel three leading rejectionists from his party could be the catalyst for this realignment. It is unlikely, though, that his leadership will be in jeopardy. But if he is forced out, the peace process will be considerably damaged. Any replacement is likely to weaken unionist support for the agreement, strengthening Mr Paisley's DUP.

This would bring its own counter-reaction among republicans and nationalists, as a more hardline unionist position would be read as a move against the equality and non-discrimination provisions of the Good Friday Agreement, as well as a rejection of devolution and power-sharing. This would strengthen republican rejectionists and boost the splinter groups such as the Real IRA. In Northern Ireland, extremism breeds extremism.

Against this prospect, the British and Irish governments, supported by the American administration, are working intensely together to sustain the Good Friday Agreement. They have made a Joint Declaration setting out exactly how all the remaining parts will be implemented, including further normalisation of security, handling of on-the-run former terrorists and further measures implementing police reforms in the province.

But these moves require final "acts of completion" by the leaders of the Provisional IRA, keeping to their word that they will never resort to violence, that the war is over and that their weaponry is redundant. Will such progress be made in 2004? It will be patchy—destabilising (but not, I predict, destroying) the peace process. □

GENERATING
A NEW ECONOMY
IN LIVERPOOL

STEVE LAVELLE
UNISYS

MARK POVALL
LIVERPOOL JOHN LENNON AIRPORT

JANE CARWARDINE
RADISSON SAS

Liverpool and Merseyside are on the move. Even before the award of the European Capital of Culture 2008 title to Liverpool there was already £3 billion worth of development in the pipeline for the Liverpool City Region. This includes Grosvenor's £750 million retail-led redevelopment of Liverpool city centre - the largest city centre regeneration project anywhere in Europe, plans for a £10 million cruise liner terminal on Liverpool's spectacular waterfront and Will Alsop's stunning Fourth Grace proposal.

Add to this the projected £2 billion economic impact of Liverpool winning the Capital of Culture award and a job creation rate of seven times the national average and it's easy to see why commentators are predicting a seismic shift in capital growth in Merseyside in the next decade. It's not surprising that companies such as Bosch, IBM, The Bank of New York, 02, Unilever, Jaguar, Atos Origin, Coutts, Unisys, Arvato Services, US Airways and a host of other internationally renowned companies are investing here.

To discover more about the competitive advantages the Liverpool City Region can offer your business
email **investment@merseyside.org.uk** or call our Investment Team on **0151 237 3933**.

LIVERPOOL 2008
EUROPEAN CAPITAL OF CULTURE

the mersey
PARTNERSHIP

www.merseyside.org.uk

makeit merseyside

englandsnorthwest
BE WITH THE BEST

long-term strategy

or short-term goals?

In the long run, short-term success cannot be our interest. Our strategy has always been to secure continuous growth. We do this by focusing on niche markets in the specialty chemicals field, by focusing on innovative pharmaceutical products. And by strengthening our presence in the U.S. – the world's largest pharmaceutical market – for example, with a new genomics research center near Boston. These crucial moves are securing our sustainable success for the future.
ALTANA. An international pharmaceuticals and chemicals group.

think on

Bigger, broader, brasher

Gideon Rachman

Brussels

As it boldly expands from 15 members to 25, the European Union will wrestle with the consequences of its ambitions

The European Union will be pulled in two directions in 2004. The political year will be dominated by a renewed drive for "ever closer union". The countries of the EU will hammer out the details of a new constitution for the Union, and formally admit ten new members on May 1st (the Mediterranean islands of Cyprus and Malta, plus the Czech Republic, Estonia, Hungary, Latvia, Lithuania, Poland, Slovakia and Slovenia). But while new political structures further the goal of European unity, the EU will also be struggling with a range of problems which threaten to divide its members as never before.

The constitution-drafting will highlight tensions over the balance of power between EU countries. Subsequent referendums on the constitution in several EU countries could provoke a political crisis, if one or more of them reject it. The enlargement of the Union will also dramatically increase the gap between the richest and poorest members of the EU, provoking an inevitable struggle over resources. Disputes over the handling of Iraq and the war on terror will ensure continuing tensions between Atlanticists and "Europe firsters" within the EU—with Britain and Poland leading the pro-American camp, and France and Germany pushing for greater European autonomy. Meanwhile, the inability of Germany and France to contain their budget deficits will lead to a full-scale row over the management of Europe's single currency.

The draft of a new constitution agreed upon by a convention led by Valéry Giscard d'Estaing, a former president of France, inevitably left many controversial details to be battled over. The biggest fight is likely to be between small and large countries. The four biggest countries in the Union—Germany, France, Britain and Italy—fear that the EU risks being swamped by small countries. The "bigs" are keen supporters of provisions in the draft constitution that would end the rule that every country has to have a European commissioner. They also want to establish a more permanent presidency of the Union, replacing the current system under which each country takes a turn for six months. And they want to reweight votes in the Council of Ministers and the European Parliament—where EU laws are made—to dilute the current over-representation of small-country interests.

The "smalls" dislike each of these changes. The most recalcitrant bargainers will prove to be Spain and Poland, medium-sized countries which both stand to lose greatly from the reweighting of votes. Over the years the Spanish have developed a reputation as fearsome negotiators, and the Poles are taking after them.

Once a deal is agreed on, a new set of problems will emerge. For the constitution to come into force, it must be ratified by all members of the Union. Several countries have said they will have referendums on the text in 2004. Tricky votes are likely in Ireland and Denmark, both of which have rejected EU treaties in the past. But an unexpected reverse could also come in the Nether- ▶

Gideon Rachman:
Brussels correspondent,
The Economist

lands, which is having a referendum on an EU treaty for the first time in its history. The Dutch have traditionally been among the most ardent builders of Europe, but are showing increasing signs of Euroscepticism.

Enlargement will radically change all EU dealings. Meetings will take longer. There is a danger that the old members will patronise and antagonise the much poorer new ones. That wealth gap will create tensions over finance. The new members will want to ensure that they get their fair share of regional aid and support for farmers, which together make up 80% of the budget. But those countries that currently do well out of the system, such as Spain, will be reluctant to see the money tap redirected. And the net payers into the system—in particular Germany, the Netherlands and Britain—will be wary of making expensive commitments.

But while some of the divisions within the EU will set new members against old, the enlargement of the Union will also create the opportunity for some new alliances. The British will be looking to the central Europeans—and the Poles in particular—to join them in supporting the idea that NATO (which includes the United States) should remain unchallenged as Europe's principal security club. The French, Germans and Belgians will try to push ahead with their idea of a more autonomous European defence. The question of how to handle America will bedevil efforts to forge a common European foreign policy.

The real crunch, however, will come over the management of Europe's single currency. In 2004 the Union will finally have to face up to the fact that the stability and growth pact, the fiscal rules designed to govern the euro, has fallen apart. The original plan was that no country would run a budget deficit of more than 3% of GDP: countries that persistently violated this rule risked being fined billions of euros. But the threat of billion-euro fines was never really credible. France and Germany are calling the rest of the EU's bluff by repeatedly running deficits of over 3%—and ignoring the huffing and puffing from Brussels.

The de facto collapse of the stability pact will be bad news politically. It will upset countries like the Netherlands and Spain, which have made significant efforts to keep within the rules. And it may damage the credibility of other allegedly solemn commitments made by the European Union. It is never good when open law-breaking (and the stability pact has the force of law) is condoned.

But the pact's death throes will be good news—at least in the short term—for Europe's struggling economies. With several countries battling recession, 2004 will not be the time to launch a fiscal austerity drive. If the big economies in the Union have the will to combine a stimulatory fiscal policy with real structural reform, Europe's economies could perk up a little. The death of the stability pact will, however, reopen the questions it was meant to have answered: how to have a single currency with umpteen different national fiscal policies, and what happens to the currency and interest rates of the euro area if individual governments run up their debts to dangerous levels? Important questions both—but ones that will not be answered definitively in 2004. □

Central Europe comes home

Robert Cottrell   *Riga*

Suddenly places like Tallinn, Ljubljana and Bratislava will be Europe's trend-setters

For five of the European Union's newcomers, May will be a doubly historic month. The Baltic three, plus Slovakia and Slovenia, will join NATO at a summit in Turkey. NATO will also welcome Bulgaria and Romania, a consolation prize of sorts for these two countries while they wait another three years or more to join the EU.

NATO entry will command less attention and less enthusiasm than EU entry among the public at large, but teenage males should have special cause to celebrate. Governments will come under pressure to shorten or abolish compulsory military service as they focus their

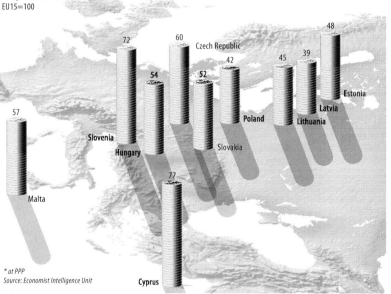

New Europe
GDP per head*, 2004
EU15=100

Slovenia 57

Malta 72

Hungary 54

Czech Republic 60

Slovakia 52

Poland 42

Lithuania 45

Latvia 39

Estonia 48

Cyprus 77

* at PPP
Source: Economist Intelligence Unit

limited resources on training the professional soldiers wanted for NATO operations. Slovakia will cut military service from nine to six months in 2004. The Czech Republic plans complete abolition by 2006.

EU entry will lose much of its shine by the time it comes around. Idealism about reuniting Europe will give way to arguments between national capitals and Brussels about EU regulations and EU budget money. Elections for the European Parliament in June will give voters the chance to issue mid-term rebukes to governments, which seem doomed to unpopularity, whether for trying to reform too much or for failing to reform enough. In their defence, most governments will be able to point to a decent economic performance, if only relative to that of the older Union members next door. The three Baltic countries will be hoping for growth of 6-7% in 2004. The Czech Republic, Hungary, Poland, Slovakia and Slovenia

Robert Cottrell: central Europe correspondent, *The Economist*

look set for growth of 3-5%.

The Baltic countries will surge ahead thanks to their low taxes, high skills and flexible labour laws. The Czech Republic, Hungary and Poland will share the same economic headache in 2004: how to manage budget deficits far exceeding 3% of GDP, the limit for countries joining the euro zone. All three say they want to adopt the EU's common currency, which means they should prepare the way by deficit-cutting. But all have weak centre-left governments whose supporters want high public spending.

Slovakia's precarious centre-right coalition government has the bravest agenda for 2004—if it survives. It wants a 19% flat rate for income and corporate taxes, the simplest tax system in Europe (save perhaps for Estonia's, where reinvested corporate profits are not taxed at all). Slovakia also intends to introduce bold spending reforms, shifting much of its health-care system to private insurance plans.

Big foreign investors are taking note. So are neighbouring countries. Cuts in direct taxes will spread across central Europe in 2004 as governments compete for investment and growth. Older EU countries will feel the pressure: low-tax Estonia sits just 80km (50 miles) across the Baltic Sea from high-tax Finland. More Finnish firms will emigrate to Estonia, on paper at least, and Finnish taxmen will look for ways of chasing them.

Some border controls will remain between central European and other EU countries, probably until 2007. But growing ease of travel will encourage more in western Europe to discover the charms of central Europe. Tallinn, the capital of Estonia, is booming already as a tourist city thanks mainly to Scandinavian visitors. Bratislava, the Prague-like capital of Slovakia, and Ljubljana, the hard-to-spell but lovely capital of Slovenia, deserve to be the vogue cities of 2004. Budget airlines will bring down dramatically the cost of flying from west European hubs to central European cities. Unfortunately, many of the ticket buyers will be gangs of youths on drinking sprees, a depressingly common hazard already in Prague and an emerging one in Tallinn. □

The EU wannabes

Heather Grabbe

Still more countries are queuing up to join the EU

Another four countries are already knocking on the European Union's door, and more will start demanding entry over the next few years. At the front of the queue are Bulgaria and Romania. They have completed the easy stages in their entry talks, and they hope to finish negotiations in 2004. But the EU wants to see them tackle corruption, economic reform and inefficient state bureaucracies before it will consider them ready. Romania and Bulgaria have set themselves a target date of 2007 for joining, but they may have to wait a year or two longer if other wannabes are nearly ready by then. The EU prefers to take in groups of countries, rather than cranking up the accession machinery several years in a row.

Croatia has a good chance of catching up with this group. It lodged its membership application in 2003, and the European Commission will deliver its response—including a recommendation on when Croatia should start negotiations—in the spring of 2004. Croatia's economy and public administration are in decent shape. But the government in Zagreb has other conditions to meet before it can start negotiations, including the handover of one man wanted for alleged involvement in war crimes, General Ante Gotovina, to the International Criminal Tribunal in The Hague.

The Union is pouring cold water on the hopes of some Macedonian and Serbian politicians to submit applications in 2004.

Heather Grabbe: deputy director, Centre for European Reform

They have to achieve greater stability before the Union can think seriously about starting an accession process.

Turkey, which applied back in 1987, is also hoping to inch closer to membership in 2004. The EU will reconsider Turkey's bid in December. If the government can show consistent improvements in respecting human rights, treatment of the minority Kurds and keeping the armed forces out of politics, the Union will probably allow Turkey to start accession talks in 2005. Those talks could last many years, however, because none of the 25 members is keen on Turkey joining rapidly. Turkey frightens many of them because its population is so large (72m and growing) and mainly Muslim.

The Union has officially offered the western Balkan countries and Turkey the prospect of eventual membership—but it has made no such promise to the other countries on its new, expanded borders. Belarus is too authoritarian, Moldova too poor, Ukraine too large (though it has fewer people than Turkey) and Russia too daunting for the Union yet to contemplate whether they could eventually become members. Are all these countries fully European? Most EU politicians would prefer to avoid giving a definitive answer. The Union gains leverage over neighbouring countries if it remains ambiguous about the question of where Europe ends, they argue.

But the EU is beginning to realise that am-

It's a long way to Brussels

biguity can be destructive if the neighbours develop unrealistic expectations. Günter Verheugen, the well-regarded enlargement commissioner, has been asked to draw up a more substantive policy for the wilder parts of Europe. He needs to come up with something more imaginative than the EU's usual recipe of aid and trade concessions. If the EU wants to stop unsuitable countries from trying to win membership, it has to offer a much more attractive runner-up prize. □

Václav Havel, former president of the Czech Republic, looks forward to a larger, livelier European Union

A new impetus for old Europe

"Expansion eastwards amounts to a final break with the vision of a United States of Europe"

The expansion of the European Union reflects the transition to democracy of the countries of central and eastern Europe, and marks the end of a chapter in Europe's history. The idea of a uniting Europe was born in response to the trauma of the second world war. Extending the Union to central and eastern Europe is its logical culmination.

The enlargement of 2004 is also about the very nature of the EU. Technically, it may be mainly about extending the reach of EU law and policies, but the historical and political significance is much greater: it heralds the Union's transformation into an entirely new geopolitical entity. For the new members, entry into the EU is a "return to Europe", of which they had always felt themselves to be a part. For "Europe", this expansion means a challenge to re-unify, since Europe had ceased to exist the moment a boundary was laid down between military blocks, cutting the age-old ties that had grown from common traditions.

"Enlargement" is usually seen primarily in terms of expanding the single European market. Yet this is a secondary aspect, an instrument for achieving the original vision of a single Europe. The essence of enlargement is a broadening of the area of commonly shared values.

The basic contours of European values—shaped by the troubled intellectual and political history of Europe, and adopted, in part, elsewhere in the world—are, I believe, clear: respect for the individual, his freedoms, rights and dignity; the principle of solidarity; the rule of law and equality before the law; protection of minorities; democratic institutions; separation of the powers of the legislature, executive and judiciary; plurality of the political system; inviolability of private ownership; private enterprise and the market economy; and the development of civil society.

All earlier expansions brought about a shift in the EU, but the current one will have a far more fundamental impact, both on the way the Union works and on its policy priorities. Expansion eastwards amounts to a final break with the founding fathers' vision of a homogeneous "United States of Europe". Few politicians in the new member-states have any direct experience of the second world war; however, they do have first-hand experience of the transition from totalitarianism to democracy. This may make them much less encumbered by the post-war historical heritage and traditional tensions between individual countries, though it does leave them impoverished for not having been involved in formulating and implementing the initial visions of the unification of Europe.

All this results in a new and more pragmatic view on numerous issues, from the broad conception of the Union to specific matters up for debate, and often irrespective of political affiliation. The new member-states may enrich the EU through their experiences of 1989 and the subsequent transformations. This may give the Union a new impetus and restore a sense of its original purpose, which is gradually vanishing under the weight of bureaucratic regulations.

National sovereignty will be one of the cardinal subjects to be debated at the national and European level. It is a highly sensitive topic in the new member-states, since the idea of freedom and independence, after decades of dominance by Moscow, was the driving force behind resistance to the communist regime. Accordingly, the concept of national sovereignty in these countries is something inviolable, and at the same time easily abused in nationalistically motivated distaste for European integration. We may therefore expect a growing emphasis on the inter-governmental approach at the expense of supranationalism. The new members will also be wary of the formation of any avant-garde groupings that might result in second-class membership for the rest.

Enlargement will bring a new dynamism to the EU's ingrained mechanisms. We may expect the formation of ad hoc coalitions on specific issues, based on national interests, traditions, culture and history. The new members will probably find common cause on matters of finance, for instance regarding expenditure on the common agricultural policy and structural funds. On other issues, there may be a variety of coalitions involving both new and old member-states. This will bring new life to EU politics.

Redefining Europe

The countries of central and eastern Europe will bring greater concerns and fears about Russia and the western Balkans. Although Russia, now closer to the Union's frontiers, will move up the EU's agenda, it can expect less conciliation and more criticism. The new member-states will be particularly sensitive to any hint of the existence of a Russian sphere of influence. If countries adjacent to the expanded EU see no prospect of joining (or at least of enhanced relations), the Union will find its neighbours growing less co-operative.

Expansion to include the countries of central and eastern Europe completes the original vision of European unification, while at the same time pushing that idea further. Turkey will become the issue of the moment, and with the integration of Turkey, thanks to its religious, cultural and historical distinctiveness, yet another chapter will begin. This will bring many new questions. Where are the frontiers of Europe, and just who might become an EU member? Is the Union defined by shared values, or is future membership determined by geography? What forms of partnership should be offered to Russia (and others that will not be members in the foreseeable future)? Only from the answers to these and other questions can the Union derive a new philosophy and structure. □

Hungarian Economic Review

An information service on business, investment and tourism from leading organisations in Hungary

Incentive tourism

Golden age II

As a multi-ethnic kingdom spanning the Carpathian basin for over 1,000 years, Hungary has long served as a meeting point for traders, craftsmen and scientists from the Balkans in the southeast to the Slavic highlands in the north and the Germanic territory to the west. This led to the development of Budapest as Austro-Hungary's commercial centre in the late 19th century opposite Vienna's primarily political role.

Indeed, Budapest's majestic Petőfi Hall, built in 1885, hosted trade shows for the electronic machinery, building material, textile, paper product, automobile, confectionary, advertising, and other industries during Budapest's "golden age" prior to the second world war, in which the hall was irreparably damaged. Later, the country's status as the most liberal barrack in the Soviet camp made it a desirable destination for cold war-era boondoggles. After Hungary's reversion to democracy in 1989, this heritage, combined with its central geographic positioning in Europe, natural beauty and cultural wealth put it back on the map of conference and business event (or incentive) tourism destinations.

"Hungary is a natural incentive destination," says Gábor Galla, boss of the Hungarian National Tourist Office. "We offer a variety of programmes incorporating historic Budapest, one of the most beautiful cities in Europe, as well as authentic Hungarian culture, arts, and gastronomy plus countryside attractions such as castles and spa resorts, all at a reasonable cost," he adds, citing General Electric, ExxonMobil, Merck and Avon as firms that regularly hold incentive events here.

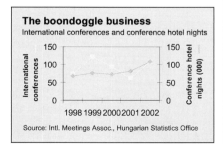

The boondoggle business
International conferences and conference hotel nights

Source: Intl. Meetings Assoc., Hungarian Statistics Office

After several years of growth, in 2002 Budapest and Hungary ranked 6th and 19th worldwide, respectively, in number of international conferences hosted, according to the Amsterdam-based International Meetings Association. Such success contributed to the continued narrowing of the gap between Hungary's ranking in international tourism arrivals (13th) and receipts (32nd) in 2002, according the World Tourism Organisation (WTO). And Hungary's 3.5% increase in international arrivals in 2002 over the prior year outpaced trends in the industry, which grew 3.1% globally and 2.4% in Europe, according to the

WTO. While the forint has appreciated by about 17% against the euro since its liberalisation in 2001, hospitality providers have cut prices, leaving the effective cost level relatively unchanged and 25–30% below that of Germany.

In recognition of Budapest's achievement and potential, the city was selected to host this year's European Society of Incentive & Travel Executives Networking and Educational Programme Conference, which showcases emerging destinations.

Mr Galla notes that the sector's growth has been enabled by a development and renovation boom that has added hundreds of hotel and conference rooms annually since 1990. Budapest alone boasts 12 five- and about 30 four-star hotels, including the likes of Marriott, Inter-Continental, Sofitel, Hilton, Kempinski, Le Meridien, and Corinthia. The landmark secessionist Gresham Palace on the Danube river and neo-baroque New York Palace in central Pest are currently being developed by hoteliers Four Seasons and Boscolo, respectively.

As of June 2003, the country's 1,421 conference rooms in commercial establishments had a capacity of 94,563 delegates, with a five-, four- and three-star breakdown of 10%, 20% and 35%, respectively. Uniquely, 9% of conference rooms are in spa hotels, where guests can enjoy a therapeutic and invigorating soak.

While the Budapest Congress Center, the country's largest, has a one-room seating capacity of 1,755 and 15 others have capacities of 400–800, international conferences held in Hungary tend to be small- to mid-size: 70% of those held in 2002 had up to 250 delegates and 85% up to 500 delegates. "But a 6,500-capacity centre is slated to open as early as 2005," says Mr Galla.

Incentive activities in and around Budapest utilise the city's unique features, including its UNESCO-protected waterfront overlooking the Danube, on which boat excursions offer spectacular views of the Royal Palace, the neo-gothic Parliament and the historic Chain Bridge linking Buda with Pest. Upriver lies well-preserved Visegrád, whose medieval fortress serves as a venue for mock battles between knights as well as renaissance concerts and period gastronomic specialties.

Under siege by incentive tourists

Sample incentive activities in Buda include folk or jazz concerts and wine tasting in the labyrinth of cellars beneath the Royal Palace; a torchlight march of Hungarian *huszár* cavalry-

men in the Palace's lookout followed by a gala dinner inside; or an exclusive reception in a 16th century Turkish bath. Activities in Pest include an open-air ride on elegant Andrássy Boulevard to City Park, where gala dinners are held in a replica of Transylvania's Vajdahunyad fortress, or to an exclusive night at the opera.

Guests enjoy operatic highlights

Recently, development has accelerated in the countryside, which has a handful of five- and about 30 four-star hotels, many of them spas. During the past few years the state subsidised the development or refurbishment of 61 spas, 12 spa hotels, 18 castles, 6 conference centres, 33 equestrian areas and 19 eco-tourism facilities. "While Budapest accounts for about 70% of incentive tourism flows, such investment will allow better utilization of the countryside, particularly for smaller conferences in intimate settings," says Mr Galla.

Sample countryside incentive activities include camping on the Hungarian plains in *yurta*, the type of tent used by original *Magyar* settlers over 1,000 years ago; a trip "100 years back in time" to the agrarian *puszta* (plain), complete with steam engine, horse-drawn carriages, horsemanship and the gastronomy of a country wedding. Gödöllő, 30 kilometres east of Budapest, boasts a royal castle used to stage dinners with period fashion shows, music and cabaret. The more adventurous can choose climbing in the Pilis mountains just north of Budapest.

Mr Galla is bullish on the impact of Hungary's EU accession in May 2004: "This will improve the awareness and image of Hungary, increase the level of trust and confidence in the country and ease border crossings." EU accession, combined with the country's natural advantages and significant tourism investment, including in the planned major conference centre to be opened 120 years after its ill-fated forerunner, will position Hungary for a second – hopefully sustainable – golden age.

HUNGARIAN NATIONAL TOURIST OFFICE
HUNGARIAN CONVENTION BUREAU
H-1012 Budapest, Vérmező út 4.
T/F 361 488 8640 / 488 8641
hcb@hungarytourism.hu, www.hcb.hu

The German question

Haig Simonian   *Berlin*

Can the country reform fast enough?

Gerhard Schröder's government will belatedly try to make up for the time it wasted in the rudderless beginnings of its second term. Legislators will be overwhelmed by welfare and labour-market measures stemming from the chancellor's "Agenda 2010" reform package, announced in 2003. The scope is impressive. According to Mr Schröder, the "biggest package of changes in German history" will bring Europe's largest economy out of the doldrums, keep welfare spending under control and address the long-term challenges of an ageing population and sharply declining birth rate.

The agenda includes bold steps to tackle unemployment (likely to flirt with 5m) and reduce crippling welfare costs by curbing benefits. Other measures aim to boost small business, slash bureaucracy and reform archaic craft industries. Local authorities are due for a shot in the arm with a thorough reform of state and communal funding. To cap it all, personal tax cuts worth more than €15 billion ($17.5 billion), due in 2005, should be brought forward by a year to build consumer confidence and boost the ailing economy.

Agreement between government and opposition on health-care reform has shown that action is

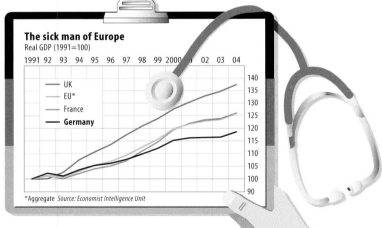

The sick man of Europe
Real GDP (1991=100)

1991 92 93 94 95 96 97 98 99 2000 01 02 03 04

— UK
— EU*
— France
— **Germany**

140 135 130 125 120 115 110 105 100 90

*Aggregate *Source: Economist Intelligence Unit*

possible, even under Germany's sclerotic political system. The cross-party health deal falls short of what is required to tackle spiralling spending. But, in a system where compulsory health-insurance contributions are split evenly between workers and employers, the measures represent a first step towards lowering crippling non-wage labour costs, one of Germany's biggest competitive handicaps.

Resistance to reform may also be blunted by uncertainties in the trade-union movement. Bitter recriminations in the mighty IG Metall engineering union, following the collapse of a pointless strike in eastern Germany in mid-2003, have weakened one of the government's staunchest critics. This may dampen hostility to reform among the trade-union cohorts in Mr Schröder's parliamentary Social Democratic Party.

2004
The rebuilding of the 16th-century bridge in Mostar, which was destroyed during the Bosnia-Hercegovina war, will be completed by the end of the year.

Still, progress will be patchy. Ironically, the long-awaited economic upswing, now likely in 2004, may sap the limited reform momentum built up in the past two years of underperformance. With a wafer-thin majority, the Social Democrats and the Greens, the junior coalition partner, cannot afford internal dissent. A revolt by independent-minded Social Democratic leftwingers, though unlikely, cannot be ruled out.

The opposition is even less predictable. Still licking their wounds after their election defeat in 2002, the Christian Democratic Union and its Bavarian sister party have yet to devise a coherent strategy. Part of their problem is the lack—or rather, excess—of leadership, with tussles between Angela Merkel, the Christian Democrats' titular chairman, Edmund Stoiber, the Bavarian leader and failed challenger for the chancellorship, and Roland Koch, a young regional baron. Yet coherence is what will be required when the reforms go before the opposition-controlled Bundesrat, the upper house of parliament, which can slow down, or even stop, many measures.

Mr Schröder will try the tactics of bullying, enticing and cajoling, familiar from his first term, to ease his legislation through. Along the way he will ditch measures liberally and even make the occasional U-turn. Such skills will be tested most severely in budgetary policy. The deterioration in public finances will prompt a further loss of credibility for Hans Eichel, the once stellar but now hapless finance minister. Confirmation that the economy was stagnant in 2003 will expose yet another set of over-optimistic ministerial forecasts and lead to further big funding gaps as tax revenues again fall short.

The tax cuts will only aggravate the problem in 2004. The government has fudged the scale of the challenge by promising to axe entrenched subsidies, including holy cows such as relief for property purchases and commuting. Experience, however, has shown that such unpopular measures seldom survive their parliamentary mauling, pointing to sharply rising debt as the most likely recourse to fund lower taxes.

That will put Germany on a collision course with the European Commission in Brussels. The 2004 budget deficit will break the rules of the EU's stability and growth pact for a third successive year. Germany's tacit willingness to join forces with partners, like France, eager to dilute the pact once and for all will become increasingly public. But it could also lead to fireworks with more financially disciplined EU member states prepared to demand formal penalties for serial infringers.

Even if Mr Schröder succeeds in pushing through the bulk of his reforms, and passes a half-decent budget, more challenges lie ahead. Further action on pensions is being taken to relieve pressure on the state system and loosen the shackles on the supplementary private schemes introduced in a half-hearted reform in the government's first term. Suggestions by a government commission to raise the pensionable age and limit the rate of increase of payments to pensioners are, however, being put aside. And deeper health reform threatens to be explosive. Further down the road lie talks on constitutional reform to rebalance the relationship between the federal government and the 16 states, and to eliminate, or at least reduce, the sort of legislative logjams inevitable in 2004. □

Haig Simonian:
Germany correspondent
for the *Financial Times*
between March 1999 and
September 2003

L'Espace Affaires - Business class. Treat yourself to a few hours of well-being.
Refined on board service, modular seat, high-tech audio-
visual equipment, exquisite dining. **www.airfrance.com**

France's creeping Americanisation

Sophie Pedder *Paris*

A growing gap between rhetoric and consumer habits

Sophie Pedder:
France correspondent,
The Economist

French voters will have their first chance to judge their president and his government since they were elected in 2002. Polls for the country's 26 regions are due in March, followed by elections to the European Parliament in June. Expect a vote of censure.

Voters are uneasy. Many opted for President Jacques Chirac only to keep out the far-right National Front. Dis-affection with the French political class lingers, despite an effort by Jean-Pierre Raffarin, the prime minister, to cultivate his image as a man of the people presiding over a government of action. The Socialist Party remains stunned by its defeat in 2002, faction-riven and lack-lustre. Extra-parliamentary movements, especially of a leftist anti-globalisation flavour, are thriving. Where will the protest vote go? Mostly towards high abstention and support for the fringes, particularly the right. Jean-Marie Le Pen's National Front could even win the regional presidency in Provence-Alpes-Côte d'Azur.

Such results will not alter the balance of power at the centre. But the elections will slow Mr Raffarin's reforms during the first half of 2004, after the surprisingly robust progress with pension reform (pushed through in 2003 despite strikes and street protests). In theory, reform of the health-insurance system will follow in 2004. France needs to curb ever-rising health costs. But resistance from doctors, chemists and drug companies, not to mention ordinary pill-popping Frenchmen, will be fierce. Many will take to the streets. So will disgruntled teachers, who will resist separate plans to reform the school system. For fear of chasing voters into the arms of the opposition, radical proposals will wait until after the elections.

Progress on reducing the yawning budget deficit

A la recherche de l'entente perdue

Steve King

Hands across the Channel

A "friendly understanding" between na-tions sounds all right, but an *entente cordiale* sounds so much better. A proper gentlemen's agreement. Something to be savoured by pot-bellied senior states-men over brandy and cigars. But it is of course nothing of the sort. Rather, it is an uneasy compromise reached after painful negotiation by people who would otherwise be at each other's throats. Politically useful, even necessary, but achieved and maintained only with much weeping and rending of garments. These will be matters for Tony Blair and Jacques Chirac—who have come to occupy opposite positions in a divided Europe—glumly to reflect upon as their respective nations celebrate the 100th anni-versary of their historic *entente* in 2004.

Negotiations between Edward VII and Emile-François Loubet, the French presi-dent, began in 1903. Nine months later, on April 8th 1904, an agreement was signed. It covered, in pernickety detail, all of the strategic sticking points, mostly colonial. Britain promised to leave Morocco to the French, for instance, and the French con-ceded Egypt to Britain (though "the post of Director-General of Antiquities in Egypt shall continue, as in the past, to be entrusted to a French *savant*").

The deal was brokered partly in response to events in the recent past: in 1898 the two imperial powers had nearly gone to war over who would control the village of Fashoda, in Sudan. But the underlying tensions were much older and deeper than that, stretching back at least as far as the outbreak of the Hundred Years War in 1337.

The *entente* supposedly marked the end of Anglo-French antagonism and Brit-ain's "spendid isolation" from continental affairs. And to some extent it did. But a century on, things appear to have come full circle. The biggest difference between 1904 and 2004 may be the scenery: Anglo-French antagonisms are no longer played out in a disputed Afri-can swamp, with the soldiers of General Kitchener and Captain Marchand rattling their sabres at one another, but in Brussels meeting rooms. Yet a workable compromise between French and British views on the future of Europe is as badly needed today as it was back then.

The main cause of the divide is simple, and it left Europe split down the middle over Iraq. Mr Chirac wants Europe to become an alterna-tive centre of power to America, whereas Mr Blair thinks that Europe's interests are best served by a close partnership with America. George Bush, meanwhile, can sit back and muse on the aptness of that old dictum,

"Love the hat, Jacques"; "Nice trident, Tony"

divide and rule.

Time, then, for Messrs Blair and Chirac—and their foreign ministers, Jack Straw and Dominique de Villepin—to crack open the Courvoisier, fire up the Montecris-tos and start hammering out a new *entente cordiale*. A united Europe needs it. □

Steve King: deputy editor, *The World in 2004*

IRELAND

The years get tougher and tougher for Bertie Ahern, Ireland's *taoiseach* (prime minister). If 2003 was his most trying year since he came to office in 1997, life will get worse in 2004. Ireland's turn to run the EU (for six months from January) will provide welcome escape for the increasingly beleaguered leader. With rising joblessness, troublesome unions and tighter budgets at home, going abroad to finalise a new European constitution with 24 other countries—the main goal of the Irish presidency, if the Italians have not already done the job—will be plain sailing by comparison.

At Europe's helm, the Irish will also want to do their bit to warm up relations between the EU and the United States. Having grown rich by exploiting the country's position at the centre of the transatlantic economy (Ireland is now the biggest per capita exporter in the world), the Irish worry about the strains over Iraq. They know that they stand to suffer more than most if the divisions deepen. They will do all they can to ensure that the warm glow of Irish hospitality is felt by all, including President George Bush, when they host an EU-United States summit in May.

But even if Mr Ahern manages some statesmanlike moments, this will help little with hard-to-impress Irish voters, who go to the polls for mid-term elections in June. His catch-all centrist party, Fianna Fail, which dominates the governing coalition, remains unforgiven for fibbing about the public finances to win re-election in 2002. Electoral losses will cause murmurings of leadership change to get louder. Defenestration, a not infrequent occurrence in Irish party politics, cannot be ruled out. If Mr Ahern is pushed, Brian Cowen, his combative foreign minister and party favourite, might just have promotion forced upon him.

KEY INDICATORS	2002	2003	2004
GDP growth (%)	6.9	3.0	3.7
Budget balance (% GDP)	-0.3	-1.5	-2.3
Unemployment (%)	4.4	5.0	5.4
Current account (% GDP)	-0.7	-1.0	-1.3

Economist Intelligence Unit

will also have to wait. Plugging the gap will be hard. The economy will grow by only around 1.7%. And the government will neither propose spending cuts ahead of elections nor slow down its programme of income-tax cuts, one of Mr Chirac's election pledges.

The second half of the year, however, could be more promising. Words such as "free market" remain taboo, but that will not preclude a cluster of measures to liberalise the economy and trim the role of the state. There will be reduced charges for companies to hire employees and an easing of the rules governing the 35-hour working week. After Air France, plans will go ahead to sell slices of France Telecom, Gaz de France and even Electricité de France. Much of the energy market will be opened to competition. Banks and insurance companies will start to sell new private retirement policies, under a government scheme to encourage personal-pension savings. Another income-tax cut is likely in the September budget.

The implementation of such measures will be eased by growing pro-reform sentiment among those exasperated by public-sector strikes. The perilous condition of the public finances could also help the government to convince voters that there is no alternative to reform. French politicians consider this sort of explanation for change to be more palatable than any suggestion that France could benefit by adopting elements of "Anglo-Saxon" capitalism. They know the force of anti-globalisation and its stablemate, anti-Americanisation, in France.

Oh-la-la-land!

The truth is that France is already highly globalised and Americanised, and will become more so in 2004. Fully 44% of the shareholdings in companies in the CAC 40, the Paris stockmarket, are already held by foreign investors, notably American funds. The public-sector unions make all the noise, but in private companies strikes are rare; as a share of the workforce, union membership in France is actually lower than in America, and will continue to drop. Outside Paris and the picture-postcard towns that tourists glimpse, the country is spread with vast American-style hypermarkets, encircled by car parks and decorated by garish billboards.

Politicians will keep grumbling about Americanisation in 2004. But ordinary Frenchmen will consume its popular culture with zeal: they will flock to the big screen for the latest Hollywood blockbuster, shop at Toys "R" Us or Gap, wear Nike trainers and munch hamburgers at McDonald's (*chez McDo*). McDonald's may be shutting restaurants elsewhere; in France it continues to expand.

Even family life is becoming more individualistic, in ways that the French find uncomfortably American. Obesity is on the rise, especially among children, thanks to the popularity of fast food. Family ties are fraying, as shown by the shocking number of deaths of elderly people, many left alone by their families over the holidays, during the 2003 heatwave. Multiculturalism is stalking the country: passionate debate will rage about secularism in France, touching explosive issues such as the right of Muslim girls to wear the veil at school.

France will continue vigorously to resist Americanisation in foreign policy. There will be some effort at a rapprochement with America after the falling-out over Iraq. But France is comfortable with its multilateralist doctrine. It will strive to consolidate the French-German axis, in order to support French influence in an enlarged EU and fortify Europe as a check on American "hyperpower". In short, in 2004 the gap will widen between the pro-American consumption habits of ordinary Frenchmen and the anti-American rhetoric of their leaders. □

> **2004**
> France's first restaurant university—a "Harvard for the art of French cooking"—will open in Rheims in October.

American in Paris

Why Italy will matter

Beppe Severgnini   *Milan*

More to do with tortelloni than Berlusconi

Italy's easiest task in 2004 is winning the European football championship. Imagine the rest. The year is going to be a tough one for several reasons. Some come from within: the slow economy, the ageing population and infrastructure, and the prime minister's unresolved conflicts of interest, especially in the media, which turns political debate into a perpetual fight. But difficulties will also come from the outside world.

First, there is Europe. The European elections in June will be a testing time for the government. As usual, no one will talk about Europe, which in Italy is basically an act of faith. The vote will be yet another referendum on the prime minister, Silvio Berlusconi.

A second external factor will influence Italy's standing in the world: the American presidential election. Mr Berlusconi has made his personal relationship with George Bush the pivot of his foreign policy. A Democrat in the White House would probably force Mr Berlusconi to move towards German and French positions, which are shared by the opposition, by the country's president, Carlo Azeglio Ciampi, and by most Italians who care about these matters.

With pension reform at last on the starting blocks, and immigration somehow stabilised (unless the influx of asylum-seekers suddenly swells), social worries in 2004 may change from previous years. A big concern will be the future of Italian cities, which have been left to fend for themselves for decades. Forty-two have a population over 100,000; three out of four Italians live in the *periferia* (city outskirts); one in four lives in a *condominio* (apartment block) built in the 1960s. Some of these dwellings are ageing badly, especially in the south. Many were built illegally and have been saved from demolition by an unwise "amnesty" declared in 2003 by the government. This worsening environment will create social tensions, a rise in juvenile crime and more alcohol and drug consumption—scourges that Italy has been largely spared, compared with some north European countries.

Other signs that Italy's society is changing fast? Think of this: 10.4m Italians, or 18% of the population, are over 60. Life expectancy is among the highest in the world (76.7 years for men, 82.9 years for women); next year Italy will have 110,000 new octogenar-

Beppe Severgnini: columnist for *Corriere della Sera* and author of "Italiani si diventa" (Rizzoli) and "Ciao, America!" (Doubleday/ Broadway Books)

2004

Genoa in Italy and the French city of Lille will share the title of European Capital of Culture.

ians. To push up the low fertility rate the government will give families a cheque for €1,000 ($1,160) on the birth of their second child.

Will it work? It is far from certain, as young couples are lured—by sex-obsessed advertising and by role-models touted by the prime minister's own television stations—towards a 21st-century *dolce vita* that leaves little space for families. Children cost money, and money will be a problem for many. The old, all-inclusive Italian middle class is about to split. Families with an average income will find it difficult to maintain their parents' standard of living, unless they can rely on traditional shock-absorbers (friends and relatives, neighbours and odd jobs, plus a comeback of old-fashioned barter).

After growing by a paltry 0.4% in both 2002 and 2003, Italy's economy will at least pick up speed in 2004, with growth of about 1.5%. One piece of good news for consumers: prices will stabilise, partly because the tax police will keep an eye on unjustified increases. Behind the smokescreen provided by the new currency, the euro, Italian prices shot up well above the official 2.9% inflation for 2003.

A word on Italy's soft power—the reason why the country will matter in the world in 2004, no matter what its politicians and financial strategists do. Tuscany will still sell its unique colours for many pounds and even more dollars. Italian cuisine, having seen off the French challenge, has become the world's benchmark and will stay so. Fashion will go through another tough year—which implies the demise of a couple of big names, but the blossoming of new talent. Fiat, at long last, will churn out attractive small cars (the new Panda, the Lancia Ypsilon), while Maseratis and Alfa Romeos will be seen again in the world's driveways: look out for the beautiful, redesigned Alfa 166. In numerical terms, exports may not increase dramatically, but the government seems determined that "Made in Italy" identifies goods produced entirely in the country (€35m has been earmarked for this).

Will the best Italian brains—now scattered across the world, and concentrated in the United States—start to trickle home? The government proposed to tax only 10% of their Italian incomes, but that may not lure them back. The reason why many leave their universities and labs is not only money. It is also lack of resources for their research, useless paperwork, nepotism, cronyism and unfair competition. Will that begin to change? If it does, 2004 will signal the dawn of a second Renaissance. But doubts are legitimate. Masochism is part of the national character—as is the happier ability to bounce back. □

Soft power in action

New reign in Spain

Guillermo de la Dehesa   *Madrid*

Ready for a subtler balance in politics and the economy

Since 1982 Spain has had only two prime ministers (compared with Italy's 12). Thirteen years of centre-left rule under Felipe Gonzalez were followed by eight centre-right years under José María Aznar. But from March 2004, when a general election is expected, there will be a new man at the helm. Admirably, Mr Aznar has kept his promise not to stand for a third term.

His annointed successor as the People's Party candidate, Mariano Rajoy, will help his chances of winning the election by making a similar term-limit pledge. A solid economic performance will also play to Mr Rajoy's advantage. Spain's GDP has been growing much faster than the euro area as a whole, and it will continue to outpace its partners in 2004. Moreover, with a budget deficit close to zero in the past four years, Spain (unlike France, Germany and Portugal) has complied with the rules of the euro area's stability and growth pact. Unemployment is down to 11%—still too high, but for the first time respectably close to the euro-area average.

Mr Rajoy, whose jobs under Mr Aznar included education and interior minister, is a subtle, affable and pragmatic politician with (until now) few enemies. He promises to continue Mr Aznar's policies. But he represents a distinct change from the more reserved and prickly Mr Aznar, who combined efficiency with an increasingly authoritarian streak. No doubt thanks to this strength of character, Mr Aznar managed not only to unite the Spanish right and attract centrist voters, but also to turn his party into a well-oiled machine responsive to his personal command. Will Mr Rajoy be able to keep that unity after Mr Aznar leaves?

The Socialist Party used to have the same kind of motivation, efficiency and electoral appeal under Mr Gonzalez. Now it seems to lack unity and focus. But José

Guillermo de la Dehesa: chairman of the Centre for Economic Policy Research

Ahoy, Rajoy!

Luis Rodríguez Zapatero, its new leader, is attractive and articulate. If he finally manages to mobilise his forces effectively, he could make it hard for Mr Rajoy to win, or at least to achieve again an outright majority. Without a clear majority, the People's Party might struggle to build the necessary coalition with regional parties, which have been upset by the limited room for manoeuvre Mr Aznar has allowed them. So although Mr Rajoy is the clear favourite, Mr Zapatero still has a chance of thwarting him with the support of regional parties.

The new prime minister cannot afford to be complacent about the economy. Its apparent soundness hides significant weaknesses. First, the composition of growth is worrying. Domestic demand is growing at almost one percentage point above GDP. The European Central Bank's monetary policy—set for the sluggish euro area as a whole—is too expansive for Spain. More than half of the growth differential between Spain and the euro area is due to a construction boom, with large investments in infrastructure by the public sector and increasing demand for housing by the private sector. Some 40% of the Spanish capital stock is invested in property.

Second, the present model of growth, based mainly on adding labour rather than on improving productivity, is also a matter of concern. Although Spain has led the way among large European countries in terms of employment creation since 1995, its productivity growth has been close to zero.

The combination of rising domestic demand and low productivity growth is not sustainable. Inflation has been growing by one percentage point above the euro-area average for some years and this, coupled with the failure to improve productivity, has led to a loss of competitiveness. To satisfy domestic demand, imports have been rising, as has the current-account deficit, which could be close to 3% of GDP in 2004. The days when Spain could look to Brussels for help are running out: because of EU enlargement, by 2007 Spain could become a net contributor to the EU instead of being a net receiver of around €5 billion ($5.8 billion) a year. Perhaps the wily Mr Aznar picked a good moment to quit. □

THE NORDIC COUNTRIES

The four Nordic countries—Denmark, Norway, Finland and Sweden—have much in common, from long traditions of consensus politics to redistributive policies and generous foreign-aid schemes. Thus in 2004 the four will be among the world elite of the "G 0.7" countries: the group of countries which fulfil the UN target of spending 0.7% of GDP on foreign aid. But many subjects divide the Nordics and in 2004 the differences between them will come to the fore.

The Finns, in an attempt further to reduce their dependence on Russian and Swedish energy supplies, will debate where to build a new nuclear-power station. They are alone among the Nordics (and in western Europe) in building new nuclear capacity at a time when environmental concerns top the political agenda in the

four countries. Swedish companies will nonetheless favour Finnish firms as business partners; in 2004 M&A activity between the two countries will be busy, especially in finance and wood products, despite the Swedish rejection of the euro in 2003.

Long the poor relations among the Nordics, the Norwegians are now ahead of the pack thanks to their oil riches. They will overtake both Sweden and Finland in the use of broadband technology. MMS (multimedia messaging services) will compete with the humble SMS, with more than 1m Norwegian MMSs being sent a month—in a population of 4.5m.

The Danes, arguably the most continental of the four, will edge away from their Nordic brethren. In a most un-Nordic fashion, excise duty on alcohol will be reduced,

and the speed limit on motorways will be raised (from 110kph to 130kph) to accommodate commuters. The government's tight immigration policy will start to bite: Sweden will receive up to 50 residence applications a month from neighbouring Danes who wish to live with their non-European partners.

GDP GROWTH (%)	2002	2003	2004
Denmark	2.1	1.2	2.1
Norway	2.2	1.1	2.1
Sweden	-0.5	2.3	2.3
Finland	1.0	1.0	2.5
Iceland	1.9	1.3	2.5

Economist Intelligence Unit

All to play for in Portugal

Dan O'Brien

Hopes of glory on the field, fears of marginalisation off it

Dan O'Brien:
Economist Intelligence Unit

For three and a half weeks from June 12th, eyes in Europe, and beyond, will look to Portugal. Euro 2004, a 16-nation soccer tournament, will be the country's first time hosting a major international sporting event. Despite the cost of six new stadiums, disruption in cities and the threat of loutish behaviour by fans, running the year's biggest show after the Olympics will give 10m Portuguese something to be proud of. All the more so if, come the tournament's end on July 4th, their ageing "golden generation" of stars—the likes of Luis Figo and Rui Costa—become champions of Europe.

But some in Europe's westernmost nation fear that, once the floodlights are turned off, their country will be forgotten. The reason: the eastward enlargement of the European Union.

Historically minded Portuguese know that half a millennium ago Europe's centre of gravity moved from the Mediterranean south to the Atlantic west when treasure and trade routes to the new world were opened up. Their country grew powerful and rich as a result. But now, having been peripheral ever since that centre moved northwards, they fear an eastward shift will cause their country to drop off the continental shelf, at least as far as foreign investors and the subsidy-dispensing EU are concerned.

Those who want to register disgruntlement with the Union will have an opportunity to do so the day after the football begins. If the prime minister, José Manuel Durão Barroso, is as good as his word, voters will have their say on the EU's new constitution in a referendum on June 13th. Despite some grumbles, they will vote solidly in favour. Being enthusiastic European integrationists has never stopped the pragmatic Portuguese from being stalwart Atlanticists, as Portugal showed in 2003 when it backed the American-led ousting of Saddam Hussein.

On April 25th the Portuguese will mark the 30th anniversary of the ending of their own dictatorship. They will not linger over celebrations. Most attention in 2004 will be on the centre-right government's efforts to revive the recession-mired economy. After two years of stagna-

Euro 2004 has cost an arm and a leg

tion, a return to modest growth should take place. But there will not be much cheer, for two reasons.

First, the government's finances are in a mess: a third year of spending cuts looms, not least to prevent another breach of the euro area's stability and growth pact. Second, further structural reforms are in store—beneficial in the long run, but unsettling at first. Thickets of labour regulations will be trimmed. The civil service and public health care will face further shake-ups. Social welfare and state pensions will be cut. Privatisation will move up the agenda. TAP, the national airline, will go back on the block after a first attempt to offload it failed in 2001. Gas and electricity infrastructure is also pencilled in for sale.

The unions will resist. They will warn of ownership falling into Spanish hands. But such fears will be brushed aside by the prime minister, a zealous reformer who rarely stops preaching to his compatriots about the need to embrace change. □

2004

A French television news channel with a focus on world affairs—a French-style CNN—is due to be launched in the second half of the year.

BENELUX

FORECAST

Virtue will start to wear thin. In sharp contrast to many other euro-area members, Belgium and the Netherlands have in recent years been able to abide by the aim of the stability and growth pact, with budgets in balance or surplus. Now the effects of weaker growth are eroding this achievement. Although they are not, like France and Germany, in danger yet of breaching the 3%-of-GDP limit, the slide into deficit is a new worry—and a reason for belt-tightening. Even Luxembourg, which for years had more money than it could spend and no debt to service, is moving into the red.

The Netherlands will hold the presidency of the European Union in the second half of 2004 and all three Benelux countries will aim to continue their tradition,

dating back half a century, of driving forward European integration. All three governments will fully support the adoption of a new EU constitution. But Europe will feel different, as what started out as a six-country club (with the Benelux three accounting for half the membership) expands to 25 members. A surprising degree of Dutch disaffection may surface in a referendum on the new EU treaty, likely to be held at the same time as elections for the European Parliament on June 10th.

To their embarrassment as fervent Europeans, the Belgians and the Dutch find themselves on opposing sides of the EU's schism over policy on Iraq, where the Dutch have provided 1,100 troops. In 2004 the two countries will try to play down their differences, since

both want to narrow divisions within the EU and NATO. Belgium has made concessions on its human-rights law to improve relations with America and ensure that NATO headquarters stay in Brussels and Mons. The Dutch government will try to help its foreign minister, Jaap de Hoop Scheffer, when he takes over as NATO secretary-general in January, to restore NATO unity and relevance.

GDP GROWTH (%)	2002	2003	2004
Belgium	0.7	0.5	1.7
The Netherlands	0.2	-0.3	0.9
Luxembourg	1.1	0.7	2.3

Economist Intelligence Unit

"Using Citrix to consolidate the complex retail IT environment that reaches across our 250 retailers in Europe dramatically improved the performance of our applications. It also cut our TCO for retail IT by over 20%."

Dr. Hartwig Faber, CIO
smart – a brand of DaimlerChrysler

access **INFRASTRUCTURE FOR THE ON-DEMAND ENTERPRISE**

smart's market success demanded timely expansion of their sales and service centers. Over 250 dealers in Europe, representing thousands of employees, needed secure access to several mission-critical applications. The key was the rapid implementation of an innovative and cost-effective, centralized access infrastructure solution. Naturally, they called on Citrix. smart, along with 99% of the *Fortune* 500, uses Citrix® software to deploy applications centrally for secure, easy, and instant access to business-critical information—anywhere, anytime, from any device. We call it the on-demand enterprise. And it's helping more than 120,000 of our customers save money and reduce IT complexity. To learn what Citrix can do for your business, visit **www.citrix.co.uk**.

30 KGS LIGHTER.
BIGGER ENGINE.
YOU DO THE MATHS.

The new BMW 5 Series from £25,455. Model featured BMW 530dSE with optional alloy wheels and Bi-Xenon headlights £33,015. For informat
The Official Fuel Economy Figures for 5 Series range. Extra Urban 51.4 – 35.8 mpg (5.5 – 7.9 l/100km). Urban 29.7 – 17.3 mpg (9.5 – 16.3 l/100k

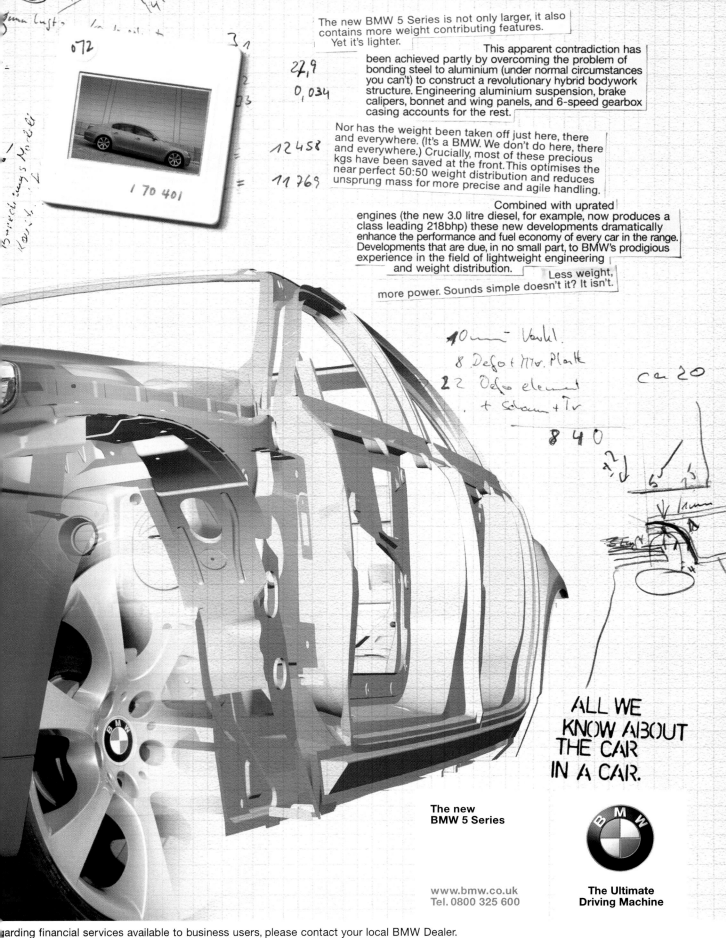

The new BMW 5 Series is not only larger, it also contains more weight contributing features. Yet it's lighter.

This apparent contradiction has been achieved partly by overcoming the problem of bonding steel to aluminium (under normal circumstances you can't) to construct a revolutionary hybrid bodywork structure. Engineering aluminium suspension, brake calipers, bonnet and wing panels, and 6-speed gearbox casing accounts for the rest.

Nor has the weight been taken off just here, there and everywhere. (It's a BMW. We don't do here, there and everywhere.) Crucially, most of these precious kgs have been saved at the front. This optimises the near perfect 50:50 weight distribution and reduces unsprung mass for more precise and agile handling.

Combined with uprated engines (the new 3.0 litre diesel, for example, now produces a class leading 218bhp) these new developments dramatically enhance the performance and fuel economy of every car in the range. Developments that are due, in no small part, to BMW's prodigious experience in the field of lightweight engineering and weight distribution. Less weight, more power. Sounds simple doesn't it? It isn't.

ALL WE KNOW ABOUT THE CAR IN A CAR.

The new BMW 5 Series

www.bmw.co.uk
Tel. 0800 325 600

The Ultimate Driving Machine

The Russian evolution

Anne Applebaum

Worrying trends as President Putin heads for re-election

To understand where Russia may be heading in 2004, begin by looking closely at two events that took place in 2003. One of them—a criminal prosecution—was widely discussed, in Russia and abroad. That affair began in June, when Russian prosecutors launched no fewer than eight separate criminal investigations into the affairs of the Yukos oil company, one of Russia's largest firms. Most assumed that the investigation had a political, not a legal basis: that the government wanted to prevent Yukos from merging with another company (and eventually with a western company) and to stop Mikhail Khodorkovsky, the Yukos CEO and Russia's richest man, from growing too powerful. He was arrested and charged with fraud in October.

By contrast, the other event, the ceremonial opening of a hydroelectric power station in the Russian far east, passed almost unnoticed. The dam, a project abandoned after the collapse of the Soviet Union in 1991, was restarted in 1998. At the opening—a festive affair with Soviet songs and emotional speeches from famous Russian writers—the president, Vladimir Putin, described the project as a "miracle". In the past five years, he said, "we have managed not only to resuscitate and recreate everything that the energy sector of the Soviet Union and of Russia was proud of, but also to make steps forward."

These two events provide clues to the thinking of Russia's ruling elite. The most powerful members of Mr Putin's entourage come increasingly from the security services or the army—the so-called "power ministries"—and their views reflect their origins. They still doubt the legitimacy of private business, and believe that large state projects should be the engine of the Russian economy. They have no qualms about changing the law on a whim. Despite the rhetoric about free markets at some of the highest levels, this particular faction is less interested in markets than in retaining power. It is wary of foreigners, foreign investment and capitalist institutions.

All of these trends look set to solidify in 2004. References to the glorious Soviet past, and the use of Soviet symbols in public, will become more common. The media, which has been gradually restricted, will grow tamer. Independent organisations of various kinds will experience harassment, either from tax inspectors or more directly from the FSB, the institutional descendants of the KGB. Foreigners will not be threatened, exactly, but they will not be welcomed either: it is unlikely, for example, that the complex visa process will be simplified.

The changes that have slowly frozen Russia's political culture are, if not reversed, bound to hurt the economy eventually. Some of this may be felt in 2004. But many foreign investors are prepared to brush their reservations aside. The opportunities—not only in Russia's energy sector, but also in its booming consumer market—will prove too big to ignore. Russian growth will slow a bit in 2004 (to some 4%, compared with 6% in 2003) as a result of lower oil prices. But only an outright collapse in world oil prices could threaten to plunge Russia back into crisis.

In electoral politics, a lot of wheeling and dealing will follow the December 2003 parliamentary elections. The Kremlin will be the most influential power-broker, whatever the technical majority among the parties. All this will be a prelude to the presidential elections in March. Television stations will support Mr Putin, just as they did in the last elections. With a record of strong economic growth, and with no serious rivals in sight, Mr Putin will almost certainly win.

Despite the signs of slippage into Soviet ways, polls show that younger Russians prefer democracy to autocracy in greater numbers than their elders. This younger generation will change political and business culture as they enter the job market and join the electoral rolls. Access to the internet will keep growing. More and more Russians will travel abroad. A clash between young people and the secretive leaders of the Kremlin's power ministries is inevitable. It may not come to a head in 2004, but watch for early signs of it. □

Putin goes back in time

Anne Applebaum:
columnist,
Washington Post

TURKEY

By the end of 2004 Turkey may have finally convinced the European Union that it deserves to be considered for membership. The decision to start formal talks would bind this Muslim country firmly to the West and help transform the West's relations with the Islamic world. But Turkey will have to tread carefully.

The Cyprus problem will be the biggest obstacle. Without a deal to resolve the island's 30-year division between Greek and Turkish Cypriots, Greece and Cyprus—a new EU member in 2004 and represented in Brussels solely by the island's Greek Cypriots—are certain to veto any talks on Turkish membership. But if the Turkish government is willing to use its considerable clout with the hard-headed Turkish Cypriot leadership

to restart settlement talks along the lines already proposed by the UN, a deal in 2004 is possible.

Another potential roadblock will be Turkey's Kurds. The Turks fear that the Iraqi Kurds will seize the chance amid post-Saddam chaos to set up an independent, oil-rich Kurdistan in the north that will then inspire calls for greater autonomy from long-oppressed Turkish Kurds, many of whom live near the Iraqi border. Turkey's paranoia about the Kurds could prompt a military showdown, in Iraq or in Turkey, and cause the EU to rethink Turkey's suitability as a peaceful member of the club.

Then there's the economy. Local elections in May could set off a round of pre-election spending that

would deepen the already cavernous budget deficit, re-start triple-digit inflation and knock confidence in the fragile Turkish lira, causing a painful recession. Uncomfortably high debt levels would make the ensuing financial mess difficult for outside do-gooders to fix—even for a country that has the potential to act as a bridge between Islam and the West.

KEY INDICATORS	2002	2003	2004
GDP growth (%)	7.8	4.0	-4.5
Inflation (%)	45.0	26.0	39.4
Current account (% GDP)	-1.0	-3.4	0.5

Economist Intelligence Unit

United States

Still the 50-50 nation

John Parker   *Washington, DC*

The contest will be close, and the campaign caustic

The 2004 election will be more than a referendum on George Bush. It will reveal whether America itself has moved away from its recent partisan balance.

Between 1996 and 2000, the balance between the parties in contests for the House of Representatives or for president was extremely close. In 1996, although the Republicans retained control of the House with 48.9% of the vote, the Democrats got 48.5%; Bill Clinton won with 49.2%. Mr Bush got 47.9% of the vote in 2000, clinching victory in the electoral college despite losing the popular vote to Al Gore (48.4%).

The 2002 mid-term elections were different. Republicans kept control of the House with 51% of the popular vote. Democrats got only 46%. Republicans will hope this five-point difference marked a fundamental shift away from the "50-50 nation" (or so-so nation, as one misprint charmingly put it). Democrats will hope the result was a blip. Which view is better founded?

For Republicans, the main domestic problem is jobs. Mr Bush, Democrats will (correctly) claim, has presided over more job losses than any president since Herbert Hoover. But the economy is improving, and Mr Bush will say his three tax cuts turned it around. By the summer of 2004, when judgments are made about the president's economic performance, growth is likely to remain respectable. Voters will have to decide whether they are more worried about jobs or more heartened by growth.

Mr Bush will also face criticism for his policy in Iraq. But even if many voters now wonder whether it was worth going to war, they are not yet inclined to cut and run. Democrats are divided between those who opposed the invasion of Iraq in the first place and those who supported it but criticise the post-war occupation. Unless the death toll of American soldiers increases from the level of about four a week, Iraq will probably not prove a decisive obstacle to Mr Bush's re-election.

Beyond these policy issues, Mr Bush and his party have some structural advantages going into the 2004 election. September 11th 2001 seems to have shifted the balance of party identification in their favour. Democratic affiliation fell sharply after the attacks, and by the autumn of 2003 there were more self-identified Republicans than Democrats for the first time since the New Deal. The defection of the South, America's most populous region, has damaged the old Democratic coalition of white southerners, industrial workers and public-service professions, and is proceeding apace. On top of all this, the campaign-finance reform of 2001 has shifted the balance of advantage towards the party that raises more money from individuals, which happens at the moment to be the Republicans. In 2003 Mr Bush raised more money than all Democratic contenders combined.

These are reasons why he will go into the 2004 campaign as the favourite. But that is a very different thing from writing off the Democrats' chances. Both the president and his party face significant new problems.

In the six months before the mid-term election, the president's personal ratings ran a huge 17 points above his ratings on the economy. By increasing Mr Bush's popularity, the war on terrorism shielded Republican ▶

2004

American expatriates will be able to cast their vote via the internet, thanks to an experimental $22m federal voting-assistance programme, which aims to avoid some of the traditional pitfalls of absentee voting.

John Parker:
Washington bureau chief,
The Economist

2004

Health-care specialists reckon that 2004 will be the fourth straight year of double-digit increases in health-insurance premiums for Americans in employer-sponsored schemes. Premiums rose by nearly 14% in 2003.

candidates from the full force of economic discontent. This is unlikely to happen again. Mr Bush's personal ratings are now about the same as his economic ones.

In the 2000 race Mr Bush was able to appeal to conservatives by promising tax cuts and to centrist voters by promising new social programmes (such as education reform). That was a time of large budget surpluses. With large and growing deficits, he will have to offer much less ambitious, small-bore policies for a second term.

Republicans benefited in 2002 from an unusually inexperienced Democratic field. Only 10% of Republican incumbents were challenged by Democrats who had previously been elected to public office. The post-war norm is 25%, and Democrats will almost certainly field more impressive challengers this time. The 2002 election provided little evidence that the balance between parties has changed fundamentally since 1996-2000.

The conclusion must be that the presidential contest will be close. Because the electorate is polarised as well as balanced, both parties will concentrate on turning out their core supporters, rather than appealing to voters in the middle. Campaigning will include lots of negative attacks, designed to galvanise party loyalists and drive down enthusiasm on the other side. There will be more attention than in the recent past on the "ground war" (efforts to get your voters to the booths on polling day) and less attention on the "air war" (television advertising designed to appeal to the maximum number of voters).

One prediction can be hazarded. The Republicans will keep control of the House of Representatives and the Senate—which might seem surprising given the narrowness of the party's control of both chambers. The reasons are technical. In the House, redistricting has left, at most, 30-40 seats truly competitive, split equally between the parties. So to win the 12 seats needed to take back the House, Democrats would have to hold all their own competitive districts and win about three-quarters of Republican ones. In the Senate, there are more Democratic seats up for grabs than Republican ones and ten of the 19 Democrats will be defending states Mr Bush won in 2000, whereas only three of the 15 Republicans will be defending states won by Mr Gore.

Narrow Republican margins are a safe bet in both chambers. A flutter on Mr Bush is more of a gamble. □

Great expectations and dangerous temptations

Zanny Minton-Beddoes

Washington, DC

America's economy will frustrate. The political reaction could be worse

For America's economy, 2004 brings great expectations. But although output will expand, the economy will not grow fast enough to make much of a dent in the jobless figures. With elections approaching, frustration in Washington will mount. Political pressure for protection against foreign imports will soar; China will become the scapegoat for all that ails American industry. Unless cool heads prevail—not easy in the heat of a close campaign—the result could be disastrous.

Begin with the expectations. In the second half of 2003 there were encouraging signs that America's economy had finally broken out of its multi-year torpor. The third quarter was a sizzler. Boosted by tax cuts, consumers stepped up their spending. Despite higher mortgage rates, the housing market remained buoyant. Even corporate investment seemed to be on the mend. The hope was that firms would finally start hiring more people. More jobs would in turn induce Americans to continue their spending, pushing the economy into a strong, sustained recovery in 2004.

Unfortunately, that logic may prove optimistic. The most striking characteristic of America's recovery—the weakness of the job market—could continue into 2004. Most post-war recoveries eventually generated rapidly rising payrolls, as firms hired back the workers they laid

Zanny Minton-Beddoes:
Washington correspondent,
The Economist

The buck stoops here % of GDP

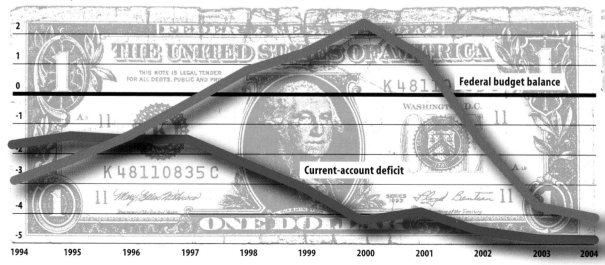

Federal budget balance

Current-account deficit

"To the future. And step on it."

"In the mid 90s, GM needed a change—and it couldn't come fast enough. Our challenge? Transform one of the world's largest corporations into a real-time, go-fast company—which meant major IT changes. From the beginning, HP Services was a critical partner providing the technology and solutions that were instrumental to our vision.

"The result? Today, we bring new vehicles to consumers in less than 24 months, versus 42 in the past. We've consolidated our information systems by over fifty percent. And we're putting better quality automobiles on the road than ever before—all while saving hundreds of millions of dollars a year through the use of precision information technology.

"HP listened, instead of talking. HP sold ideas, instead of pushing product. HP over-delivered, instead of over-promising. As a result, GM is racing toward the future—a real-time, go-fast company."

—Ralph Szygenda, Group Vice-President and CIO, General Motors

General Motors demands more from IT and HP makes sure they get it.

+ hp

= everything is possible

www.hp.com/go/demandmore

hp invent

The big dug

Light at the end of the tunnel for Boston's commuters

"Yellow dinosaur steamshovels were grunting/as they cropped up tons of mush and grass/to gouge their underworld garage", wrote Robert Lowell after the city council built a car park beneath Boston Common. One wonders what the Beantown bard would have made of the Big Dig, the vast highway, bridge and tunnel project which has turned a large chunk of Boston into something like a demilitarised zone for the past 12 years.

The main point of the Big Dig is to replace a section of highway along the downtown waterfront, and to improve access at other points nearby. At the moment traffic jams last for ten hours a day and the accident rate is four times the national average. Work began in 1991. The budget grew faster than the dirt piled up, from $2.8 billion to $14.6 billion by the time it's all done. Construction should be finished in early 2004, with landscaping to follow.

The Big Dig is the single largest civil-engineering project in American history and perhaps also the only one to have an ice-cream sundae named after it. Brigham's, a Boston ice-cream-parlour chain, has introduced its own version of the Big Dig, with four scoops of Oreo-cookie ice cream, walnuts, hot fudge, peanut-butter sauce and whipped cream with a cherry on top. □

2004

Sales of DVDs in America could hit $25 billion, more than five times those of VHS cassettes.

▶ off during the cyclical downturn. This recovery, by contrast, is marked by higher productivity rather than more jobs, as firms squeeze more output from fewer workers.

Faster productivity growth was a hallmark of the late-1990s boom. Output per worker grew by an annual average of 2.6% between 1996 and 1999, up from 1.5% in the previous four years. This rise fanned much of the hype about a new economy in America.

The real surprise, however, has been productivity's performance since the economy flagged. Output per worker soared, even as the economy slowed and stayed sluggish. Between the middle of 2002 and the middle of 2003 productivity rose over 4%. Even if only part of the recent rise is permanent, its consequences will be big.

In the long term, higher productivity is unambiguously good news, implying more profits, higher wages and better standards of living. But in the meantime, higher productivity means that the economy must grow even faster to produce more jobs. If productivity growth remains over 3%, the economy will have to grow by well over 4% to make much impact on the jobless figures.

And that is a tall order. Consumer spending, which for several years has been the bulwark of American demand, is likely to flag next year. For the past three years America's households have kept their wallets open despite the faltering economy, helped by steep cuts in interest rates, the extraction of equity from their homes and several rounds of tax cuts.

That will change in 2004. There will be one more small boost from Uncle Sam early in the year, as Americans receive rebate cheques for the taxes they paid in the first six months of 2003, but fiscal policy overall will be much less stimulative. Nor is there much chance of another mortgage-refinancing boom. Take away these sources of stimulus, and add a dollop of job uncertainty, and the chances are that America's households will save more and spend less.

A period of modest spending and higher saving is exactly what America needs after the debt-financed excesses of recent years. But the combination of modest economic growth and stagnant labour markets makes for ugly politics. Jobs will be the Democrats' clarion call in the presidential campaign. Manufacturing has been particularly hard hit, with almost 3m job losses, concentrated in swing states such as Ohio and Kentucky.

The politics of protectionism

The White House will feel enormous pressure to act. But it has few policy tools left. With a probable budget deficit of over 4% of GDP in 2004, and the prospect of huge deficits down the road, there is no more room for big tax cuts—or large spending increases. The Bush strategy of boosting demand with fiscal stimulus will come to an end. Washington will be filled with recriminations over the government's spectacular slide into red ink.

One remaining avenue is a cheaper dollar. A cheaper dollar would boost American exporters and shift Americans' consumption from imports towards domestic goods. A gradually declining dollar would, ideally, be an important component in the elimination of America's imbalances, particularly its huge current-account deficit (over 5% of GDP). Although the dollar has already fallen from its peak in early 2002, it has further to go.

Given the political pressures at home, team Bush will be tempted to speed that process up by talking the dollar down. As 2003 progressed, there were increasingly loud shouts for China to allow its currency to appreciate. The Chinese yuan has been fixed to the dollar since 1994. In September the G7 group of rich countries, at America's behest, called for "more flexible exchange rates". While 2004 should see a weaker dollar and stronger Asian currencies, that shift must come gradually.

The problem in 2004 will be that the economic goal—a gradual decline in the dollar—will jar with the political pressure for a quick fix. The clamour for tariff protection, particularly against China, will rise. In 2003 legislation was introduced in both houses of Congress demanding draconian tariffs on Chinese goods unless the currency was revalued. Protectionist proposals will proliferate in 2004. The mood in Congress will mirror that of the mid-1980s when Japan was blamed for hollowing out the titans of American industry. The economic dynamic is different today. America's big firms benefit from investment in China; it is smaller manufacturers that are screaming. But the politics will be frighteningly similar: 2004 could see a dangerous retreat from free trade. □

"Our members must feel like more than a 16-digit number."

"As one of the leading credit card and financial services providers in Europe, Barclaycard knows every transaction matters. Which means we can't afford to be anything less than perfect — authorizing over 1.5 billion transactions annually.

"With the help of HP, we've met our goal of 100% uptime since January 2000. Having prescribed a backbone of NonStop servers, HP Services helped Barclaycard create a dynamic system capable of supporting our 10 million cardholders and delivering a multi-currency one-stop shop for our global clients.

"Retailers get 100% uptime. Customers get a relationship they can trust. And we get 20% annual growth and lifetime cardholders."

—Steve Adams, IT and Operations Director

Barclaycard demands more from IT and HP makes sure they get it.

+ hp

= *everything is possible*

www.hp.com/go/demandmore

hp invent

The new American job

Lionel Barber   New York

Have brains, will travel

The American worker has seen hard times these past three years. Almost 3m private-sector jobs have disappeared since President George Bush took office. When the great American job-creating machine at last starts to crank up again, what type of jobs will it be churning out?

The big winners in 2004 are likely to be the cutting-edge, creative types. According to Richard Florida, Heinz professor at Carnegie Mellon University and author of "The Rise of the Creative Class", creative-class people account for more than half of the total payroll in the United States, whether they are bohemian entertainers, "super-creators" in bio-technology, electronics and software, or knowledge-based professionals.

The shift towards a more flexible, knowledge-based workforce will accelerate in 2004 as American companies adjust further to the demands of a global marketplace. Inevitably, competitive pressures will mean more outsourcing of jobs that can be done more cheaply out-

Lionel Barber: United States managing editor of the *Financial Times*

side the United States—and louder complaints about software engineering being outsourced to India and the competitive threat from China. The relentless search among American corporations for more efficiency and cost-savings is bad news for those workers caught in the middle. These are the people who are either unskilled or who have the wrong skills, and those who find it hard to shift career.

Think of the Willy Lomans, the door-to-door salesmen who were on their way out even before the arrival of eBay and internet auctions. But also think of the Organisation Man, the middle-ranking white-collar executive who took orders from above and executed those commands without questions. He wore the right suits, had the right house, had the family. He fitted in. Douglas Breeden, dean of the Fuqua Business School at Duke University in North Carolina, says these qualities no longer meet the needs of a knowledge-based society or a modern corporation. The accent is on web-friendly workers who can think flexibly, work in teams and who are comfortable thinking across disciplines. Organisation Man will be more dispensable than ever.

What about jobs lower down the ladder? There is some room for optimism in the retail industry as consumers feel better about eating out in restaurants and stepping back into the clothing stores. Hotels also expect ▶

Hail to the Indians

Kate Galbraith

A final museum on the National Mall in Washington, DC honours the first Americans

On the first day of autumn 2004 the heritage of America's original inhabitants will take centre stage as the Smithsonian's National Museum of the American Indian opens in Washington. The $200m domed structure, built with limestone from Minnesota, will have ample outdoor surrounds. The mid-western plains it isn't, but a sprinkling of trees and large "grandfather rocks" hauled in from Canada will suggest the ancientness of the land.

Appropriately, the museum will occupy a prime spot on the National Mall, wedged between the Capitol and the much-loved Air and Space Museum (which is itself opening a huge hangar housing America's first space shuttle beside Dulles Airport). It will fill the mall's last building space. Other projects, such as a prospective museum of African-American history, will have to go elsewhere.

The new museum will not be trouble-free. News reports will replay grumbles from the original architect, a part-Blackfoot Canadian who was dismissed in 1998 owing to

what museum officials say was his inability to stick to timetables. The museum's holdings—highlights from the 800,000 objects gathered from America's far corners by an early 20th-century banker-turned-collector

named George Gustav Heye (some are already on display at the smaller Heye Centre in New York)—will fall under continued scrutiny by tribes. Plucking curiosities from old Indian graves was acceptable a century ago; now such practices stir retroactive outrage. In 1990 Congress passed a law requiring sacred objects and human bones to be sent back if tribes ask for them, provided ownership can be shown. Museums around the country have struggled to comply. Sometimes they have trouble pinpointing the origins of certain objects, which may have passed through the hands of long-dead traders.

The museum and its southern Cheyenne director have worked hard to honour sensitivities. They have made sure that the building faces east, as is traditional; that the café will serve native food; that there will be an outdoor firepit and amphitheatre. Many tribes, impressed, will contribute artefacts to the opening exhibitions—Inca gold from South America, an ice-fishing vehicle from Canada, pottery from New Mexico. A worthy showing, from the first Americans. □

Kate Galbraith: correspondent for Global Agenda, *Economist.com*

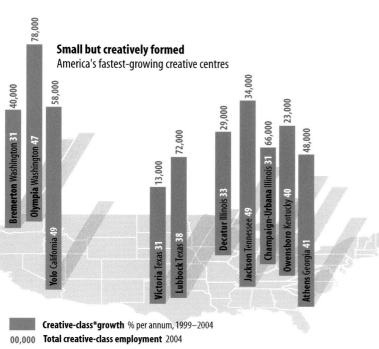

Small but creatively formed
America's fastest-growing creative centres

Bremerton Washington 31 — 40,000
Olympia Washington 47 — 78,000
Yolo California 49 — 58,000
Victoria Texas 31 — 13,000
Lubbock Texas 38 — 72,000
Decatur Illinois 33 — 29,000
Jackson Tennessee 49 — 34,000
Champaign-Urbana Illinois 31 — 66,000
Owensboro Kentucky 40 — 23,000
Athens Georgia 41 — 48,000

Creative-class*growth % per annum, 1999–2004
00,000 Total creative-class employment 2004

*Includes high-tech but excludes service and manufacturing workers
Source: Kevin Stolarick, Carnegie Mellon University

some boost in demand as people start to rediscover their desire for travel. But a more promising source of jobs is likely to be the health-care sector, thanks in part to Congress's big boost to Medicare. Demand for nurses and orderlies should rise, too, as Americans grow older and need more care, either in their own homes or in retirement communities.

This may increase the opportunities for part-time work rather than full-time jobs which require full pension rights and expensive health-care cover. Disputes between companies and unions over pensions and health-care entitlements have become the new battleground in wage negotiations, as corporations encourage workers to be more self-reliant and more comfortable about investing their savings in retirement plans. Older workers will also choose to stay in the labour market.

The creative class will be comfortable in the new competitive environment. They will seek out the best places to work, not just by industry but also by geography. More than 40 years ago, the introduction of air-conditioning fundamentally changed the demographics of the United States. Suddenly it became tolerable to work in offices in the south and south-west. Cities such as Albuquerque, Atlanta and Phoenix exploded in growth and population. In 2004 the same lure of a better quality of life will encourage high-value workers to move to mountain states such as Colorado, Idaho and Utah. They will also seek desert locations in Arizona and Nevada, where the price of property and state taxes are lower than in overcrowded California. On a smaller scale, a similar phenomenon is unfolding on the east coast: senior professionals are choosing to commute rather than live in high-priced New York.

These trends in the American job market put a premium on brains and location. In 2004 the overall growth in employment may still be frustratingly slow. But the American worker who is both creative and flexible will do just fine. □

2004

Cheryl Stearns, an American pilot, will attempt to break the high-altitude skydiving record by ballooning to 130,000 feet and parachuting back to earth in a pressurised space suit.

Joseph S. Nye junior: dean of Harvard's Kennedy School of Government and author of "The Paradox of American Power" (Oxford University Press). Assistant secretary of defence for international security affairs, 1994-95

America's soft learning curve

Joseph Nye

In 2004 Americans need to become more adept at soft power, argues a star from the Clinton Pentagon

Not since ancient Rome has one nation loomed so large in global affairs. With America accounting for nearly half the world's military spending, no opposing coalition can create a traditional military balance of power. The four-week military campaign in Iraq in 2003 was dazzling. Yet it was extremely damaging to America's attractiveness in many parts of the world. Anti-Americanism has increased. Polls show that America's attractiveness plummeted in Europe and reached single digits in some Muslim countries.

The world is puzzling over America's global role. Some see an American empire where the United States can act unilaterally and others have no choice but to follow. However, this view misunderstands the profound ways that world politics changed during the last decades of the 20th century. George Bush entered office committed to a traditional realist foreign policy that would focus on great powers like China and Russia, and eschew nation-building in failed states. But after September 11th 2001 his administration issued a new national security strategy that declared that America was "menaced less by fleets and armies than by catastrophic technologies in the hands of the embittered few." Now "weak states, like Afghanistan, can pose as great a danger to our national interest as strong states."

The rhetoric of the new strategy attracted considerable criticism, but the Bush administration was correct in its change of focus. September 11th showed that globalisation is more than just an economic phenomenon. It has been shrinking the natural buffers that two oceans provided to America. At the same time, technology and the information revolution have elevated the importance of transnational issues and empowered non-state actors to play a larger role in world politics. In 2001 a surprise attack by a transnational terrorist group killed more Americans than the state of Japan did in 1941. This "privatisation of war" represents a major historical change in world politics, one whose potential impact on America's cities could drastically alter the nature of our civilisation. This is what Mr Bush got right.

However, the Bush administration has done far better on the ends than on the means. A tug of war has existed between unilateralists and those who favour a more multilateral approach. The unilateralists believe that the nature of the new threats is so dire that America must escape the constraints of the multilateral structures it built after the second world war. They deliberately resisted the use of NATO after the allies invoked Article 5 (which considers an attack on one member to be an attack on all) in September 2001. They sought to minimise the role of the UN in Iraq before and after the war. And they talk of Europe in a way that divides "old" from "new". In secretary of defence Donald Rumsfeld's view of alliances, the issues ▶

Land of the free, home of the bar code

American border control goes high-tech

In the fifth century BC, Nehemiah, a lowly cupbearer, asked the Persian king for permission to travel to Judah. The king agreed and gave Nehemiah a letter to "the governors beyond the river". This primitive passport did the trick. Nehemiah enjoyed a safe and successful business trip.

Two-and-a-half millennia later, he would find that a letter from the Persian king cuts no ice with immigration officials, especially American ones. From October 2004 all foreign visitors to America must have either a machine-readable passport or a visa. That applies to everyone, including travellers from the 27 countries which are currently part of America's visa-waiver programme.

The new American visas will contain biometric data, probably in the form of fingerprints and a digital image of the traveller's face. Eventually, the American government would like to see this kind of data included in all passports. Such high-tech travel documents are hard to fake and can be scanned straight into security databases.

But there are drawbacks too. The full programme, called US VISIT, would be one of the biggest IT projects in American history. Critics say it could cost anything from $3 billion to $10 billion to set up. Others worry about the impact stricter visa and passport rules will have on tourism and trade.

And then there's the awkward question of whether the new measures will do much to keep terrorists and other undesirables out. "Security, like a chain, is only as strong as the weakest link," says Bruce Schneier, a security consultant and author of "Beyond Fear: Thinking Sensibly About Security in an Uncertain World". "Building Fortress America is not going to make anyone safer." □

▶ should determine the coalitions, not vice versa.

Unfortunately, the unilateralist approach will undercut America's ability to implement its new strategy and meet the new challenges that were revealed on September 11th. The unilateralists focus too heavily on America's military power and pay too little heed to "soft power". The willingness of other countries to co-operate on the solution of transnational issues such as terrorism depends in part on their own self-interest, but also on the attractiveness of American positions. Soft power lies in the ability to persuade rather than coerce. It means that others want what you want, and there is less need to use carrots and sticks.

Hard power, the ability to coerce, grows out of a country's military and economic might. Soft power arises from the attractiveness of a country's culture, political ideals and policies. When America's policies are seen as legitimate in the eyes of others, its soft power is enhanced. Hard power will remain crucial in a world of states trying to guard their independence, and non-state groups willing to turn to violence. But soft power will become increasingly important in preventing the terrorists from recruiting supporters from among the moderate majority, and for dealing with the transnational issues that require multilateral co-operation for their solution.

One of Mr Rumsfeld's rules is that "weakness is provocative". He is correct up to a point. But legitimacy is also a form of power. Humans live not only by the sword, but also by the word. The 1991 Gulf war was widely regarded as legitimate, whereas legitimacy in the 2003 war was contested. Unable to balance American military power, France, Germany, Russia and China created a coalition to balance American soft power by depriving America of the legitimacy of a second UN resolution.

Not by hardness alone

Although this "soft balancing" did not prevent the United States from entering Iraq, it did raise the price America paid. When Turkish parliamentarians regarded American policy as illegitimate, they refused Pentagon requests to allow the fourth infantry division to enter Iraq from the north. Inadequate attention to soft power had a negative effect on the hard power America could bring to bear in the early days of the war. Similarly, the administration's resistance to a significant role for the United Nations in the reconstruction of Iraq is estimated to have cost America both lives and money—more than $100m, or about $1,000 per American household. Hard and soft power sometimes conflict, but they can also reinforce each other. As America wrestles with the reconstruction of Iraq in 2004, the unilateralists will have to learn that soft power is not weakness; it is a form of strength.

Americans—and others—face an unprecedented challenge from the dark side of globalisation and the privatisation of war that has accompanied new technologies. This is sometimes summarised as a "war on terrorism". Like the cold war, it will be prolonged. The cold war was won, however, not just by military containment but by western soft power that transformed the Soviet block from within. That is why 2004 should be the year that Americans learn better to understand and apply soft power. □

The mood in Malaysia

The right software can transform your infrastructure into an on-demand environment.

The best way to survive any business crisis is to avoid it altogether. That's why our management software is designed to make your business more responsive than ever. It lets you align your IT to fit your business needs. And it's seamlessly integrated. As a result, you can maximize your resources and increase profitability. To find out more about transforming your IT environment for business success, go to ca.com/management1.

Computer **Associates**®

Colin Powell, America's secretary of state, predicts that anti-Americanism will subside

The power of good intentions

"The United States has a rare opportunity to enjoy excellent relations with all the world's major powers simultaneously"

I t's nice to be liked, for nations as well as individuals. But it's more important to act responsibly. Not everyone approves of the foreign policies of the Bush administration, and this concerns us. But not as much as whether we are meeting our obligations to the American people and to international security more broadly.

Some critics of American foreign policy never tire of repeating the caricature that President Bush acts on a shoot-from-the-hip unilateralist impulse. This simply is not the case. When the president's strategy was laid out publicly in September 2002, some observers exaggerated its references to pre-emptive action. Many who did not read the document got the impression that it is mostly or only about pre-emption.

It isn't. The National Security Strategy focuses above all on alliances and partnerships. It stresses the promotion of freedom and dignity through them. Its policy emphasis includes both free trade and new initiatives in economic development assistance, and efforts to stem the proliferation of weapons of mass destruction. It demands American efforts to solve regional conflicts and, not least, it prioritises developing strong, co-operative relations with other major powers.

With the help of many allies, we are succeeding in the global war on terrorism. That success is owed in part to the victories of American and allied military forces in Afghanistan and Iraq. We are working hard to transform those military victories into lasting political achievements, and our efforts will neither falter nor fail. Success in the war against terrorism is owed, too, to diplomatic accomplishments in enhancing law enforcement co-operation and intelligence sharing.

Partnerships, not polarities

Less well appreciated, however, we are also succeeding in other important domains of the president's strategy. The United States has a rare opportunity to enjoy excellent relations with all the world's major powers simultaneously. Of course, we have an important advantage in being blessed with many close friendships, reflected in our key alliances. Why belabour terms like multipolarity when there are no poles among nations that share basic values?

The greatest challenge lies in fully integrating an increasingly democratic Russia and a modernising China into the mainstream of democratic, free-market institutions. It also means bringing an economically developing India closer to the global councils of the major powers.

Our relationship with Russia has been dramatically transformed for the better. We are radically reducing our strategic-weapons arsenals, and in Moscow we now have a partner in combatting terrorism and the spread of weapons of mass destruction worldwide. The new relationship that is developing between Russia and NATO, too, has real substance. We are closer than ever to

a Europe whole, free and at peace.

India has been a democracy since independence in 1947, and with recent reforms it is becoming a true market economy. It still faces many challenges. We want to help India overcome them, and we want to help ourselves through closer association with one of the world's most venerable cultures. At the same time, we have improved our relationship with Pakistan, a country with domestic challenges of its own. Those twin improvements helped us when a major war on the sub-continent seemed a distinct possibility in 2002. With the help of allies in Europe and Asia, we mobilised to head it off.

We have continued to improve relations with both India and Pakistan, and we aim to turn that parallel improvement into a triangle of conflict resolution in South Asia. We do not wish to impose ourselves as a mediator, but we are trusted increasingly by both sides. We deploy that trust to urge conciliation through peaceful means alone.

Sino-American relations are better than they have been in many years. We believe that it is up to us, together, to shape our common future, and we do not conceive that future in zero-sum terms. The National Security Strategy says it directly: "We welcome the emergence of a strong, peaceful and prosperous China." We co-operate where our interests coincide. A key case in point is Korea.

When we do succeed in resolving the problem of North Korea's nuclear-weapons programme, we will have demonstrated that American diplomacy is designed to satisfy not only American national interests, but the interests of international security as a whole. We will show that the equities of other powers can be best advanced along with American ones, not in opposition to them. We will have strengthened global peace, and we will have used a strategy of partnerships to do so.

Our need to respond with military force to the events of September 11th inevitably makes some people abroad uncomfortable. There has been a rise in anti-American sentiment, tied particularly to the war in Iraq. But these feelings will subside as Iraq's reconstruction proceeds. We are working hard to ameliorate other discordant issues, too.

We fight terrorism because we must. We seek a better world because we can, because it is our desire to do so. That is why we devote ourselves to democracy, development, health and human rights. Those are not mere high-sounding decorations for our interests. They are our interests. They are the purposes that our power serves.

American motives are as well-intentioned today as they have ever been. Because this is so, I know that America's reputation for honesty and compassion will be restored in places where it is today impugned. As we strive to preserve, defend and expand the peace that free peoples won in the 20th century, I believe we will see America vindicated in the eyes of the world in the 21st. To this the world in 2004 will bear witness. □

Latin America emerges from its gloom

Michael Reid

After the storms of the past few years, the delights of political calm and quickening economic recovery

The uptick in the United States, stronger prices for commodity exports and cheap foreign financing should combine to help Latin America's economy grow by around 4% in 2004. This will be its best performance since 1997. With no national elections scheduled in any of the larger countries, for once there is little danger of politics blowing the region off course.

The year will start with a one-day Special Summit of the Americas in Mexico City in January. The heads of government of 34 Latin American and Caribbean countries will meet George Bush and Canada's prime minister, Jean Chrétien (who will be making his farewell appearance on the international stage before he steps down in February in favour of Paul Martin). Mr Bush will use the summit to show Latino voters back home that, yes, he does care about Latin America, and to put his weight behind the Free-Trade Area of the Americas (see next story). The Latin Americans, or some of them at least, will use it to show off an emerging political consensus, led by Brazil's president, Luiz Inácio Lula da Silva.

Latin America's "neo-liberalism" of the 1990s foundered on financial turbulence. Now several governments in the region are groping towards a kind of pragmatic social democracy, Latin-American style. Out are the privatisations and market reforms of the 1990s; in their place is a bigger role for the state, as regulator and promoter of industrial development.

The shift to the left is nuanced, and not region-wide. One exception is Colombia. There Álvaro Uribe, an austere conservative, will continue his American-backed crackdown against drug traffickers and the FARC guerrillas. He will hope to secure the disbanding of some right-wing paramilitary groups during 2004. The FARC's leaders and Mr Uribe will again try to kill each other. The president's supporters will seek to change the constitution to allow the president to stand for a second term in 2006, but in Colombia, traditionally wary of over-mighty executives, that will be a hard sell.

Another exception may be Venezuela, where 2004 could see the end of President Hugo Chávez and his Bolivarian revolution—if (a big if) the centre-right opposition stays together and avoids mistakes. The populist Mr Chávez may succeed in delaying a recall referendum that the opposition hopes will be held in February. If and when it comes to the vote, he is likely to lose the referendum and the presidential election that would follow.

Elsewhere, leftish candidates may do well in two out of four presidential elections, all in smaller countries in the region. In Uruguay's October ballot, Tabaré Vasquéz, a doctor and former mayor of Montevideo from the left-wing Broad Front, will face a strong challenge from Alejandro Atchugary, an orthodox former finance minister from the ruling Colorado party. Mr Vasquéz will prevail. Like Lula's Workers' Party in Brazil, which it closely resembles, the Broad Front would govern pragmatically.

In May, Panamanians will probably elect Martin Torríjos, the son of Panama's nation-building *caudillo* of the ▶

2004

The Brazilian government will distribute 3.4m condoms to high-school pupils as part of a programme to prevent teen pregnancy and the spread of AIDS.

Michael Reid:
Americas editor,
The Economist

1970s, General Omar Torríjos. But in El Salvador, which votes in March, the conservative Arena party is likely to hang on to power—mainly because the former guerrillas of the FMLN have chosen as their presidential candidate Shafik Handal, a veteran Communist ill-placed to win votes in the centre. And in the Dominican Republic, whose previously buoyant economy has been damaged by a huge bank fraud, voters may punish President Hipólito Mejía and elect Leonel Fernández, a neo-liberal former president.

Attention in Chile will focus on municipal elections in October. This will be a dress-rehearsal for a presidential vote in 2005, which could see the right return to the Moneda palace for the first time since democracy was restored in 1990.

Increasing political fragmentation means that the governments that do best will be those that are most skilful at coalition-building, negotiation and legislative compromise—and that are blessed with a constructive opposition. Lula in Brazil is likely to fare better on this score than Vicente Fox in Mexico. Having spent 2003 taming an inflationary blip and persuading investors of its commitment to responsible policies, Brazil's government will go for growth in 2004. It will benefit from booming agri-business, as South America helps supply China's insatiable demand for food. Lula's popularity will help his Workers' Party make gains in municipal elections in October. It might even hang on to the mayoralty

of São Paulo, a tough city to govern well.

Argentina, too, will benefit from its farm exports. Agreement early in the year with creditors could usher in an acceleration in its recovery from its financial collapse and debt default of 2001. But don't hold your breath. The talks may drag on throughout the year, delaying a revival of investment. Still, President Néstor Kirchner has a chance to emerge as the undisputed leader of Peronism, sidelining his political godfather, Eduardo Duhalde.

Mexico's growth prospects are uncomfortably dependent on those of the United States. Mr Fox will make little headway with vital reforms aimed at lowering energy and labour costs. He will have better luck with political reforms.

Despite these variations, economic performance across the region will be more uniform than in recent years. Statistically, growth will be highest in Venezuela (close to 8%), but that is simply a rebound from a disastrous year marked by political conflict and a two-month general strike. Chile, emerging from a sluggish period, will overtake Peru as the fastest-growing economy on Latin America's Pacific seaboard.

Yet Latin America will fall well short of East Asian growth rates. Gone is the investor excitement of a decade ago that brought foreign capital cascading into the region, released by free-market reform and privatisation. But gone too, with luck, is the turbulence that saw capital flood out of the region again in the past few years. □

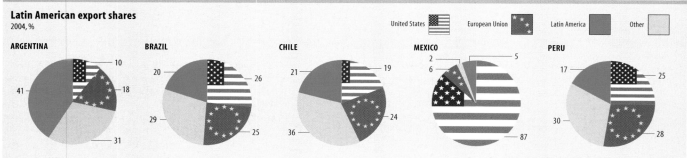

Latin American export shares
2004, %

United States European Union Latin America Other

ARGENTINA   BRAZIL   CHILE   MEXICO   PERU

Sources: Economist Intelligence Unit; Banco Central de Chile; Banco Central do Brasil

The Americas trade carve-up

Michael Reid

A sorry climax is in store for a grand idea

Free trade from Toronto to Tierra del Fuego: the grand idea is supposed to come to fruition in 2004. Yet the chances are that ten years of talks about a Free-Trade Area of the Americas (FTAA) will culminate in December 2004 in a motley handful of bilateral trade deals, ranging from the unhelpful to the unambitious.

Blame that partly on the conflicting interests of the two principal players in the talks, Brazil and the United States, but above all on rising protectionism and the hold-ups in the Doha round of world-trade talks. Brazil has long wanted the United States to dismantle its farm subsidies, its ad hoc barriers to farm trade and its aggressive use of anti-dumping

duties. The Americans want Brazil to open up services and government procurement to international competition.

That clash had been finessed by both sides agreeing to shunt these issues into the Doha round, originally due to finish at the same time as the FTAA but now likely to drift on and on. That delay will make agreement hard when the trade ministers from 34 countries in the Americas meet in Brazil for their final horse-trading session, perhaps in November 2004.

Both sides have been working on alternative strategies. The United States hopes to have wrapped up a free-trade agreement with five small Central American countries by the start of 2004. The Americans can be expected to offer similar talks to Colombia

and perhaps Peru and the Caricom group of Caribbean countries in 2004 if the FTAA talks go badly.

Brazil has a harder hand to play. It has tried to line up a united South American block in favour of an "FTAA-lite", restricted to issues of market access and tariff-cutting. But Argentina and Uruguay, two of Brazil's partners in Mercosur (South America's would-be common market, which also includes Paraguay), may prefer a wider agreement. The European Union will be watching closely: in separate talks with Mercosur, it is likely to match any such tariff concessions. Whatever emerges from this whole unedifying process is likely to have more to do with discriminatory commercial preferences than with genuine free trade. □

Canada's new man

Jeffrey Simpson   *Ottawa*

Peace and prosperity at home, but work to do abroad

Canadians sometimes bridle at their reputation for being a bit dull. They will live up to that reputation in 2004, however. Which is no bad thing.

The economy, the fastest-growing in the G8 for the past three years, will chug along nicely. The spectre of Quebec breaking up or disrupting the country has disappeared. And the already ten-year rule of the Liberal Party will continue, as the popular former finance minister, Paul Martin, takes over in February from the prime minister, Jean Chrétien. Mr Martin is expected to call an election that will return the Liberals with a large majority.

Four other parties run candidates against the Liberals, but none is remotely strong enough to form a serious national threat. Canada is in effect a one-party state, a kind of friendly political dictatorship presided over by the centrist Liberals, the most electorally successful political party in the western world, having governed Canada for 70 of the past 103 years. If political continuity defines boring, Canada is the western world's most boring democracy.

Mr Martin was finance minister for nine years before leaving the cabinet in frustration at Mr Chrétien's stubborn refusal to retire. On Mr Martin's watch, Canada turned a serious deficit into surpluses or balanced budgets. He speaks French and English perfectly, and combines fiscal prudence with a reforming instinct on social policy. His biggest political problem will come from within his own party. Dozens of backbenchers are itching for cabinet posts. So are big-name candidates Mr Martin hopes to entice into politics—which means many noses out of joint when he forms a cabinet.

He will inherit an economy expected to grow well above the Japanese and European rates in 2004, if a bit slower than the United States. Canadians, whose GDP per head increased by an impressive 20% from 1996 to 2002, will grow richer still. A stronger American economy will

Jeffrey Simpson: national affairs columnist, *The Globe and Mail*

Onwards and upwards for Martin, at last

increase Canadian exports and swell Canada's already large trade surplus. The Canadian dollar, which rose sharply against the US dollar in 2003, might creep higher, thereby pinching profits for export-dependent industries. But those industries had benefited from an almost 40% decline in the currency's value against the US dollar over the past 25 years, so their moans will ring false.

Mr Martin, having slain the Canadian deficit, will keep the nation's fiscal accounts in the black. Balanced budgets are now considered imperative across the political spectrum. That puts Canada in a unique position within the G8, where all other countries are in the red.

Mr Martin will also inherit a quiescent Quebec. The province's restless grappling with its place in Canada produced 30 years of constitutional dramas. But French-speaking Quebeckers, even those who still favour independence, do not now expect to see their dream realised any time soon. The provincial election in 2003 replaced the separatist Parti Québécois with the Liberals under Jean Charest, a former federal politician passionately committed to a united Canada.

Constitutional peace; political continuity; balanced budgets; strong economic growth: where's the catch? Mr Martin's chief worry will be relations with the United States, which have soured under Mr Chrétien. Canada refused to go along with the invasion of Iraq. Almost every policy or cause of the Bush administration—social conservatism, tax cuts for the wealthy, ballooning deficits, a muscular foreign policy and marginal regard for international institutions—is unpopular in Canada.

Yet Canada sends 85% of its exports to the United States. Security against terrorism requires close co-operation. The two peoples generally like each other. Getting on with the United States is not an option for a Canadian government, but an imperative.

Mr Martin has to find the right balance between improving relations and keeping his distance, given the Bush administration's unpopularity in Canada. He also needs to work out how to replenish Canada's foreign capabilities. Budgets for aid, defence and diplomacy have all fallen. The gap has never been wider between Canada's international aspirations and the shrunken reality. □

ARGENTINA   *FORECAST*

The worst of the turbulence in Argentina is over; even so, it will still not be a smooth ride in 2004. After the boom years of the 1990s, when foreign investment flooded in and Argentines could dream again of the days when theirs was among the world's richest countries, Argentina suffered a crippling recession from 1999-2002. Buenos Aires, once the "Paris of South America", became a newly "Latin-Americanised" capital as urban poverty, street vendors and rubbish-pickers proliferated. A 10.9% fall in GDP in 2002 took average real incomes back to their lowest level in a decade.

An export-led recovery is under way but a return to the heyday of the 1990s is not in prospect. Following ten years of a fixed exchange rate, a newly competitive currency will attract tourists to the country's many

national parks and ski resorts. Agricultural exports will grow too, albeit constrained by restricted access to rich-country markets. Home to one of the developing world's best-educated workforces, Argentina is also well placed to foster knowledge-intensive industries such as software, consulting and medical equipment.

But confidence was shattered by a widespread violation of contracts in the chaos of 2001-02. The rapid economic opening of the 1990s is now widely criticised in Argentina, and progress on structural reforms will be tortuous. One of the priorities for Néstor Kirchner, the country's president since May 2003, will be building public trust in the discredited political class. A centrepiece of this effort will be a move to re-open hundreds of cases of human-rights abuses committed

during the 1976-83 military dictatorship. As important to voters will be Mr Kirchner's delivery on promises to clean up corruption and reduce crime. These are formidable challenges, and Mr Kirchner's support is fragile. Argentina is out of intensive care but still on the critical list.

KEY INDICATORS	2002	2003	2004
GDP growth (%)	-10.9	5.0	4.9
Budget balance (% GDP)	-1.5	1.9	1.0
Unemployment (%)	18.8	16.2	14.5
Current account (% GDP)	9.2	7.9	6.2

Economist Intelligence Unit

Don't worry, there'll be another one along shortly.

Heathrow to Hong Kong. Non stop. Three times daily. That's more than any other airline.

A total of 21 opportunities to experience our New Business Class, every week.

Now you're really flying.

Based on Winter 2003 timetable. New Business Class is being progressively introduced. Completion March 2004.

www.cathaypacific.com

CATHAY PACIFIC

The billion-person question

Simon Long

Delhi

2004

A $12 billion upgrading of India's "Golden Quadrilateral", the road network that links Delhi, Mumbai, Calcutta and Madras, is due to be completed by the end of the year.

Simon Long:
India correspondent,
The Economist

Will India, the world's biggest democracy, keep its cool?

India's glory—the regular, peaceful and democratic transfer of power by parties ruling a poor country of more than a billion people—is not without its dangers. One is that in a calendar crowded by state and national elections, painful reform, however necessary, is deferred in order not to upset potential voters. Another is that some politicians are tempted to stoop to crude populism, including the stoking of communal tensions. In 2004, the year of a general election, India is at risk on both counts.

The timing of the polls is, within limits imposed by the independent Election Commission, in the gift of Atal Behari Vajpayee, the prime minister. Mr Vajpayee will face some pressure from members of his own Bharatiya Janata Party (BJP), which leads a coalition government of 20-odd parties, to call them early. The economy will enter 2004 in party mood: the best monsoon for at least five years has cheered farmers and urban consumers alike; prices are stable; foreign-exchange reserves are bulging; and the rupee, after weakening steadily for years, is enjoying a new bout of strength.

Industry will grow at a respectable 6-7% in 2004. More spectacular successes will distinguish the services

sector: India is set to consolidate its place as the world leader in the relocation of "information-technology enabled services". From its strong bases at both the high end of the business (writing and developing software) and the low end (telephone call-centres), India's outsourcing expertise will spread into new areas, especially in the financial-services industry. This may provoke some protectionist rhetoric in America and Europe. But the globalisation of services will prove as unstoppable as that of manufacturing.

The government, the theory goes, will bask in the glow of plentiful rains and a strong economy. But in his budget, at the end of February, Jaswant Singh, the finance minister, will find it hard to add to the festive spirit. He will refrain again from the desperately needed fiscal overhaul: cutting subsidies, broadening the tax base and privatising state-owned enterprises. But, having been generous in 2003, he will be constrained by the size of India's budget deficit (at least 11% of GDP if state governments are included) from indulging in cruder votegrabbing. Then, suppose in July and August the monsoon fails? Better, say some in the BJP, to cut and run.

Mr Vajpayee, however, is not that type. He also has his eye on his place in history: as the first prime minister not from the Congress Party (now the main opposition) ▶

▶ to last a full five-year term; and, with less hope of success, as a statesman who tried to make peace with Pakistan. So the prime minister will probably sit it out, leaving the elections until the last possible moment, in October.

And he will probably win. But it will be a close-fought battle, in which the BJP will have to overcome three main obstacles. The first is that Congress looks much more like a potential party of government (and its leader, Sonia Gandhi, more like a potential prime minister) than they did in the last elections in 1999. Mrs Gandhi herself remains derided by intellectuals in Delhi, and sneered at by the BJP's Hindu nationalists for her Italian origins. But opinion polls suggest many voters like her.

Second, the collapse of the BJP's coalition with the Bahujan Samaj Party (BSP) in the government of India's most populous state, Uttar Pradesh, is a serious blow to its electoral strategy. The BSP under Sushri Mayawati, who quit as Uttar Pradesh's chief minister in 2003, has solid support among *dalits* (once known as "untouchables") in that state and others in the northern "cow belt" that is crucial to electoral success at the national level.

Third, incumbency itself is a big hurdle in Indian politics. All governments disappoint. Mr Vajpayee's has disappointed more than most. Until 2003, economic performance was lacklustre at best. One good year will not dispel all the bad memories. Moreover, restrained by the interests of a disparate coalition, the BJP has done little to advance the programme, known as *hindutva*, that inspires its activists and their most fervent supporters.

All these obstacles can be overcome. The BJP remains more likely to be able to cobble together a parliamentary majority with the help of small, regional and caste-based parties. Congress's most serious handicap is its lack of a coherent set of policies. It has tended to take some of its supporters, such as members of the Muslim minority, for granted. So in some state elections it has campaigned not as the party of Nehruvian secularism, but as a kinder, gentler BJP, on a "soft" *hindutva* platform.

That is not a winning strategy. The BJP will burnish its own Hindu credentials. It will push *hindutva* measures such as a federal law banning cow slaughter. Above all, it can be expected to revisit the issue which launched it as a national party: the dispute over the site in Ayodhya of the Babri mosque, demolished by Hindu fanatics in 1992 because they believed it was built on the ruins of a temple marking the birthplace of the god-king Ram. For many Hindus this remains an unfinished drama with an inevitable conclusion: the construction of a superb new temple. Contentious archaeological evidence will give the issue new life as the elections approach.

That does not bode well for communal harmony. Nor does the likelihood that the conflict in Kashmir will drag on, while Indian cities will be scarred by acts of terrorism blamed on Muslim extremists and, behind them, Pakistan's intelligence services. This will thwart Mr Vajpayee's peacemaking. He may make one last push, by attending a regional meeting in Islamabad in January. But as Indian hardliners glower, and Pakistan realises he will not talk about the one issue they want to discuss—the status of Kashmir—relations will go back into cold storage. □

2004

The third and final stage in the construction of the Three Gorges dam on the Yangzi gets under way in China.

Tiger v dragon

Simon Long

Delhi

India and China will be wary of closer ties

To meet the target set by its current five-year plan (2002-07), India would need to achieve an improbable average annual growth rate of 8%. That is the minimum required to provide jobs and the chance of prosperity to its swelling population. Such a growth rate would also give India's statesmen another cherished prize: bragging rights over China.

Since living standards in China overtook India's more than a decade ago (see chart), the Chinese economy has grown roughly twice as fast as India's. As a destination for foreign direct investment, China has in recent years proved five times as popular as India.

Indian reactions range from denial ("lies, damn lies and Chinese statistics"), anger ("it's easy if the government's a dictatorship") and paranoia ("they will take all our jobs") to a perverse sort of pride ("we may be slow and cumbersome but at least we live in a democracy"). In some quarters, however, 2004 is billed as the year when Sino-

Chasing the dragon

— Nominal GDP*, \$bn — GDP* per head, \$

CHINA

INDIA

1990 92 94 96 98 2000 02 04

*at PPP

Source: Economist Intelligence Unit

Indian relations move beyond the mutual suspicion that has characterised them ever since they fought a border war, which China won with embarrassing ease, in 1962.

A visit to China by India's prime minister, Atal Behari Vajpayee, in 2003 brought home how much the two countries have in common, both in fear of an American-dominated world order and in economic as-

pirations. The worry that China might one day dominate even markets where India has a seemingly secure niche—such as IT services—yielded for a while to the potential for co-operation. The world's most successful centres of, respectively, low-cost manual labour and low-cost English-speaking services ought to have complementary strengths.

Business, not brotherhood

Sadly, politics will still get in the way. Two-way trade will continue its healthy growth (from a very sickly base) but a new era of Sino-Indian "brotherhood", as Jawaharlal Nehru called it in the 1950s, is not about to dawn. Even as Mr Vajpayee was in China, the People's Liberation Army was making its presence felt across one sector of the disputed border. The achievement of recent years has been to set such issues to one side, while relations in other areas are "normalised". But what is normal, on both sides, is a lack of trust, leading to a cautious hesitancy about closer ties. □

2004

North Korea prepares to link its domestic intranet, the Kwangmyong, to the global internet, using the Hermit Kingdom's hitherto unused domain designation, ".kp".

All quiet only on China's western front

Dominic Ziegler   *Beijing*

China's Communist Party longs for calm, both at home and abroad, but distractions are guaranteed

Those who have long predicted a resurgent China strutting menacingly around a regional stage will have a fretful time of it in 2004; but the rest of us can relax a bit. For the time being, China will attempt to prove itself a pretty impeccable neighbour, and (if it handles the potentially perilous North Korean situation well) even the model of a world citizen. At bottom, too many challenges at home demand the full attention of those claiming to run this vast, chaotic land. For China's rulers, the fewer international distractions the better—particularly if they have the potential to disrupt the insatiable quantities of raw ingredients, notably oil and money, needed to continue the country's economic transformation.

So, good relations with America. In Asia, China will in 2004 do much to bury old grievances with neighbours, even if it reserves the right to dig some of them up later. It will undertake never to use force in territorial disputes with ASEAN neighbours over the South China Sea, under which oil and gas lie. Having already settled land-border disputes with Vietnam and Russia, China will even make noises about resolving border issues with India, over which a nasty war was fought in 1962. However, its chief territorial dispute—with itself, over Taiwan—will remain on hold.

For China, by far the sternest diplomatic test of 2004 will be North Korea, whose regime is kept alive on imports of Chinese oil and whose nuclear posturing is a more immediate challenge to the world's security, after September 11th, than Iraq, Afghanistan or Iran ever were. Until now, Kim Jong Il's defiance—admitting that his country is building nuclear weapons that it may test at any time—has been possible because China ▶

Dominic Ziegler: special correspondent, *The Economist*

NORTH KOREA   *FORECAST*

In 2004 the Agreed Framework, concluded between the United States and North Korea to defang the North Koreans' nuclear-weapons programme, is ten years old. America will prefer not to celebrate the birthday. But the North's leader, Kim Jong Il, will feel more festive. Unlike in 1994, he boasts two nuclear programmes: the original one, which is based on plutonium, and a new one based on uranium.

The outlook for dialogue this time round is mixed. North Korea is unlikely to abandon its nuclear programmes—or indeed its thriving export trade in unsavouries such as missiles and drugs—without specific security guarantees from America and promises of lots of aid. The Americans will be reluctant to be seen to reward North Korea for misbehaving.

An Iraq-style attack on North Korea is also unlikely. Bristling with chemical and biological weapons and only minutes away by MIG from Seoul, where a quarter of the South's population lives, North Korea would be a far riskier proposition than Iraq proved to be.

The North will miss no opportunity for mischief-making, playing the United States off against the other interested parties—South Korea, China, Japan and Russia—if only to buy more time for its nuclear programmes. Being on North Korea's doorstep and so vulnerable to its misdemeanours, these four countries will take a more cautious approach than America towards North Korea.

The nuclear issue also threatens to snuff out recent tentative North Korean economic reforms. It would take little in the way of hostility from outside, perceived or otherwise, for the already paranoid Pyongyang regime to stop creeping marketisation. After a dire decade of decline, the economy is growing again. Engagement and showing North Korea the material gains that accrue from co-operation may be the best way of ensuring that the reforms—and dialogue—continue in 2004.

KEY INDICATORS	2002	2003	2004
GDP growth (%)	1.2	0.7	1.5
Merchandise exports ($bn)	1.0	1.5	2.1
Merchandise imports ($bn)	1.9	2.0	2.3
Population (m)	22.4	22.5	22.6

Economist Intelligence Unit

Minding their own business

In China, 2004 will be the year when ordinary folk at last see the Communist Party start to get out of their bedrooms. Thanks to new rulings, couples will no longer have to ask their work unit in order to marry—a preposterous notion almost anywhere else in the world except North Korea. And if husband and wife are both products of China's one-child policy, they may officially have two children, not one (this to ease the coming and rapid greying of China). For urban Chinese, two children are probably as many as they want. In the countryside, the one-child policy is as often honoured in the breach as in the observance. □

blocks any attempt to haul North Korea before the UN Security Council for sanctions. While no love is left for its old ally, China's fear has been that pressure applied on North Korea might bring about the regime's collapse, with dire consequences for China, not least through a flood of refugees.

Some of the subtler minds among China's leaders recognise how short-sighted this is, and privately regret China's own history of weapons proliferation. These minds now want China to push a tougher line on North Korea—joining the Americans, South Korea, Japan and Russia to insist not just on the verifiable dismantling of Mr Kim's nuclear and other military programmes in return for massive injections of aid and guarantees of non-aggression, but also on a clear commitment to Chinese-style reforms to its hopeless economy. The same minds argue that if Mr Kim fails to respond to these offers (or responds, as ever, by breaking his word), then stronger measures against North Korea, including force, must be contemplated.

At home, 2004 will bring extraordinary signals of change in the way Chinese are able to go about their lives. On the economic front, some sort of guarantee for private-property rights will be enshrined in the country's constitution in March—an attempt to limit the depredations of the state and to allow private enterprise, now a crucial part of the economy, to gain a more secure hold.

Communist means of social control are also being radically loosened, and this will accelerate next year. Household-registration rules will be eased further to encourage educated Chinese to move in search of work. The tens of millions of poor country migrants looking

Robert Ward:
Economist Intelligence
Unit

for work in the cities, the butt of arbitrary police oppression, will be protected by new regulations forbidding their repatriation or their mass detention in camps, hitherto a giant blot on China's reputation. Increasingly, work units and local officials will have to give up the final say over who gets to have a passport: individuals from more and more cities will have the automatic right to one. Travel restrictions to Hong Kong have been greatly eased, and will be relaxed further. This will be the year when mainland Chinese really start to see the world.

Why will President Hu Jintao and his colleagues sanction such momentous changes? A mix of reasons. Helping the lot of migrant workers furthers aims to develop poorer parts of the country: despite official campaigns to drum up investment in poor regions, it is returning migrant workers who inject the most capital. Rules freeing up travel to Hong Kong are an attempt to boost the troubled economy of China's special territory. On the face of it, many parts of the state's coercive apparatus, set up when every aspect of personal life was governed by the Communist Party, appear to be losing the will to govern. Yes, even armed bureaucratic dictatorships want to be popular.

Whatever the reasons for these changes, they will, at every level, generate demand for more. To take just one instance: many informed Chinese know that Hong Kong's free press, by forcing an admission from an obfuscating central government that there was a serious SARS crisis in China, saved many hundreds of lives in 2003. By the same token, many of the 8m mainland visitors to decent, civil Hong Kong in 2004 will take back a desire for a kind of life which does not exist on the mainland. Do the changes imply an unswerving path towards liberal government and civil rights? On the contrary, they open the gap between people's expectations and a leadership only imperfectly operating the levers of power. There lies the scope for popular disappointment. So the final prediction for 2004: it will be the year when the natives start to get restless. □

Ageing trailblazer

Robert Ward

Time to start learning from Japan again

In 2004 Japan marks the 100th anniversary of the outbreak of the Russo-Japanese war, when it first thundered on to the global stage. Japan's victory in the war stunned the world, not least by triggering revolution in Russia and offering those who cared to look a grim glimpse of modern warfare. A century later, Japan will show, albeit in a reassuringly quieter way, that it has lost none of its ability to surprise or educate. This time, as then, the world will do well to look and learn.

Japan's politics will surprise, if only because of its perversity. The ruling Liberal Democratic Party (LDP) will remain the democratic world's most reviled yet successful political party; by 2004 it will have been in power for 47 of the past 49 years. Oddly, this will owe much to the prime minister, Junichiro Koizumi. When he took power in April 2001 he promised to destroy the party in the cause of reform. Instead, he has strengthened it. Not ▶

only has he made the party more nimble by bashing and weakening its once formidable factions, but his maverick style resonates well with the 50% of voters who claim no party affiliation. Thanks to Mr Koizumi, the party looks more confident than at any point since it split and briefly fell from power in 1993-94.

Having won a convincing victory in the late 2003 party leadership election, and followed that with an early general election, Mr Koizumi's next big political test in 2004 will be the mid-year upper-house election. Since the LDP lost its majority in the chamber in 1989, voters have tended to use upper-house elections to punish the party for its policy mistakes and other misdemeanours. Although Mr Koizumi's enemies in the party will crow if the LDP fails to regain its majority, Mr Koizumi is a realist and will be happy with simply maintaining the status quo. If he achieves this, the dearth of credible challengers to his authority within the party suggests that his position may be safe until the end of his term as party leader—and hence, by tradition, as prime minister—in 2006.

Sealing his political authority will allow Mr Koizumi to focus on what really interests him: revamping Japan's security policy. This will take priority over economic reform. In any case, with economic growth likely to purr along at 1-2% in 2004—a whizzy rate of expansion by recent standards—the pressure for wrenching economic change is now off. Those economic reforms that he does pursue will be mainly political in nature, directed at undermining his opponents within the party and their support groups outside it.

One driving force of Mr Koizumi's revamp will be the military threat from North Korea, which is already bristling with chemical and biological weapons and may soon have nuclear ones too. Unless North Korea shows signs of compromise on its nuclear programme, Japan may feel in 2004 that it has little choice but to commit formally to building a ballistic missile defence (BMD) system with the United States. This will be a risky move. It will please the United States (which will then be able to share financial and technological burdens) and the Japanese public (which fears the North Korean threat). But it will also irk China, which views BMD as a threat to the potency of its military. In the worst case, it could trigger a regional arms race, as China beefs up its guns and bombs in response.

The implications for Japan's security policy of com-

mitting to BMD are also enormous. Not only will it tie Japan more closely than ever into the American security umbrella in terms of the interoperability of military hardware, but it also threatens to compromise Japan's self-imposed ban on collective self-defence. Mr Koizumi wants to update Japan's so-called "peace" constitution, which is the world's oldest unamended constitution, and has instructed the LDP to come up with a blueprint for constitutional reform by late 2005. He may well feel that committing to BMD will help force the issue. Going for BMD will also make Japan into a useful global prototype for the United States, as a successful roll-out of the technology might in time persuade other allies to join the system.

Grey heaven

While Japan blazes a trail in security policy, it will maintain its global lead in another area—the ageing of its population. In 2004 one-fifth of the population will be 65 or over and there will be more than 20,000 centenarians. (Mr Koizumi himself turns a well-preserved 62 in January.) The increasing burden of providing pensions and health care for the growing elderly cohort will ensure that Japan's public finances remain by far the worst in the developed world in 2004. The need to safeguard the financial assets of its pensioners, most of which sit in inflation-vulnerable bank deposits, will also constrain monetary policy, preventing the Bank of Japan from taking radical measures that might reverse years of deflation.

Yet where policymakers struggle, corporate Japan will thrive. Japanese companies will be world leaders in catering for the grey market. A trip to downtown Tokyo already reveals a pensioners' paradise, with shops brimming with gadgets for the elderly, such as electronic goods with extra-large buttons and displays or even beer cans and shampoo bottles with Braille lettering. The market for pensioner-friendly goods is already reckoned to be worth more than ¥2 trillion ($18 billion); future growth will be exponential.

Although Japan has one of the world's most rapidly ageing populations, other countries such as China and South Korea and most of western Europe are closing the gap and would do well to learn from Japan's experience. In 2004 Japan will show these countries and others that, while ageing brings problems, going grey can also be a good thing. □

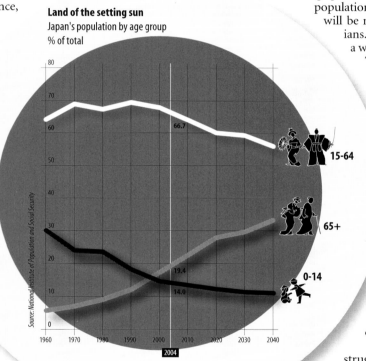

Land of the setting sun
Japan's population by age group
% of total

Source: National Institute of Population and Social Security

66.7 — 15-64

65+

19.4

14.0 — 0-14

2004

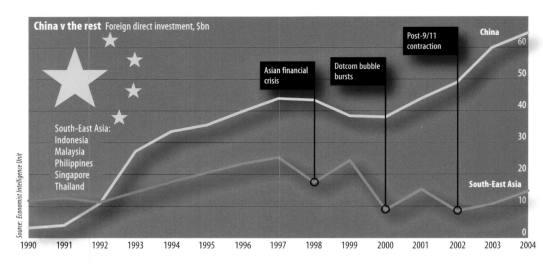

China v the rest Foreign direct investment, $bn

China

Post-9/11 contraction

Asian financial crisis

Dotcom bubble bursts

South-East Asia:
Indonesia
Malaysia
Philippines
Singapore
Thailand

South-East Asia

Source: Economist Intelligence Unit

60 · 50 · 40 · 30 · 20 · 10 · 0

1990 1991 1992 1993 1994 1995 1996 1997 1998 1999 2000 2001 2002 2003 2004

Cheer up, South-East Asia

Christopher Lockwood

Christopher Lockwood: Asia editor, *The Economist*

Brighter times ahead, despite uncertainties from bombs and ballot boxes

Few regions are less the master of their own destinies than South-East Asia, whose economies are highly sensitive to investment flows and the demand for manufactured goods from far away. The region includes some of the world's most trade-dependent countries.

This was wonderful in the 1990s, when a *tsunami* of western capital rolled over the region and its electronics industry. From 1997, though, the process went into reverse: the Asian financial crisis was followed by a meltdown in global demand for high-tech goods as the dotcom bubble burst in 2000, then by the post-September 11th contraction. The respiratory disease SARS added its malign influence in 2003. In the meantime, the giant sucking sound of foreign direct investment (FDI) heading to China has starved the South-East Asian economies of fresh capital. In 1995 Malaysia alone attracted about $5 billion in FDI. By 2003 that figure was below $1 billion—a fiftieth of what China gets, whereas at the beginning of

the 1990s both received about the same amount.

But 2004 will be a happier year in much of the region. Growth rates in all the main South-East Asian economies—Thailand, Indonesia, the Philippines, Malaysia and Singapore—will accelerate. American companies are starting to invest again, boosting demand for things such as memory chips, in which South-East Asia specialises. American consumer sales are strengthening, too, which again will tend to be felt disproportionately in South-East Asia, as it was in the early 1990s. America, though, is only part of the picture. Japan will at least be growing. And China, besides competing for foreign investment, is starting to play a significant role in the economies of South-East Asia.

China is drawing in imports at a remarkable rate, up by almost 50% in 2003. Many of these come from South-East Asia. Chinese people are travelling abroad as tourists in increasing numbers, as political reforms make it easier for them to get passports. Nearby South-East Asia is a logical destination—cheaper than Europe and America, and home to a large Chinese diaspora. Chinese tourist arrivals in Malaysia have risen threefold in the past five years. China has also become an exporter of capital, in the form of direct investment of its own, to the region.

The weakness of China's currency, the yuan, which is likely to remain pegged to the US dollar despite American pressure, will be a concern across the region; unless revalued, it could prompt a round of competitive devaluation. Another worry common to most of the South-East Asian economies is their growing public-sector debt, acquired since the crisis of 1997. Though not particularly high by global standards, it is in almost all cases heading upwards. Most regional governments need to start squeezing spending.

But the main difficulties faced in several of the South-East Asian countries are political rather than economic. Affecting the whole region is the spectre of Islamic fun-

---

PAKISTAN

FORECAST

Economically, Pakistan will be one of Asia's success stories in 2004. Growth will be among the fastest in the region, underpinned by inflows of foreign funds and a big debt-rescheduling package. Inflation will increase, but this is because of industrial bottlenecks and increased sales taxes, not food-price rises.

If this economic strength persists, Pakistan's political environment will eventually improve. But not in 2004. Relations between the president and army chief, General Pervez Musharraf, and the opposition, led by an alliance of Islamic parties, will remain strained. The opposition wants General Musharraf to give up his army job but he is loth to do so: his strength comes from his military role, not the presidency. If the dispute is resolved, the Islamic parties, which already govern

two of Pakistan's four provinces, may join the central government. How would the world take to Taliban sympathisers helping to run Pakistan? Provided General Musharraf remains the real power in the land, Pakistan will be left to its own devices.

General Musharraf's relationship with his prime minister, Zafarullah Jamali, is also fraught. The president would like to see parliament run more effectively. He may decide to replace Mr Jamali with the commerce minister (and owner of the Pepsi-Cola franchise in Punjab), Humayun Akhtar Rehman.

Pakistan may hold peace talks with India over the Kashmir dispute. They will achieve little, except perhaps the establishment of another bus link between the two countries. Pakistan's clandestine relationship with

North Korea and disputes with Afghanistan will strain its friendship with the United States, while the country's poor security environment will ensure that there is little interest from western companies in its nascent privatisation process. Given the number of potential threats Pakistan faces, just muddling through the year without a crisis will count as success.

KEY INDICATORS	2002	2003	2004
GDP growth (%)	2.8	5.8	5.5
Budget balance (% GDP)	-4.6	-4.6	-4.1
Unemployment (%)	7.8	7.7	7.7
Current account (% GDP)	4.5	3.3	2.8

Economist Intelligence Unit

Afghanistan's perilous addiction

Jonathan Ledgard

Kabul

Nice progress. Shame about the opium

The Buddhas of Bamiyan will not get rebuilt in 2004. Nor will much else in Afghanistan. The country will limp through the year. But there will be many successes.

More Afghans will have access to clean water, medical care and schooling than ever before. Refugees will return, particularly from neighbouring Iran. The economy will grow by a third or more. The national currency, the afghani, will remain stable against the dollar. Warlords will wear suits and ties more often. An Islamic constitution recognising at least some rights for women will win approval. An uncomfortable alliance between moderate, royalist-leaning Pushtuns and the Panjshiri hardmen running the defence ministry will survive. A dapper but listless Hamid Karzai will carry elections in the summer.

Afghanistan will receive plenty of cash from donors, not least from a Washington administration in election mode. Too much of this money will be siphoned off outside Afghanistan by unqualified consultants. Corruption, insecurity and inertia will mean few improvements in the disaffected Pushtun south, where they are most needed.

An insurgency of neo-Taliban—a grouping of former Taliban commanders, al-Qaeda stragglers, tribal malcontents and drug traffickers—will continue to blow up mountain passes, raise the flag over isolated villages, and murder Afghan and foreign aid workers in cold blood. But it will have less

Jonathan Ledgard: Afghanistan and Central Asia correspondent, *The Economist*

A budding narco-state

room for manoeuvre. Pakistan will make some effort to flush out neo-Taliban from its territory. The fledgling Afghan National Army will produce more soldiers of a better quality than expected. They will combine with American-led commandos and air power to kill increasing numbers of neo-Taliban. The insurgency will not be defeated but nor will it spread.

Peacekeepers will not venture outside Kabul. Instead will come—mostly to safe areas—small cadres of foreign troops known as provincial-reconstruction teams, who will be brought under NATO command in 2004. They will have some success in improving security and in helping donors to rebuild

infrastructure.

Such successes mean little. Afghanistan will not address the elephant in the corner of its room—the drug business—to the peril of the region. In 2004 Afghanistan will take another step towards narco-statehood: a third of the economy will be drug-related. Some 90% of the heroin shooting into veins in Europe in 2004 will be Afghan in origin. Afghan opiates will have a street value of $25 billion. Revenue from that bonanza will allow drug-enriched commanders to buy influence in the summer elections. Afghanistan will lack the money, and the world will lack the political will to wean impoverished farmers off opium. □

---

damentalism and terrorism. This is at its most deadly in Indonesia, where tourism has been savaged by the Bali and Jakarta bombings. The Philippines, too, will suffer more bombings, kidnappings and fighting in the southern provinces in 2004. But even areas terrorism has not yet reached are fearful. The region-wide crackdown on extremism has served to illustrate just how extensive are the tentacles of groups like Jemaah Islamiah, an outfit that has been linked to al-Qaeda, with cells reported in Thailand, Cambodia, Singapore and Malaysia, as well as Indonesia, where it is strongest. But police work and, crucially, regional co-operation on security issues has become more impressive, and will intensify as well.

Several countries face other kinds of political uncertainty. Presidential elections are due in the Philippines and in Indonesia, and a general election is due in Malaysia. Indonesia's president, Megawati Sukarnoputri, is likely to win her election, though critics fear the price for this will be to make her even more beholden to the army.

In the Philippines, the failed mutiny in 2003 may have made it less likely that President Gloria Macapagal Arroyo will win re-election in May 2004; if so, her successor will be less of a technocrat and more of a conventional politician. The result of Malaysia's election, by contrast, is not in any doubt: UMNO will continue to rule as it has since independence in 1957. But unless Abdullah Badawi, who took over as prime minister when Mahathir Mohamad's 22-year rule came to an end in 2003, can halt and preferably reverse the slow advance of the Islamic opposition PAS in the northern states, his tenure will be brief, as a destabilising leadership challenge can be expected.

One of the biggest stories in 2004 will come from the poorest and newest member of ASEAN, the Association of South-East Asian Nations. Myanmar's harsh treatment of opposition in general, and of Nobel peace laureate Aung San Suu Kyi in particular, will see tightening sanctions, and the threat of economic meltdown, though ASEAN is likely to rebuff all calls for its first expulsion. □

2004

South Korea will decide on the location of its new administrative capital city, probably in Daejeon, in the south-east of the country.

Lucky 13 in Australia

Robert Milliken   *Sydney*

The boom goes on, as John Howard aims for re-election

John Howard, Australia's prime minister, once suggested he might retire after he turned 64 in July 2003. Instead, in the elections expected in the second half of 2004 he will be seeking a fourth mandate for his conservative coalition government. His decision to stay on confounded pundits who believed Mr Howard would prefer to go out undefeated, like his hero, Robert Menzies, the founder of the Liberal Party which Mr Howard leads, rather than risk the political tide turning against him. It also upset Peter Costello, the finance minister, who had expected to inherit the leadership seamlessly and to bring a more progressive stamp to the Liberals.

But the pundits reckoned without Mr Howard's determination to relish his political success. He spent 22 years in politics before he finally became prime minister in 1996. Having won three elections, Mr Howard now rules the Liberals with almost absolute authority. And the portents for a fourth win are good.

The Labor Party rules in all six Australian states. But at the federal level, Simon Crean, its second somewhat lacklustre leader since it lost power in 1996, is struggling to make an impression; another leadership change before the election cannot be ruled out. Labor will focus on domestic issues where the government is vulnerable: health and education. As queues at public hospitals lengthen and universities grow even more overcrowded, Labor will undertake to pour federal money into revamping both systems.

Still, times are good. The economy will grow by about 3.3% in 2004, notching up a 13th year of uninterrupted expansion. The groundwork was laid by the former Labor government's reforms, but Mr Howard can claim to have driven the prosperity forward. Exports have flourished, thanks to a weak Australian dollar, and Australians themselves are feeling richer than ever on the back of a housing boom that has fuelled much of the expansion. In Melbourne, the second biggest city, house prices have soared by 91% since 1997.

The long boom brings problems, too. Australians have saddled themselves with worryingly high debt. If the Reserve Bank, the central bank, raises interest rates in 2004, many will be squeezed, and blame the government. After eight years in power Mr Howard's government has been tainted by sleaze involving some ministers, including Mr Howard himself, being caught misleading Parlia-

> **2004**
> The world's last transcontinental railway line will open in Australia in January. The journey from Adelaide to Darwin will take nearly two days.

The wisdom of Solomon?

Robert Milliken: Australia correspondent, *The Economist*

ment. In normal times this could be enough to turn the public mood against the government. But these are not normal times. The Bali bombings of October 2002, in which 88 Australians were among the 202 people killed, and the Marriott Hotel bombing in Jakarta in August 2003 brought home to Australians that "the lucky country" is no longer far removed from terrorism. Mr Howard has made security and the war on terrorism vote-winning issues (much as Mr Menzies did with the fight against communism 50 years ago).

Australia's alliance with America has become pre-eminent in the Howard government's foreign policy. The prime minister sent a small military contingent to the war in Iraq, against strong public opposition, and has much kudos riding on negotiations for a free-trade agreement with America which may, or may not, come to fruition in 2004. But many Australians feel uneasy about being seen as America's "deputy sheriff" in the Asia-Pacific region, a tag that stuck from an interview that Mr Howard gave in 1999. George Bush's remark in October 2003 that he saw Australia as a "sheriff" in the region hardly helped. Malaysia, for one, said it reinforced the view that Australia had become America's puppet.

Having appeared to take little interest in Pacific affairs for seven years, Mr Howard's decision in 2003 to send an Australian-led regional military and police force to restore order to the Solomon Islands showed he had read the signs that Australians feel more comfortable with the role of doing good works in their own neighbourhood. With a so-called "arc of instability" to its north among other Pacific island states, such as Papua New Guinea, Australia's role as a Pacific power is likely to expand. Some of the island nations themselves may resent this; but the argument that an Australia-New Zealand military presence saves these states from becoming terrorist havens plays well with Australian voters.

In Asia, China will be the country Australia courts most in 2004. For a short time in 2003 China outstripped America as Australia's second-biggest trading partner (after Japan). It is a major source of overseas students, and the government supports China's role in containing North Korea.

About 120,000 immigrants will arrive in 2004. They are the answer to Australians' disinclination to produce enough babies to replenish their ageing population, and to the calls of business leaders for more (skilled and enterprising) immigrants. One of the few commodities the new arrivals will find scarce in this land of sunshine and abundance is water. The Murray and Darling rivers have been almost strangled from drought and overuse. Whoever wins the 2004 election will face the thankless task of finding a way to get them flowing to the sea again. □

Anwar Ibrahim, a former deputy prime minister of Malaysia, writes from prison (where he is serving a 15-year sentence on charges of abuse of power and sodomy) of Asia's road to true democracy

A passion for freedom

"Genuine democrats are emerging, inspiring the young to value freedom and dignity"

Malaysians had their first taste of democracy when national elections were held in 1959. Less than two decades later, I had my first taste of political imprisonment for highlighting the plight of the marginalised rural masses. The Internal Security Act used against me, and thousands of others, was introduced by the British as a weapon against communist terrorists. The communist threat is now history, but the law remains and is used today to suppress all shades of dissent.

Malaysia is not the only Asian country that claims to espouse democracy while punishing dissenters. In much of the region, democratic space remains cramped by draconian legislation, the slavishness of media organisations, the collusion of judges with politicians and the bias of enforcement agencies against government critics.

When Benigno Aquino, the iconic Filipino political prisoner, was assassinated, and the ensuing "people power" ousted the dictator Ferdinand Marcos, pro-democracy activists saw it as a turning point for the region. The region's autocrats should have seen the writing on the wall. Instead, political oppression continued. As I write, the world is still in the dark as to the fate of Asia's shining democrat, Aung San Suu Kyi.

For a while, in the wake of Asia's financial crisis in the late 1990s, democrats again saw light on the South-East Asian horizon. Even within the power establishment, there were voices that spoke of the necessity for political reform, partly as insulation against future economic convulsions. And indeed Indonesia and Thailand made substantial progress towards democratic maturity.

This new optimism was shattered when New York's twin towers crumbled. In that act of utter barbarism, the ground shook beneath the democratic foundation that South-East Asian activists have been building with their investment of courage and sacrifice. Ironically, the epicentre of this tremor is not terrorism itself, but the war against terrorism, which is being waged in the name of freedom and democracy. Instead of harnessing democratic energy in the region, it has strengthened the hand of authoritarianism.

Re-energised authoritarian regimes gloat over the so-called wisdom of repressive laws and acts. Under pressure from the United States, they have since tightened the screws on dissent by describing dissenters as terrorists or Taliban. To appease their domestic audiences, however, they make strident anti-American noises, accusing the Bush administration of hypocrisy and double standards. Their spin doctors write of imperialistic designs, condemn America's treatment of suspected terrorists and accuse it of human-rights abuses—all the while ignoring the stench in their own backyard.

Before the collapse of the Berlin Wall, a few countries in South-East Asia could boast that they were, in comparison with eastern Europe,

democratic. They had multi-party systems and regular elections while the east Europeans were stuck with single-party dictatorships. But the tree of democracy planted when these countries achieved independence was never nurtured to health and strength. On the contrary, it was poisoned and mutilated to near death. Democracy can never grow without genuine democrats; until the habits of the heart are strengthened into a passion for freedom and a distaste for fanaticism.

Grounds for hope in 2004

There is reason yet for optimism. Toughened by imprisonment and other forms of oppression, genuine democrats are emerging in South-East Asia, inspiring the young to value freedom and dignity. Civil-society activists are pushing the boundaries of democratic space. To circumvent restrictive press laws, web-based newspapers have mushroomed, creating avenues for a free exchange of ideas. Talented young writers, passionate about their own freedom, are publishing their own independent magazines and producing other *samizdats*.

Reports are seeping through the prison walls into my cell that educated youths—graduates of local and western universities, and even of theology from Cairo's al-Azhar University—are congregating and discussing Kant's "What is Enlightenment?", dissecting Popper's "Open Society" and debating Hayek's "Road to Serfdom".

In this context, the non-interference doctrine of the Association of South-East Asian Nations (ASEAN) is anachronistic. The group's continued relevance must be predicated on its preparedness to summon the courage to shift towards democratic engagement. That is the most viable way of co-operation against terrorism, particularly Muslim militant cells in the region. It is also the most effective means of ensuring economic collaboration. ASEAN must look north to Japan, South Korea and Taiwan, where economies became stronger after receiving a shot in the arm from democratisation. And there is India, Asia's biggest democracy and culturally the most vibrant—a country that looks set to become a superpower if it can rein in its Hindu zealots.

The countries of the region must firm up their democratic institutions; they must ensure free and fair elections and uphold the supremacy of the law. The region needs to move from opaque crony capitalism towards open, transparent governance and a market economy. Constitutionally entrenched rights are crucial. As globalisation penetrates deeper, institutions and practices that are not compatible with it will come under increasing strain.

A genuinely democratic South-East Asia will generate the creative political judgment that is necessary for embracing both modernity and cosmopolitanism. □

Is your business prepared for fast-changing world markets?

Rely on viewswire.com to keep you up to speed on developments in 195 countries.

ViewsWire provides the most timely and comprehensive country analysis available.

More than 300,000 executives worldwide already rely on ViewsWire from the Economist Intelligence Unit for timely analysis and forecasts on 195 countries. Every day we look at key economic, political and industrial developments around the world and tell you what they mean for your business. ViewsWire keeps you ahead of critical international business issues such as:

- What's the next move for the US in the Middle East and how will it affect business?
- How have global alliances realigned following the war in Iraq?
- Which emerging markets present the most favorable environments for foreign investment?
- Where are Latin American economies headed while chaos reigns in Argentina?

ViewsWire will help you make your international business decisions and manage your activities in today's fast-changing world markets. No other provider of international business intelligence can boast the breadth of coverage and depth of analysis that we offer. Over 100 in-house analysts contribute to the service and we draw on the unparalleled resources of the rest of The Economist Group. We also include selected content from a range of highly respected content partners such as the BBC, the *Financial Times*, the World Bank and the OECD.

Six reasons to subscribe:
1. Get daily analysis of recent events and their impact on your business.
2. Draw on a comprehensive database of key economic data and country forecasts.
3. Make use of our rich range of political, economic, financial and business background information.
4. Get coverage of tax, financial and trade regulations—as changes occur.
5. Stay on top of changing operational risks in 60 countries through our risk channel.
6. Track the latest trends in a range of industries and see our analysis and five-year forecasts through our new industry channel.

FREE trial and a 15% discount on your new subscription

To apply, go to viewswire.com/discount and complete the request form. Please include the **promotion code vw15** in the "Enquiry box".

Or contact our offices:
New York: +1 212 698 9745
London: +44 (0)20 7830 1007
Hong Kong: +852 2802 7288

Only qualified organisations are eligible for this offer. Please note that this special offer applies to new subscribers only and is valid until March 31st 2004.

An Economist Group business

Economist Intelligence Unit | The Economist

Turning the region around

Xan Smiley

The invasion of Iraq changed just about everything. In 2004 its implications will spread across the Middle East

2004

After more than 20 years of bloody civil strife in Sudan, a peace deal is likely to be brokered between the government in the Muslim north and rebel groups in the Christian south.

Change in the Middle East could be as seismic as it was at the end of the 1980s and early 1990s in eastern Europe and the Soviet Union, with one big difference. As the Soviet empire imploded, hope outweighed fear. In the Middle East, fear still has the upper hand.

But all is not gloom. Despite a horribly messy and bloody start to the business of rebuilding Iraq, the good signs are as many as the bad. It is in the Middle East's other hottest spot, Israel-Palestine, that it is far harder to see progress towards peace. In any event, the American removal of Saddam Hussein in Iraq has totally changed the region. It is as though a huge rock has been thrown into a fetid pond. The ripples are reaching across the entire Arab world, as well as to Iran and Kurdistan.

If democracy can take root in Iraq, the implications for the rest of the Arab world, where there is not a single real democracy, will be immense. Moreover, if some kind of federal arrangement can also take hold, that too would show people elsewhere in the region that government does not have to be centralised in order to be effective.

The Kurdish north has prospered, relatively speaking, and the Kurds seem likely to remain sensible enough not to demand secession. The Shia Muslim world is in ferment, but most Shias in Iraq, where they will become the most influential group in the country, seem ready to keep theology and government fairly separate. The Sunnis, who had run the show since the creation of Iraq in the 1920s, have been the post-Saddam losers. But they may become more acquiescent if a decent degree of security can be re-established, if oil production can surpass its pre-war level, and if public services, in particular electricity and water, can do the same.

The Americans will allow a wider share of the burden of nation-building and security to be spread among other countries, under the aegis of the United Nations, though with the United States still insisting that it plays the leading role. Iraqis will take up their responsibilities for their own governance sooner than was predicted. Drafting a constitution will be difficult but is a prerequisite to a ▶

Xan Smiley:
Middle East and Africa editor, *The Economist*

genuine handover of power to Iraqis. A referendum on a constitution should, with luck, occur in 2004.

A striking improvement in Iraq would have a good knock-on effect, even in Israel-Palestine. However, even if Iraq is not doomed to deteriorate in 2004, hopes for settling Israel-Palestine will be a lot feebler. Whether or not the road map roughly charted out by George Bush and others is formally chucked in the bin, its timetable to establish a viable Palestinian state by 2005 will almost certainly be put to one side, and the fearful cycle of repression and violence between the two warring sides will continue.

Meanwhile, the Israelis will keep building a giant wall of separation roughly between Israel proper and the occupied territory of the West Bank in order, they hope, to keep Palestinian terrorists out of Israel. This will fuel resentment, poverty and despair among Palestinians, as they are penned into enclaves and see more of their land being taken over in the supposed interests of Israeli security. The wall will not follow the line that divided the two halves of Israel-Palestine in 1967 but will make protective loops around the larger Jewish settlements in the occupied territory. An embryonic Palestinian state would thus be severely squeezed and chopped. Despite the wall, the bombs in buses and cafés will go on.

Of the nearby states, Egypt will continue to stagnate under the rule of the ageing Hosni Mubarak, while Jordan, whose King Abdullah adroitly got into the Americans' good books during the war in Iraq, will be perkier. Yet even there, with Palestinians making up more than half the population, the king's position can never be deemed totally secure while the Israeli-Palestinian sore festers. Syria's regime, under Bashar Assad, is increasingly weak. Lebanon has both a presidential and general election in 2004. It, too, is shaky: its economy is feeble and its sectarian balance fragile.

The country facing the most unsettling changes in the wider region may be Saudi Arabia. That, once again, is largely thanks to America's occupation of Iraq and the vibrations that can be felt by its immediate neighbours.

Saudi Arabia may well witness further ructions and threats to the ruling House of Saud. The ailing King Fahd is not expected to see out 2004, though people have been predicting his demise for years. If he does pass on, the big question will be whether his anointed successor, Prince Abdullah, himself 79, will have the nerve, skill and foresight to arrange for a new generation to succeed him in due course, rather than let power pass in turn, as tradition has previously demanded, to a series of ageing brothers. The establishment of a rich, broadly democratic and Shia-led order in Iraq would spell danger to a Saudi Arabia that proves unable to reform.

In this sea of uncertainty, it is obvious that al-Qaeda and its associated groups are bound to see a grand opportunity to display their lethal clout against the Americans and anyone co-operating with them. It will not be possible simply to defeat such enemies, as Mr Bush sometimes declares. In 2004 and beyond, they will have their occasional brutal successes. The sensible aim is to contain them and above all to change the environment in which they thrive, which is why the creation of a more or less just and peaceful order in Iraq is overwhelmingly the biggest task in hand. □

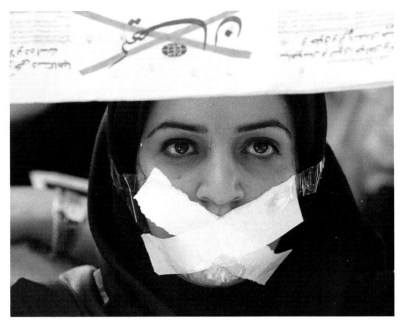

On edge in Iran

Christopher de Bellaigue   *Tehran*

Fading hopes of reform, but new overtures to the West

Christopher de Bellaigue: writer for *The Economist* and the *New York Review of Books*

After several years of painful decline, Iran's reform movement will stretch out to die in 2004. Iranians will be convinced of their inability to influence the decisions that are taken in their name, and their semi-democracy will more closely resemble the authoritarian regimes that proliferate elsewhere in the Middle East. But this will not provoke the popular explosion that Iranian exiles and Americans desire. It will exacerbate existing apathy, cynicism and despair.

In February Iranian voters will replace the reform-minded parliament that has been frustrated, ever since its triumphant election in 2000, by powerful conservative adversaries. Until the last gasp of the outgoing assembly, an appointed upper house and monitoring body called the Council of Guardians will veto any enlightened legislation to come before it. Conservative judges will threaten sitting deputies. The "house of the people" will be declared an illusion.

Ignoring charges that it is acting despotically and illegally, the Council of Guardians will disqualify dozens of incumbent deputies, blacklisted for their "radicalism", from re-election. Hundreds more reformist candidates, supporters of President Muhammad Khatami, will also be prevented from standing. Mindful of the value of high voter turnouts, the conservative supreme leader, Ayatollah Ali Khamenei, will summon voters to the booths. A large number, perhaps a majority, will ignore him.

Judging by the 2003 council elections—when only 12% of voters in Tehran cast a ballot—turnout will plummet from the almost 70% of the electorate that went to the polls in 2000. While weakening the regime as a whole, this will favour the conservatives, whose support among perhaps 15% of Iranians will win them more seats than

2004

Al-Jazeera, a Qatar-based television network, plans to launch a new documentary channel in February. The channel will go free to air in the Middle East; westerners will have to pay to watch it.

it should. The next parliament will be full of less reform-minded unknowns. They might support whichever conservative emerges as the establishment's choice to replace Mr Khatami after he stands down in 2005.

In its booming economy Iran will have the means to keep its young and restless population off the streets. (There will be periodic unrest, as there has been since 1999, but it will be localised and small-scale.) Minor structural reforms will burnish Mr Khatami's reputation as a cautious economic moderniser. The challenge he faces is to carry on pumping money into food subsidies and job-creation schemes while preventing inflation, around 16% by the end of 2003, from reaching crisis levels. Unemployment will peak at about 18% of the workforce, but the central bank will fight a losing battle to tighten monetary policy.

The government's failure to wean the economy off its dependence on oil revenues will leave Iran vulnerable to price fluctuations. When the oil price is high, as it has been for the past four years, Iran powers ahead. Unless Iraq's oil exports soar, or the world recovery proves illusory, the economy will grow by at least 5% in 2004. The car industry will exemplify the dynamism of the internal market. Iran will produce 1m cars, 250,000 more than in 2003. Almost all will be sold domestically.

Nuclear questions

Amid the depressing politics and mixed economics, it is unlikely that Mr Khatami will make good on his repeated threat to resign in the face of conservative obstructionism. Were he to go, his dwindling band of supporters argue, that would remove the sole remaining obstacle to despotism. The president will be swayed by what he regards as the paramount need for unity at a time of unprecedented international pressure. He came to power to reform the Islamic Republic, not dismantle it, and he has no desire to go down in history as Iran's Gorbachev.

The international pressure comes over Iran's controversial nuclear programme, which it claims is solely for

Khatami is no Gorbachev

peaceful purposes, but which America and others suspect is about making bombs. Iran was told to curtail its nuclear programme or face punishment at the hands of the United Nations Security Council.

Determined to deny him international prestige, Mr Khatami's hardline opponents had opposed his efforts modestly to increase co-operation with the International Atomic Energy Agency (IAEA). In October 2003, however, the same conservatives, after getting Mr Khamanei's authority to resolve the issue, made concessions of their own. Not only did they accept toughened inspections of suspected nuclear sites; they also agreed to suspend "temporarily" a programme of uranium enrichment and to give the agency a full account of Iran's past nuclear misdemeanours.

Some, especially in America, doubt whether Iran will make good on these undertakings. The Iranians are focused on driving a wedge between America, which wants Iran to give up its nuclear programme entirely, and other countries that are content with improved co-operation with the IAEA. That divide may widen in 2004.

The deal, and the way that Mr Khatami was sidelined as it was being struck, have increased the impression that, among Iran's competing factions, the conservatives alone are capable of taking strategic decisions. In 2004 they will try to strengthen their grip on foreign policy. If the nuclear deal holds, Iran will be denuded of the nuclear ambiguities that might have acted as a deterrent to Mr Bush's hostility. This increases the likelihood that the conservatives will make overtures to their American arch-enemies. On at least two occasions in 2003, impeccably connected conservatives bypassed Mr Khatami and contacted Americans close to the Bush administration, with offers of a deal.

The Americans' rebuttal of these offers was founded on two things: their reluctance to confer respectability on the unelected parts of Iran's theocracy, and their suspicion that no single Iranian faction can deliver strategic policy change. That view may now need to be re-examined. Expect more overtures in 2004. □

America's hopes of nurturing pluralism in the Arab world will bear some fruit in the Gulf. Quietly, if hesitantly, Gulf rulers have been reforming. This process will accelerate in 2004, particularly as oil prices fall and the financial handouts traditionally made in place of democratic accountability dwindle.

Bahrain now has a functioning parliament, though only half the electorate bothers to vote and the Shia opposition groups shout loudly of injustice and corruption; at least they are no longer tear-gassed into silence. In Qatar a new constitution has been approved by referendum, paving the way for a 45-seat legislature, with two-thirds of its members to be elected in 2004. The new constitution will vest ultimate authority in the emir, Sheikh Hamad bin Khalifa al-Thani, but this is still a giant leap for a country that in the 1980s was the epitome of a smug and profligate Gulf autocracy.

Dubai will, as usual, set the economic pace. The small emirate with limited oil but limitless energy will open a financial free zone—beyond the control of the central bank. Bahrain, the main financial centre in the Gulf, will look on nervously. Still, the signs are good that Bahrain will become only the third Arab country to sign a free-trade agreement with America. Qatar will push ahead with its natural gas-based industrialisation. And after ten years of prevarication, Project Kuwait will finally take wing in 2004, allowing foreign firms a direct stake in exploiting the country's northern oil reserves.

Saudi Arabia's relations with Qatar are close to breaking point following America's decision to move its troops and military control centre there. To show America that they have the resolve and wherewithal to deal with their own Islamist militants, the Saudi authorities will "uncover" a series of anti-western plots.

There will be some political progress in the kingdom—elections to city councils are planned—but modern tools are just as likely to be used to amplify archaic messages. The religious police now have a website, on which they exhort Saudis to beware of the dangers of "Jewish" Barbie dolls.

GDP GROWTH (%)	2002	2003	2004
Bahrain	5.1	4.9	5.4
Kuwait	-2.0	4.2	1.1
Oman	2.0	1.1	1.6
Qatar	4.6	8.5	5.0
Saudi Arabia	1.0	3.9	1.4
UAE	1.8	5.2	4.1
Economist Intelligence Unit			

Islam and democracy: the great experiment

Noah Feldman

Iraq's democratic progress—or the lack of it—will reverberate across the Muslim world

Noah Feldman: assistant professor of law at New York University and author of "After Jihad: America and the Struggle for Islamic Democracy" (Farrar, Straus & Giroux)

A year ago, the prospects for democracy in the Muslim world depended solely on incremental developments in the politics of individual countries. Free elections in Turkey, for example, had brought to power an Islamic-oriented party which was, and still is, governing democratically with less military interference than many expected. Quasi-free elections in Morocco

Nice idea, but will it catch on?

and Pakistan had shown that Islamic parties would win votes when autocratic rulers gave them a chance to take part. In Iran, meanwhile, it was becoming clear that President Mohammad Khatami lacked either the will or the capacity to stand up to the hardliners and translate his two overwhelming electoral victories into meaningful change. Gradual movement was the order of the day, with a step back for every one or two forward.

The Iraq war changed all that. As Baghdad fell, the Anglo-American coalition declared its commitment to establishing what would be the first legitimate Arab democracy, and one of a handful of constitutional democracies in majority-Muslim countries. This was a tall order, with even the most basic preconditions of law and order necessary to construct democracy in Iraq still lacking. But Iraq will be perceived as the natural experiment for the possibility of building democracy from scratch in a country where Islam plays a significant role in public life. Incrementalism is out the window. Either the Iraqi experiment will succeed, in which case the reverberations will encourage democratisation in other Arab and Muslim countries, or it will fail spectacularly, dealing a terrible blow to the fragile beginnings of Islamic democracy.

The progress in Iraq will be relatively easy to judge. A constitutional convention should be in place by autumn 2004. The Iraqi people should have a constitutional draft to debate, alter and (one hopes) approve by the end of the year, paving the way for proper elections.

If a free constitutional debate occurs, broadcast live in Arabic on satellite television, it will mark a watershed in the history of Islam and democracy alike. Democratically inspired clerics and laypeople, head-scarved women and coat-and-tie secularists will debate not only federalism and Kurdish self-government but the very relation between Islam and the state. Viewers will be treated to disquisitions on Islam and sex equality, the treatment of non-believing citizens, the funding of mosques and a host of other issues that until now have been purely theoretical in most of the Muslim world. Behind all this lies a basic question: can a state be at once truly democratic and in some sense Islamic in character? The answer will be in the doing: a lively debate followed by a ratified constitution and elections will do much to refute the canard that Islam and democracy are incompatible.

Success in Iraq would still be a one-off instance of foreign intervention, unlikely to be repeated elsewhere in the Muslim world because of its enormous cost. Yet the presence of nascent democracy in Iraq would affect autocratic Muslim rulers, fearful of intensified American pressure. It would influence also ordinary citizens in Muslim countries, who would quickly come to see in a prosperous, democratic Iraq a model for themselves.

The mere presence of a democratic Iraq could eventually push Iran over the edge towards reform. It would not be surprising to see Saudi Arabia creating a consensus-based selection process for its consultative assembly, still some way from the legislatures that are becoming increasingly common in other Gulf emirates but an improvement over the wholly appointed body that currently exists. The Jordanian monarchy, which held long-delayed elections in 2003, could liberalise further.

Conversely, if security is not restored in Iraq, and if the constitutional process stalls, autocrats in places such as Egypt and Algeria will appear to be vindicated in their insistence on a Hobson's choice between their rule and anarchy. The cautious liberalisations in the Gulf, in Jordan and in Morocco will be reined in. Indonesia's powerful army will be tempted to use the continuing threat of al-Qaeda terror to keep the president, Megawati Sukarnoputri, on a short leash. President Pervez Musharraf will have all the evidence he needs to maintain authoritarian control of Pakistan's corrupt politics, and America will continue to support him.

The real losers, should the Iraqi experiment collapse, will include not only the Iraqi people but Muslims elsewhere who have increasingly been arguing in recent years that democracy is as suitable to their beliefs and cultural conditions as it is to Sweden or Sri Lanka. Although patience should be the watchword in nurturing democratic development anywhere, the harsh reality is that hopes for an Islam that is capable of accommodating democracy (and vice versa) will rise or fall with the fate of constitutional self-government in Iraq. Regardless of the fact that Iraq is distinctive, it will become the prism through which the debate about Islam and democracy will be refracted—with vivid colour—in 2004. □

2004

Work will begin on Atlantis, a vast $650m resort on The Palm, Jumeirah, one of two palm-tree-shaped islands off the coast of Dubai. The islands have been created from scratch in one of the world's biggest land-reclamation projects.

Celebration time in South Africa

Adam Roberts   Johannesburg

But there are clouds over the anniversary festivities

Get ready to party in April, when South Africans mark ten years of democracy. In the first all-race elections, Nelson Mandela, as leader of the African National Congress (ANC), was elected president. His successor, Thabo Mbeki, will lead this year's song and dance, but Madiba, the clan name by which Mr Mandela is fondly known, is sure to grab the limelight.

Does the anniversary matter? It is a good excuse to push South Africa's claim to be the world's fastest-growing tourism spot: safari parks, beaches and vineyards will be busier than ever as a global television promotion campaign gets into swing. Most likely that will be helped by FIFA's decision in May on which country will host the soccer World Cup in 2010. It is promised to Africa, with South Africa the favourite.

More seriously, the celebrations coincide with a general election. The ANC hopes this will lift voters' enthusiasm, but interest is lagging. Unhappy voters in troubled, corrupt and poor provinces such as the Eastern Cape, the heartland of the ruling party, may not vote at all. That makes it less likely that the ANC will get control of two-thirds of parliament, the share needed to make changes to the constitution. Still, the ruling party is sure to win this third all-race election so easily it could sit in office alone. But it will retain allies like the Zulu-based Inkatha Freedom Party, for the sake of political calm in KwaZulu-Natal province. An alliance with unions and communists will also continue, though they are unhappy with the government's solidly liberal-capitalist policies. The rump of the movement which imposed apartheid, the New National Party, will shrink further as white voters switch to the opposition Democratic Alliance.

After the election the real political fun begins. Mr Mbeki stays on as president until 2009, and must pick ministers and his deputy, the presidential successor-in-waiting. Jacob Zuma, deputy since the last election, is tainted by allegations of corruption. Look instead to the foreign minister, Nkosazana Dlamini-Zuma (Jacob's ex-wife). If she gets the job she will be by far the most powerful woman in Africa.

Policies will not change much, but watch the fight against AIDS. In 2004 all state hospitals should start giving patients anti-retroviral drugs: roughly 11% of the population (about 5m people) have HIV, so many lives could be prolonged and children saved from becoming orphans. Drugs will eat up a rising share of public spending, even if prices fall as the first cocktails of generic pills are made locally. But it will be worth it. The cost of not treating AIDS is becoming ever more obvious: there will be a sharp rise in mortality as South Africa moves towards the "death phase" of the disease, when more people die than there are new infections. Average life expectancy at birth will drop to 50 years and then below. The government will continue to drag its feet; Mr Mbeki will barely

Adam Roberts: Southern Africa correspondent, *The Economist*

2004

Botswana will finish putting up a 300-mile-long electric fence on its border with Zimbabwe, designed to stop an influx of illegal immigrants and sickly livestock.

mention AIDS. One small glimmer of hope: stigma will gradually decline as more people openly get treatment.

The other big domestic issue to watch is black empowerment. The mining, energy and financial sectors already have "charters" setting out how much capital should eventually go to non-whites. But in early 2004 a new law for all firms will come into force. They must show what they do to train, employ and generate equity for black South Africans. Foreign firms will get some exemptions, but any company that wants a government contract, or needs a licence to operate, will have to comply with new rules. But true empowerment requires more jobs: black unemployment is stuck at roughly 50%.

Yet Mr Mbeki will be more interested in foreign affairs. He will shuttle around Africa to broker peace deals and boost his plan for continental economic recovery. Over 3,000 South African soldiers serve as peacekeepers in the rest of Africa—mainly in Burundi, the Democratic Republic of Congo and Liberia—and pressure to bring some home will grow as the army struggles to cope.

Mr Mbeki's doctrine of quiet support for negotiated change in Zimbabwe will probably get a boost, if only because no other strategy is working. He said in June 2003 that the crisis in Zimbabwe will be over by June 2004. That is too hopeful, unless he can somehow persuade President Robert Mugabe to leave. If he does, expect a surge of investment as South African firms pile into Zimbabwe, as they do elsewhere in Africa.

Mr Mbeki might be seen as a canny expansionist of South Africa's interests in the continent. But he would do better to concentrate more of his efforts at home, especially on AIDS. Otherwise, the 20th anniversary party a decade from now will be a much gloomier affair. □

The mourning after HIV/AIDS in South Africa, '000

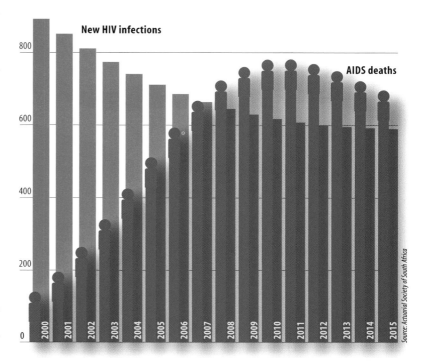

Source: Actuarial Society of South Africa

The gradual return of Iraqi crude will help bring down the price of oil, possibly by as much as 30%.

Africa's extremes

Douglas Mason

The very good, the very bad and Malawi in the middle

Sub-Saharan Africa will end 2004 as it has ended most years over the past decade: underperforming economically and wracked by bad governance and declining living standards. The UN will report that many African states have yet again fallen in the global ranking of human development: since 1990 real incomes per head have fallen 0.4% a year on average. Yet a small but growing number of countries will grasp the opportunities available to consolidate macroeconomic stability, attract investment and aid, increase growth and reduce poverty—proving that good governance can produce results in Africa as easily as elsewhere.

Mozambique's economy will grow by 8%—close to its average rate for the previous 11 years. Ghana, Tanzania, Uganda, Botswana, Cape Verde, Rwanda, Mauritius and other relatively well-governed countries will achieve steady growth, and reduce poverty. Africa will also feature disproportionately among the world's fastest-growing economies, with four countries in the top ten. That will include the fastest-growing of all, Chad,

African drums
Oil production
'000, b/d

Main producers
Nigeria 2,500 / 2,000 / 1,500 / 1,000 / 500
Angola
2000 01 02 03 04

Emerging producers
Equatorial Guinea 400 / 300 / 200 / 100
Chad
2000 01 02 03 04

Declining producers
300 / 250 / 200 / 150 / 100 / 50
Gabon
Congo-Brazzaville
Cameroon
2000 01 02 03 04

Marginal producers
Democratic Republic of Congo 60 / 50 / 40 / 30 / 20 / 10
Côte d'Ivoire
2000 01 02 03 04

Sub-Saharan Africa total
4,500 / 4,250 / 4,000 / 3,750 / 3,500
2000 01 02 03 04

Source: Economist Intelligence Unit

with a startling 58% growth rate in 2004 (from an extremely low base), as it pumps up as the continent's newest oil producer.

Africa will gain from its role as a growing—and relatively stable—supplier of oil, particularly to America, which has been quick to spot a strategic opportunity. Africa's oil exports will rise by 14%, led by Nigeria and Angola but with increasing attention on emerging producers such as Equatorial-Guinea, Chad and, later, São Tomé. Oil will help counter Africa's global marginalisation, although critics will point out, correctly, that ordinary Africans will benefit little from the capital-intensive oil sector, which employs few people, has few links to the rest of the economy and tends to fuel corruption. Angola's corruption-prone, oil-rich government—which has requested a programme from the IMF, despite having refused to implement its previous one—will be a test of the Fund's resolve to make an African government take poverty reduction seriously.

Several of sub-Saharan Africa's long-running wars and civil conflicts will move towards resolution. Peace will return to the Democratic Republic of Congo, defying expectations that this multi-country and multi-party conflict could be insoluble. Although its cumbersome new government comprising dozens of different groups—five of them armed—will inevitably be a fractious affair, it will do just enough to keep the agreement together as preparations for elections begin near the end of the year. Donors will pour in money, adding to the more than $2.5 billion already pledged or disbursed, underpinning a post-war boom.

Post-conflict recovery, albeit imperfect, will continue in Sierra Leone, validating the risky intervention by Britain's Tony Blair and UN peacekeeping forces. Liberia, rid of its warlord president, Charles Taylor, should begin a workable if messy peace, ending the baleful influence of this bandit state which has spread war and instability throughout West Africa for a decade. Mr Taylor, now in exile in Nigeria, may become Africa's first head of state to be extradited for war crimes.

Even the tragedy of Zimbabwe under its appalling but wily president, Robert Mugabe, will enter its endgame. The chances are that Mr Mugabe will be gone, or sidelined, by the end of the year. Like so many other despots, his grip on power will appear unassailable up until the moment it slips.

But the good news will have its limits. Côte d'Ivoire will deteriorate further. President Laurent Gbagbo will be caught between two intransigent factions: his own army and the rebels. Doing enough to satisfy either would reignite war or spell his own end. Four decades of peace and prosperity are an increasingly distant memory. Comoros and Burundi, where the Tutsi-dominated army has yet to allow a Hutu head of state to serve a full term in office, are at risk of coups in 2004.

Between the extremes of Africa's success stories and its war zones, the majority of sub-Saharan countries will muddle through. Africa's most typical country in 2004 will be Malawi. It has never been at war, has had only one change of government in 40 years, and experiences economic stagnation, declining living standards and the ravages of the HIV/AIDS pandemic. President Bakili Muluzi will step down in December, reluctantly accepting defeat in his attempt to secure an unconstitutional third term.

More African countries will hold democratic elections in 2004 that can be termed free and fair, even if they are predictably won by incumbent governments. Botswana's government will be returned to power in October, as will Ghana's president, John Kufour, who—as is now more common in Africa than before—heads a government that displaced a long-entrenched one and is completing a first, relatively successful term in office. Mozambicans will vote for the third time since emerging from civil war in the early 1990s. The dark continent has plenty of light as well as shadows. □

Douglas Mason: Economist Intelligence Unit

A world without alliances

François Heisbourg

The Atlantic alliance will have a new secretary-general in 2004. But do alliances like NATO matter any more?

2004

Watch this space. France, Germany and Belgium will continue to like the idea of an independent EU military headquarters, perhaps in the Brussels suburb of Tervuren, despite noisy objections from America and Britain.

In strategic terms, the network of permanent defence alliances set up after the second world war between America and its European and Asia-Pacific allies belongs to the past. This is the result of basic and lasting changes in the international system, not simply a consequence of the Bush administration's assertiveness. The "death of the alliances" is the direct effect of the end of the cold war and the emergence of new security threats.

In the new setting, America is the sole superpower. It will actively resist the long-term emergence of any peer competitor, whether this is an ascendant China or the EU positioning itself as a rival. The White House formalised this objective in its National Security Strategy in September 2002. More generally, the "mission determines the coalition", as Donald Rumsfeld, the secretary of defence, put it shortly after the September 11th attacks. The permanence of alliances is no longer of the essence; mission performance is. This is because the constant, existential threat from the Soviet Union has given way to a shifting set of threats and challenges. As for Europe, it has ceased to be an area of major strategic concern for America.

This move from alliance-centred policies towards ad hoc coalitions is not specific to America. It is a general phenomenon, with America's partners following a similar script. Witness the alliance-splitting policies of both "old" and "new" Europe during the Iraq crisis.

Personalities, it is true, have magnified these trends: the loosening of alliance ties and the expendability of unity have taken on an unnecessarily acrimonious character. But the underlying changes are more important. So whatever the results of the 2004 presidential election, it is unlikely that America will return to the multilateralist system which prevailed, with varying degrees of intensity, from 1941 (with the Atlantic Declaration and Pearl Harbour) until 2001 (with George Bush's inauguration and the terrorist attacks of September 11th).

This does not imply that America has no strategic alternatives. After all, pre-1941 America experienced phases of both engagement and disengagement, expansion and isolationism. America has the option of retreating into its shell. If the military, budgetary and political costs of remodelling the Middle East prove to be unsustainably high, the American body politic could, quite rationally, emphasise its own territorial protection rather than bear the cost of its overseas commitments.

NATO, the most durable and intimate manifestation of the system of permanent alliances, is particularly challenged. Already it has ceased to be a war machine. The Kosovo air campaign was NATO's first and last major war. With less than 8% of America's military force earmarked to NATO, operations with a significant American force component will necessarily be run by an American chain of command, not by NATO. Although NATO has ▶

François Heisbourg:
director, Fondation pour la Recherche Stratégique

▶ been a formidable lever for democratic reform in the post-communist countries aspiring to membership, this is now becoming a wasting asset as the alliance expands to most of central and eastern Europe. NATO also remains an essential provider of interoperability and standardisation between the armed forces of its members. But it will be difficult to keep America interested in this "service provider" function of NATO if the Europeans continue to fall behind in defence spending. Finally, NATO operates increasingly as a UN regional organisation through its peacekeeping and peace-support operations in the Balkans and, most recently, in Kabul.

This shrinking set of tasks corresponds to only a fraction of the overall transatlantic relationship, and—strategically speaking—not to the most important part of it. Real-world security challenges such as the Iraq crisis or, just over the horizon, Iran and North Korea, are not dealt with primarily in alliance councils. Strategic relations with China or Russia are not handled in alliance mode by either America or its European and Asian partners. Nor is the fight against global terrorism conducted mainly through the alliance system. Strategically important policies such as crisis-management in Africa or peace initiatives in the Middle East are shaped and implemented outside traditional alliance relationships.

This withering of permanent alliances will become more apparent in 2004 as the United States enters election-year introspection. Lord Robertson, an energetic former British defence secretary, steps down as NATO secretary-general on December 31st 2003, to be replaced by Jaap de Hoop Scheffer, the Dutch foreign minister. Competition for the job was lacklustre. No wonder. □

A year of optimism

Our global snapshot of expectations for 2004

Cheer up: 2004 will be a better year than 2003—at least according to Economist.com users. Optimists outnumber pessimists by almost four to one in a global poll of Economist.com readers for *The World in 2004*. Only 12% believe the year ahead will be worse, all things considered, compared with 44% who think it will be better (and 44% who reckon it will be about the same). As for their personal economic situation, more than half the respondents expect to be better off in 2004; fewer than one in ten expect to be worse off.

The online survey, conducted from September 12th-15th, drew 1,702 responses from around the world. Nearly half the respondents came from North America, but all the world's main regions were represented, with 22% from Asia-Pacific, 21% from Europe and 10% from the rest of the world. Not everyone, of course, may be as cheerful as the relatively sophisticated folk who log on to Economist.com. It is striking, though, that the broad optimism was shared by respondents all around the world. In Latin America and Asia-Pacific, half of all respondents think 2004 will be better than 2003. Even in the gloomiest region, sub-Saharan Africa, optimists outnumber pessimists by more than two to one.

One reflection of the relatively upbeat mood: people expect to be flying more. Two respondents out of every five reckon they

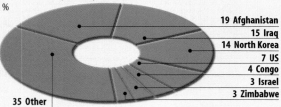

Compared with 2003, do you expect to be:
%
- 38 About the same
- 9 Worse off
- 53 Better off

In which country would you least like to live in 2004?
%
- 19 Afghanistan
- 15 Iraq
- 14 North Korea
- 7 US
- 4 Congo
- 3 Israel
- 3 Zimbabwe
- 35 Other

will be taking more flights in 2004 compared with 2003; just one in seven thinks they will fly less. Bulls outnumber bears, with 30% expecting to invest more in the stockmarket in the coming year and 7% expecting to invest less. Two respondents in five expect to buy a new mobile phone in 2004.

The poll suggests there is neither complacency nor panic about the nasty things that could happen over the coming year. The risks are acknowledged: 39% expect a collapse in house prices; 33% expect a renewed outbreak of SARS; 23% expect there will be a major terrorist attack on the scale of September 11th 2001. But in all cases those who think these things will happen are comfort-

ably outnumbered by those who think they will not.

Also unlikely, in the view of at least 85% of those asked, is regime change in places like Iran, North Korea and Cuba. What about regime change in the United States? There the verdict is closer: 53% expect George Bush to be re-elected, 47% do not.

We also asked where people would most and least like to live in 2004. The most popular country (chosen by 25% of respondents) is the United States, followed by Canada (12%), Australia (8%) and Britain (7%). People naturally tend to prefer countries close to home. Brazil is favoured among respondents from South America and Australia is the top choice among those from Asia-Pacific.

More revealing is where people would least like to live in 2004. Afghanistan comes top, with 19% of all responses. Nearly half of all respondents chose one of the trio of Afghanistan, Iraq and North Korea. Even among Economist.com users, though, 7% picked the United States as the country they would least like to live in—ahead of places like Congo and Liberia. Among respondents in North America and Europe, the figure was only 5%. But in all other regions, at least 10% picked the United States (in South America, the score was 17%, just behind Iraq's 18%). A revealing tinge of scepticism among the broadly optimistic view of 2004. □

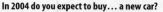

In 2004 do you expect to buy... a new car?
%

- 25 Yes
- 75 No

...a new personal computer?

- 37 Yes
- 63 No

...a new mobile phone?

- 41 Yes
- 59 No

What if...

Warner O'Doom

Five risks to look out for in 2004

What if the worst comes to the worst? With luck, and proper management, it shouldn't. The global economy appears to have turned the corner. But remember the risk manager's mantra: "Expect the unexpected". With that in mind, we asked a seasoned risk expert to scour *The World in 2004* for major mishaps that might upset global markets. Here's his pick of five top risks to look out for in 2004.

Warner O'Doom: guiding spirit of the Country Risk Service at the Economist Intelligence Unit

World recovery fails to take hold

If you believe the financial markets, the world economy is on the mend. Stockmarkets are well off their lows, inflation—not deflation—is back on central bankers' lips, and long-term bond yields have spiked far higher and faster than all but the most savvy bond trader had predicted. But while financial markets point to recovery, the excesses in the real economy are getting worse.

American consumers' debt levels are at an all-time high and the current-account deficit of the United States plunges deeper into the red each month. The EU and Japan, despite some recent hopeful signs, are mostly spectators in the race to re-ignite world growth. For the United States, the pay-off from low interest rates and high budget deficits is likely to come in 2004, when the Bush administration is expecting the recovery finally to take hold. But the global imbalances may be so massive that they cannot be fixed by American policymakers alone. If this proves to be the case, the only way out will be through another American-led world recession.

Iran or North Korea overplay their hands

In 2004 Mr Bush will hope to turn his attention to domestic issues ahead of national elections. Iran and North Korea may see his preoccupation as an opportunity. Iran made conciliatory moves in October 2003, but doubts about its intentions remain. If Iran decides to push ahead with its nuclear programme or creates too many conditions on a proposed UN inspections regime, or if North Korea decides to follow through with its threat to test nuclear weapons, they risk a world nuclear crisis as serious as anything since the 1962 Cuban missile affair.

Mr Bush has shown himself to be a risk-taker and, if he decides the stakes are too high, he may respond forcefully to these provocations. For Iran this could lead to a surgical strike on the country's nuclear facilities. For North Korea it could mean threats of American military action that would spread panic from Seoul to Beijing, and from Tokyo to Moscow.

2004

A new $4 billion global satellite navigation system, called Galileo, will be developed by several European countries with help from China. The first of its 27 satellites is due to be launched late in the year, with the rest to follow by 2008.

World trade talks collapse

After the debacle at Cancún in September 2003, the Doha round of world trade talks could collapse entirely in 2004. The failure would probably spell no less than the end of an era that has seen world trade rise 22-fold since 1950. The death of this post-1945 consensus on freer world trade would almost certainly push countries to join emerging trading blocs that would seek one-off deals favouring key partners while excluding others. The across-the-board costs of this less efficient world trading regime would be a permanent downgrade in the potential growth rate of the global economy. But the real losers would be the world's poorest, the very group that the Doha round is intended to help. They would be the least sought-after in the contest for carving the world into competing trading blocs.

SARS reappears with a vengeance

During the first six months of 2003, Severe Acute Respiratory Syndrome (SARS) caused more than 700 deaths worldwide and brought a number of Asian economies to the brink of recession. But the worst fears surrounding the outbreak were never realised, and after three months in the headlines, the disease subsided. But SARS may reappear in 2004. SARS-like diseases have rarely been known to vanish and the source of the virus is still unknown. In China, where SARS originated, some of the health precautions imposed by the authorities at the height of the crisis have been relaxed. At worst, an outbreak in 2004 could occur with an intensity far exceeding the initial outbreak. If the disease takes hold in places where public-health systems are rudimentary—sub-Saharan Africa, for example—it could kindle a global pandemic, killing millions and bringing the world economy to a standstill.

World financial accord ends in disarray

Weak banking systems have been at the heart of many of the financial crises in recent years. A new global safety rulebook for banks, known as Basel 2, already delayed but due to be approved in 2004, is supposed to cushion the world's banking system from future crises. But plans to finalise the new standard could become bogged down.

Financial lobbying groups have stepped up their offensive against it. The world's regulators cannot even agree: the United States has pronounced that only a handful of the largest American banks will be judged against the Basel 2 standard; the EU authorities are planning across-the-board implementation. The array of forces against the accord, and the sheer complexity of the proposals, threaten to strangle the project.

If Basel 2 died, global bank capital standards would still be in operation. But these would be the rules set out in the 1988 Basel 1 accord, which helped trigger the credit bubble that led to the 1997 Asian crisis. Hardly a recommendation for stabilising world financial markets. □

2004

China will stage its first Formula One grand prix in Shanghai. Canada, meanwhile, has been dropped from the calendar, due to its ban on tobacco advertising.

Hard choices on human rights

Michael Ignatieff

All the world's national-security challenges come from regimes that are also rights violators. How to respond?

The key question in human rights in 2003 was: when can human rights be used to justify regime change? From that question a second will follow in 2004: does regime change actually improve human rights? Sceptics will say that regime change in Iraq brought only chaos; defenders of American policy will keep saying give Iraq time.

Human rights always had a central place in Tony Blair's justification for the Iraq war. Although they played less of a role in George Bush's speeches, once weapons of mass destruction failed to turn up, rescuing 26m Iraqis from tyranny and torture was the best argument for regime change left standing. Yet there is nothing that bothers human-rights activists more than their doctrine becoming an alibi for imperialism. In September 2002, when Mr Bush cited Amnesty International reports of

Michael Ignatieff: director, Carr Centre for Human Rights Policy, Kennedy School, Harvard University

Intervening with flowers in Myanmar

Iraqi torture and human-rights abuse in the case he made for action against Iraq at the United Nations, Amnesty issued a press release which thundered: "Not in the name of human rights." Amnesty pointed out that the United States had not denounced Saddam when he was gassing the Kurds or shooting down the Marsh Arabs.

This was true enough, but great powers are rarely consistent about human rights. America (and most other countries) is bound to have one standard for its friends and one for its enemies, even one standard for Saddam when he was an ally and another when he became a *bête noire*. Denouncing the hypocrisies of the powerful is easy, if necessary, work. The harder question for human-rights activists is where they should stand when the hypocrites actually decide to topple a rights violator.

Staying neutral is one option, and some human-rights organisations—such as Human Rights Watch—do not take a position for or against the use of force in defence of human rights. Others, like Physicians for Human Rights, were prepared to endorse force as a last resort, but not in Iraq. Yet these positions put human-rights organisations in a peculiar position: denouncing the rights violations of bad regimes and then staying neutral when somebody sends in the tanks to topple them. However hypocritical the track record of the regimes doing the regime change, most human-rights organisations know that invasion offered Iraqis their best chance at creating a rights-respecting country.

Many countries, one question

Iraq will not be the only, or even the most important, human-rights issue in 2004. But the issue raised by Iraq—when do tyranny and abuse justify intervention?—will be the key dilemma in Zimbabwe, where President Robert Mugabe's senescent regime takes a once-rich land to the edge of famine; in Myanmar, where a dictatorial junta is clinging to power rather than cede it to the people's choice, Aung San Suu Kyi; in Iran, where democratic forces remain choked off by a regime that combines medieval religious repression with 21st-century pursuit of weapons of mass destruction; and North Korea, where a regime that cannot feed its own people uses nuclear ▶

Unlucky strikes

From the Dingle Peninsula to the Land of the Thunder Dragon, misery for smokers

At least one thing will unite Europe and America in 2004: the common crusade against smokers. Smoking has already been banned in public places in around 100 American cities, including New York and Boston. Turkish tea houses, Greek taxis, Spanish buses and Italian restaurants have done the same. Ireland will be next, when a smoking ban takes effect in all public places on January 1st 2004. Opponents (particularly bar owners and restaurateurs) say this will lead to layoffs and destroy the pub's role in social and cultural life.

Though the European Commission cannot dictate tobacco policy to member states, officials reckon they have a good chance of pushing through an EU-wide ban on lighting up in restaurants and cafés by touting it as a health-and-safety measure to protect workers from passive smoking. This could take a while, and will meet with noisy protests. In the meantime, the commission is banning smoking at its headquarters in Brussels and Luxembourg. It has also declared

that, from 2004, warning labels must cover a whopping 30% of the front and 40% of the back of cigarette packets. What little remains of those iconic packet illustrations (swirling-skirted dancers, placid dromedaries) may soon be overshadowed by EU-approved snapshots of cancerous lungs and other diseased organs.

Europe hasn't seen such anti-tobacco hysteria since the 17th century, when Pope Urban VIII issued a bull prohibiting smoking and James I fulminated against "a custom loathsome to the eye, hateful to the nose, harmful to the brain, dangerous to the lungs".

American and European smokers can, as they huddle in darkened doorways and gloomy alleys outside restaurants and bars, at least console themselves with the thought that things are even worse in one tiny pocket of Asia. The Himalayan kingdom of Bhutan wants to become the first nation to outlaw smoking completely. The sale and smoking of tobacco was banned in all but two provinces in 2003. Now the king has decreed that the entire country will be tobacco-free by 2004. □

blackmail to keep itself afloat. Force may not be prudent in all or even any of these cases, but some threat of force may be the only factor which will push these regimes towards compliance, both with non-proliferation regimes and with human-rights conventions.

It is a significant fact that all the world's national-security challenges come from regimes—such as North Korea and Iran—which are also rights violators. This ought to tell the United States that human-rights hypocrisy is a luxury powerful states can no longer afford. If bad human-rights behaviour is a good predictor of international dangerousness, then it does not pay to cosy up to dictators, even when they promise you stability, bases and regional order. America only has to look at the price it has paid, long-term, for turning a blind eye to the rights violations of Saddam. If that is the case, America and its allies may want to think about how future administrations are going to regard the cosying up to regimes

like Uzbekistan, which, because they provide bases for the American war on terror, believe they can get away, literally, with murder at home. Human-rights violators make unreliable friends and potentially dangerous foes.

Getting tough with Saddam started out as popular politics for an American president, but it is anything but popular in the international arena. Nearly 60 years after the creation of the Universal Declaration of Human Rights in 1948, there is still no international consensus about when rights violations in one state justify other states to intervene. For 60 years believing in human rights was easy; it was the apple pie of international relations. Not any more. The conflict between human rights and state sovereignty now divides the two intervening states, Britain and America, from much of the rest of the world. If the Iraq experiment fails in 2004, it will also determine the future likelihood of interventions—and the use of human rights to justify them—for years to come. □

A global response to cyber-terrorism

Craig Mundie

How to stop the internet becoming a weapon of mass disruption

The internet has done wonders for communication and productivity. It has also proved a honey pot for hackers and other criminals. Solving that problem is the high-tech industry's next big challenge.

In less than ten years, e-mail and the web have become indispensable tools. But every silver lining has its cloud, and the internet's is crime. Internet crime comes in many flavours, from traditional scams made easier by universal online connectivity to cyber-crimes and cyber-terrorism—deliberate attacks on the confidentiality, integrity or availability of data and systems on a national or global scale. The sheer pervasiveness of computers controlling critical infrastructures (telecommunications, transport, finance, electricity) suggests that the risks we face from cyber-terrorism will proliferate in 2004.

In 2003 we saw an escalation of the impact of computer hacks on business and personal computing. Hackers are no longer merely demonstrating computer skills to their friends; they are disrupting commerce and communications, and inflicting billions of dollars of damage. The global nature of the internet adds another dimension: the disruption of networks could seriously affect national and global security and economic prosperity.

So what is to be done? The two most critical proactive steps involve vendors, who must build more secure products that are easier to manage, and computer users, who must deploy these products in secure ways. Neither is a small task. At Microsoft, we have made what we call trustworthy computing our top priority. We are retraining our workforce to create products that are secure by design, secure by default and secure in deployment. We are working to make our products as secure as possible. But responding effectively to new threats takes time.

Computer users also have to take action if cyber-crimes are to be prevented. Just as we lock up our homes and cars, and keep our credit cards in a safe place, we all

need to keep our computers secure—especially as they are now such a critical part of our lives.

There are structural challenges too. Information technology has proliferated far faster than educational institutions have been able to produce skilled systems administrators to manage them, and far faster than the general population could be educated in information technology. As a result, many successful cyber-crimes occur because a network has been misconfigured. Recent advances in automation, such as automatic patching and virus updates, help to some extent. But users of IT systems are accustomed to, and require, incredible flexibility—so locking down systems and removing user-configurable options in the name of security may not be widely accepted. We therefore need to achieve "security usability": products must provide both flexibility and easy-to-implement security features.

Governments also have critical roles to play. As large ▶

Craig Mundie: senior vice-president and chief technical officer, Microsoft

The world's worst: Turkmenistan

Stalinism in one country

Where will be the worst place to live in 2004? Twice before we have put the question to the analysts at the Economist Intelligence Unit. They correctly predicted that Afghanistan would be especially dire in 2001, and Liberia in 2003. This time the world's worst prize goes, perhaps surprisingly, to Turkmenistan.

At first sight, Turkmenistan cannot compete with the war-torn countries in Africa or with dreadful places like North Korea. It weathered the collapse of the Soviet Union without major strife, and has observed a doctrine of permanent neutrality since 1995. However, Turkmenistan suffers from a peculiarly insidious ill: its 63-year-old president, Saparmurad Niyazov, "Turkmenbashy" the Great, Father of the Turkmen.

Foreign articles tend to treat him as a hilarious joke. They laughingly recount his decisions to name cities, bays, household objects and all manner of things after himself. They point out his love of pomp and his unnaturally black hair (which came upon him quite suddenly in the late 1990s). Yet there is a far more sinister side to this cult of personality. Even during the Soviet period, Turkmenbashy the Great—then plain Comrade Niyazov, who in 1985 became first secretary of the Turkmen Communist Party—ensured that *glasnost* and *perestroika* passed the Turkmen republic by. Since independence in 1991, Turkmenbashy has slowly brought about a return to Stalinist rule.

The only polls ever held in independent Turkmenistan—the presidential election in 1992 and a referendum on extending Turkmenbashy's term of office in 1994—achieved Soviet-like results of over 99% support. Citizens have few rights left. In April 2003 restrictions on political assembly were extended to the most innocuous events: people in the capital, Ashgabat, have to register with the authorities not just public meetings but also private functions such as weddings and funerals. Turkmenbashy exercises control through the secret police, the KNB. It uses torture and psychotropic drugs on its prisoners, and stages show trials in which the perceived enemies of the state confess and beg for forgiveness from the great leader.

All foreign influences are deemed nefarious. Opera and theatre are banned. Any foreigner wanting to marry a Turkmen must pay $50,000—although this is unlikely to affect many, since entry into Turkmenistan is now practically impossible. Leaving is also extremely difficult, and banned outright for women under 35 unless they have had at least two children. Those with one or none, it is understood, have failed to fulfil their duty to perpetuate the Turkmen race.

Since September 11th 2001 Turkmenbashy has positioned himself on the side of the winners, supporting the war against terrorism and nicely forgetting years of cordial relations with the Taliban. As a result, while other nasty regimes come under intense American scrutiny, Turkmenbashy carries on undisturbed with the business of self-glorification and oppression. He is fortunate in the country's vast reserves of natural gas, which provide him with a fast-growing economy and enough income to sustain his regime without international assistance.

But Turkmenistan's export revenue is not

Father of the Turkmen gets magic-carpet treatment

widely shared. Much of it is diverted into the Foreign Exchange Reserve Fund, which is under Turkmenbashy's personal control. Turkmenbashy lives in palaces and oversees showy construction projects—including several giant gold statues of himself—but most of the population lives at subsistence level.

In 2004 the regime's worst features will intensify: ever-widening purges; heightened religious persecution, extended to Muslims under the pretext of combating terrorism; and the final disconnection of Turkmen citizens from the outside world as ethnic Russians are forced to leave or sever links with Russia. A worthy winner, indeed. □

▶ users of IT, governments can prioritise security, from purchasing decisions to implementation and a continued emphasis on R&D in security technology. Governments may also have access to information on potential cyber-criminals and the threats they pose to our networks.

We also need to focus on factors that could deter on-line criminals, many of whom still believe that hacking is a harmless pastime. A widespread lack of traceability and authentication means that most criminal conduct cannot be tracked to its source. This, in turn, means that arrests are too infrequent. Better security will help, reducing the number of successful attacks and allowing law-enforcement agencies to focus on the more determined adversaries who circumvent security for a criminal purpose. But better accountability is ultimately the key.

Building traceability into the internet and creating robust biometric authentication has huge implications for privacy that require vigorous debate. But the question is not whether we want accountability or anonymity on the internet in general, but whether we want them in a particular application. In online banking, for example, the bank wants robust authentication. So does the consumer. Most people would also agree that anyone attempting to access critical systems of a power plant or telecoms network should be strongly authenticated in ways that expose the identity of unauthorised users.

These questions must be addressed on a global basis. Close co-operation will be needed between the technology industry, governments and all the stakeholders in the ongoing process of making the internet an even more positive force, while denying cyber-terrorists the opportunity to use it for their own purposes. □

Ernesto Zedillo, director of the Yale Centre for the Study of Globalisation and a former president of Mexico, suggests how to rescue the Doha round of trade liberalisation

Doha or die

"It may be easier to agree on something more important: a grand vision"

The seeds of the Doha round's breakdown were sown from the moment it was launched in Qatar in 2001, then nurtured all the way to the WTO meeting in Cancún in September 2003. It was, to paraphrase Gabriel García Márquez, a chronicle of a collapse foretold.

True, there was enough enthusiasm for international co-operation—especially after the tragedy of September 11th—for the round to be started at Doha. It was even baptised as the WTO's Development Agenda. Developing countries were persuaded to go along with the round because, they were told, it offered the only way of addressing many long-standing issues, particularly the rich countries' obscene agricultural protectionism.

But from the start there were reasons to be sceptical about the sincerity of the developed countries' commitment towards the success of the round. For one thing, the EU and Japan accepted the negotiations on agriculture only after loading the agenda with other issues of much less importance for developing countries and forcing an all-or-nothing approach for the conclusion of the talks. The United States then ruined its liberalising credentials with the introduction of steel tariffs and a subsidy-laden farm bill, and further dented its trade leadership when in December 2002 it blocked a deal to ease poor countries' access to essential medicines by amending the trade and related intellectual property rights agreement. It took eight additional months to get the deal unblocked.

By far the biggest disappointment, and the fundamental cause of the round's derailment, was on the agricultural front. Real negotiations never even took place, before or at Cancún. Countries produced their proposals but failed to show any willingness to compromise.

The EU was the worst (but not the sole) offender. It was not until June 2003 that it announced some lukewarm reforms to its common agricultural policy; on its own it failed to produce a proposal fully consistent with the Doha round's mandate on agriculture. A few days before the Cancún meeting, the United States and the EU came together to form a coalition, but unfortunately for the wrong purpose: perpetuating agricultural protectionism. The proposal from the Europeans and the Americans was, on the one hand, very imprecise about their market-access offer and, on the other, very precise in shielding their massive subsidies to farmers from significant reform.

It backfired, not surprisingly. It gave rise to the formation of a coalition of countries led by Brazil, India and China, which produced their own agricultural proposal and remained both militant and monolithic right to the close of the meeting. Not even a last-minute gesture by the EU—agreeing to drop the investment and competition multilateral agreements from the Doha agenda, by no means a minor step—could bring the negotiations back on track.

Will the disaster be mended in 2004, the year when the round was originally meant to be concluded? It is unlikely, if not impossible.

Obviously, the Doha round would immediately be resuscitated if countries started negotiating seriously about agricultural liberalisation. This would require, first, a meaningful move on the part of rich countries towards capping the value of their farm subsidies (and decoupling them from production), as well as significantly lowering their barriers to imports. It would also require a big effort on the part of developing countries to become serious trade reformers in line with their long-term interests.

The developing countries were right to resist the EU-US farm trifle. But this will be a pyrrhic victory if they persist in seeing the round's raison d'être as an endeavour to get as many concessions as possible without having to open up further to international trade themselves. They will severely damage their development prospects if they continue to be more inclined to fight for exemption from WTO obligations than to secure freer access to all international markets.

A compass for trade negotiators

Despite the huge economic advantages of achieving global trade liberalisation, let us not expect any specific progress in market-access negotiations in 2004. Domestic politics will not become more propitious for serious agricultural reform in Europe and Japan, and will be less so in the United States, because of the presidential elections. It will also take some time for developing countries to cool down from Cancún.

A more realistic and promising strategy to rescue the talks would be for WTO members to go back to discussing principles rather than details. Paradoxically, in such a politically charged year as 2004, instead of arguing about reciprocal market concessions, it may be easier to agree on something more important: a grand vision for the multilateral trading system, one that fosters growth and development.

By temporarily avoiding the negotiation of details, WTO members may be able to agree that, in a conveniently distant long term, the trading system must deliver the total removal of barriers to all merchandise trade, a substantial and across-the-board liberalisation of trade in services, and the enforcement of the principles of reciprocity and non-discrimination. Perhaps they could also agree that the most useful WTO would be one focused solely on trade liberalisation and relieved of other global economic governance tasks, which could be better accomplished by other multilateral or regional entities. Were these ideals to be adopted, negotiators would then have a compass to start navigating the rough waters of trade talks once again. □

Interview with a fungus

The essay competition run by Royal Dutch/Shell and *The Economist* has reached its fourth year. This time the question posed was "Do we need nature?" Nearly 6,000 people, from all over the world, offered answers. The first prize of $20,000 was won by Diane Brooks Pleninger from Anchorage, Alaska, whose essay, printed here in slightly abridged form, inverted the question neatly and informatively

You're watching the spores channel...

D.P. *Good evening, viewers. Our guest is Pilobolus crystallinus, author of the award winning bestseller, "Do We Need Mankind? A Fungal Perspective". Mr Pilobolus is a member of the kingdom Fungi, class Zygomycetes. He is a scholar, lecturer, dung-dweller and author. Welcome, Mr Pilobolus.*
P.c. Thank you, Diane. Good to be here.

D.P. *Mr Pilobolus, your most recent book raises tantalising questions about the future of the biosphere and the role that you and other inhabitants will play in it. Tell us how you came to write it.*
P.c. The book resulted from a series of symposia I attended over the past two centuries under the sponsorship of the World Federation of Fungi, on the topic, "What Does Nature Need?" The Academy of the WFF is constituted of one delegate from each family of fungi. I was fortunate to represent the *Pilobolaceae.*

D.P. *The 19th, 20th and 21st centuries have been a revolutionary period in the biosphere. How have fungi been affected by the events of modern history?*
P.c. The modern history of the fungi, which I date from about 400m years ago, has been a remarkable success story. The fungi occupy two vital niches in nature whose importance has never been challenged. In one niche, we are drivers of the carbon cycle, elite teams of detritivores whose mission is to digest organic matter and return the component parts to the ecological system. Without our work, life on earth would long since have ground to a halt for lack of raw materials. In another niche, we act in partnership with the roots of plants to extend their reach into the soil environment and enhance their uptake of water and nutrients. These partnerships are called mycorrhizas—*myco* for the fungus, *rhiza* for the root. Animals in turn feed on plants and benefit from this arrangement. So the fungi play two very distinct roles worldwide, and both roles are critical to maintaining the biosphere.

D.P. *When does mankind come into your history?*
P.c. Mankind comes into our history about 20,000 years ago, at the time they discovered the uses of alcoholic fermentation. We credit the genus *Saccharomyces* with this development. Ancestral spores of that yeast settled in a pot of gruel prepared by a group of hominids whose existence up to that point was best described as nasty, brutish and short. This began what we call the honeymoon period in the relationship of man and fungus. Unfortunately, it didn't last long.

D.P. *What happened to end it?*
P.c. Two things. Agriculture was one. Monocropping and animal husbandry led to concentrations of plant and animal populations that were vulnerable to certain of our members, particularly the smuts, rusts, mildews and blights. Some crops and herds proved to be sensitive to basic fungal metabolites. For instance, my colleague *Claviceps purpurea* produces the biochemical ergot. Ergot causes gangrene, madness and death in humans. However, there is no credible scientific evidence that it evolved in *C. purpurea* with harm to megafauna in mind. The same may be said of *Aspergillus flavus*, which occurs on nuts and grains. The aflatoxins produced by *A. flavus* are among the most powerful poisons and carcinogens on earth. To *A. flavus*, they are merely metabolic by-products, with a touch of self-defence function as well.

The other change for the worse resulted from transportation. The rapid movement of species allowed no time for immunities to develop in local populations. Many fungal species have been vilified for causing mass exterminations of elms, chestnuts, potatoes and other plants. This mirrors the unhappy experience of animal and viral microorganisms implicated in plagues and epidemics. The real culprits, of course, are the humans who transport exotics from continent to continent.

D.P. *As you see it, what has been the human purpose during recent centuries?*
P.c. With the advantage of hindsight, I think we can summarise it as a failed experiment in individualism. The idea of the individual—and there is no fungal equivalent—arose during a period of rapid change in human society. In the abstract, individualism looked defensible, even appealing. The ideal individual was to be educated and enlightened, someone we'd all like to know. However, as a practical matter, the culture of enlightened individualism reformed itself after a brief period into a cult of personal freedom. Over the next several centuries, unbridled personal freedom and chance distributions of natural resources led to the creation of certain wealthy and isolated colonies of humans. Their prosperity excited envy and the rest of the world did what they could to emulate them. Large populations of humans moved from a very simple experience of the natural world to the expectation of a lifestyle similar to what the exploiters were enjoying. This clamour for plenitude put enormous stress on the biosphere.

D.P. *As we know, humans failed to reverse this trend. Can you explain their failure to act?*
P.c It certainly wasn't for want of trying. If you visit the media archives of mankind—and we fungi are able to do so freely in spite of their efforts to exclude us—you will see that environmental issues were at the forefront of concern in all the wealthier nations for the past century and a half. Treaties, regulations, protocols, public opinion were used to stem the tide of harmful practices. But population growth outpaced the effectiveness of trade boycotts and outran the ability of the media to cultivate public awareness of environmental issues. And population growth added to the pressure on the biosphere as more and more people demanded ▶

higher standards of living.

A couple of analogies can help us visualise what was happening. One is the problem of the universal solvent. If there were such a substance, what would you keep it in? The phenomenon of affluence turned out to be a sort of universal solvent. Nothing could contain it. More insight is provided by the old canard about bread and circuses, which refers to the stultifying effects of amusement. Poor-quality information tends to ferment into low-grade entertainment. Under the sulphurous glare of continuous, worldwide news broadcasts, human institutions—government, military, religious, culture itself—became subjects of human amusement. This unrelenting, self-referential entertainment left a large part of mankind chronically inebriated and fundamentally uneducable.

D.P. Many times in your book, you mention what in earlier centuries would have been called "values"—altruism, moderation, that sort of thing. How do fungi define ethical values? Or perhaps you call them spiritual values?

P.c. (Laughs.) Much of what others consider spiritual, we call secular. This does not mean we are without a theology. There are two major systems of mycotheism in the fungal world. The more recent religion is only about 50m years old, but it has a strong representation among the younger orders. The older religion is more widespread, although it is also more rationalised from the original texts. Overall, 99.4% of fungi are adherents of one or the other faith. But the important thing to note is that there are no tensions, no doctrinal disputes between the two theisms. The core principle of both religions is identical.

D.P. And that principle is…?

P.c. Whereas the root principle of virtually all the religions of mankind is behaviour modification, our core religious value is species recognition. The fungi comprise nearly a million and a half species and uncounted millions of mating types. The pressures that result from diversity of this magnitude cannot be overstated. We have long recognised that the best way to maintain order in the system is to encourage institutionalised mycotheism. As a result, we are widely considered to be the polity most capable of reaching consensus among ourselves and acting in concert upon that consensus.

D.P. How do you describe the present relationship between nature and mankind?

P.c. I can only speak for the fungi, who characterise mankind as expendable. My chapter, "Many Keystones, One Arch", explores the uses that mankind has made of the fungi, which range from antibiotics and immunosuppressants to papermaking to bread, beer, cheeses and wines, and the familiar delights of mycophagy. Our members observed and recorded millions of human-fun-

You need us, we don't need you

gus interactions over a period of two centuries. Again, humans cannot escape our observation. We are everywhere: on their skin, in their homes, underground, in the stratosphere. After intensive analysis of these data, the Academy was not able to identify even one indispensable human-fungus transaction. No obligate parasitism, no essential relationships, no *sine qua non*. I ask readers to remember this important fact as they learn the startling outcome of our deliberations.

D.P. Without revealing the ending to your book, can you speak briefly about the last chapter?

P.c. Recently, the Academy convened a plenary forum to review our findings on the place of mankind in the world ecosystem. We evaluated the state of the biosphere, giving due weight to mankind's most recent energy policies, bioengineering innovations, developments in agriculture, industry and transportation, the efforts made towards environmental remediation and detoxification of hazardous and radioactive wastes. We considered the question of just how much perturbation of the natural order we should tolerate from human activities. We agreed that the biosphere presently stands at 9.6 on a scale of disturbance from zero to ten. Based on these findings, the Academy adopted a position statement which we presented to the WFF. I have taken the title of that statement for my last chapter, "The Knot of a Thousand Tyings". I'd like to read from it, if I may.

D.P. Please do.

P.c. "Our members do not recoil from the future. We believe that life on earth is embarked on a unique trajectory, one that will not be repeated. We believe that the outward journey has entailed a long and intricate interweaving of the interests of all living things. We believe that the homeward path will entail the systematic unweaving of those threads. We believe we are eminently suited for a role in this process." □

The full version of this essay, and the seven other prize-winning entries, can be found at www.shelleconomistprize.com

The judging panel comprised:

Richard O'Brien, jury chairman and strategy consultant at Outsights;

Peter Warshall, editor at large, *Whole Earth* magazine;

Christine Loh, co-founder and CEO, Civic Exchange;

Sally Feldman, head of the School of Media, Arts and Design, University of Westminster;

Adrian Loader, director of strategic planning, sustainable development and external affairs, Shell International;

Bill Emmott, editor, *The Economist*

The world in figures: Countries

LEAGUE TABLES

Oil producers will dominate the top places in the global league of economic growth. Two emerging oil producers, Chad and Equatorial Guinea, will be the world's fastest-growing economies; Chad surges, from a very low base, thanks to a new pipeline. Next come Liberia and Iraq, both rebounding from conflict. Four African countries and four former Soviet republics are among the top ten. The ranking is based on the 150 countries whose GDP is forecast in the Economist Intelligence Unit's *CountryData*. It excludes countries that lack proper data—such as Afghanistan, where the best guess is that the economy will grow by a third or more in 2004.

THE WORLD'S FASTEST

		GDP growth, %
1	Chad	58.0
2	Equatorial Guinea	23.0
3	Liberia	20.0
4	Iraq	19.0
5	Kazakhstan	10.1
6	Georgia	10.0
7	Turkmenistan	10.0
8	China	8.2
9	Azerbaijan	8.0
10	Mozambique	8.0

Only two countries are expected to see their economies shrink in 2004. They are Turkey (where a currency crisis looms) and Robert Mugabe's Zimbabwe.

THE WORLD'S SLOWEST

		GDP growth, %
141	Côte d'Ivoire	1.3
142	Switzerland	1.2
143	Paraguay	1.2
144	Kuwait	1.1
145=	Haiti	1.0
145=	Seychelles	1.0
147	The Netherlands	0.9
148	Gabon	0.6
149	Turkey	-4.5
150	Zimbabwe	-6.2

2004 forecasts unless otherwise indicated. Inflation: year-on-year annual average. Dollar GDPs calculated using 2004 forecasts for dollar exchange rates.
Source:

Economist Intelligence Unit

london@eiu.com

EUROPE

MAIN EVENT: EU enlargement. Ten new members join the Union on May 1st.

WILD CARD: Referendums on a new EU constitution. Will voters rebel?

AUSTRIA

GDP growth: 1.6%
GDP: $274bn
Inflation: 1.3%
Population: 8.2m
GDP per head: $33,360

Do not expect the government to last out 2004. Tensions have been rising between the centre-right Austrian People's Party and the far-right Freedom Party (FPÖ). Who's to blame? The FPÖ's erstwhile leader and perpetual troublemaker, Jörg Haider.

The government has given up trying to balance its budget; it expects a deficit in 2004, and for some years thereafter as it pursues tax and pension reforms. The economy will not improve much either. Slow growth in the bigger surrounding economies will hold Austria back.

To watch
Fallout from EU enlargement. No one is closer to the frontline than Austria, which expects enlargement to create investment opportunities for its businesses. But Austrians worry about rising immigration and job losses.

BALTIC STATES

GDP growth: 6.3% (aggregate)
GDP: $40bn
Inflation: 2.0%
Population: 7.1m
GDP per head: $5,540

EU and NATO membership beckon for all the Baltic states in 2004. Investment will drive the economies in all three countries. In Estonia the government looks secure, but Lithuania's government will become increasingly unstable ahead of October's parliamentary elections; a new grouping, the Liberal and Centre Union, will probably form the next government. Tension within Latvia's four-party coalition government will rise, mainly over the pace of economic reforms, but not to breaking-point.

BELGIUM

GDP growth: 1.7%
GDP: $317bn
Inflation: 1.2%
Population: 10.3m
GDP per head: $30,810

The main priority of the government will be to create jobs. But proposed incentives for employers to add workers will be constrained by the government's heavy debts. Some progress will be made in opening the telecoms and energy markets, where Belgium has been a laggard. The economy will improve slowly, along with its neighbours.

BULGARIA

GDP growth: 4.7%
GDP: $23bn
Inflation: 3.3%
Population: 7.7m
GDP per head: $2,980

Expect the general election to be brought forward to 2004. The ruling coalition led by the Simeon II National Movement still commands a majority in parliament, but divisions within the SNM are deepening, and defections are rising. The opposition Bulgarian Socialist Party, focusing on unfulfilled SNM promises, would probably win an early election.

Bulgaria will join NATO in 2004. EU membership is a more distant prospect. A 2007 target date has been set, but if the EU struggles to absorb the ten new entrants of 2004, Bulgaria's application could be delayed.

To watch
Organised crime. The EU has demanded legal reforms, and none too soon. Allegations of links between prominent SNM politicians and organised crime will keep the pot boiling.

CZECH REPUBLIC

GDP growth: 3.6%
GDP: $95bn
Inflation: 1.8%
Population: 10.2m
GDP per head: $9,250

The coalition government has been buffeted by heavy fiscal winds: the Czech Social Democratic Party, which leads the coalition, is pushing for unpopular spending cuts. The government will want to hold together, if only to allow smooth entry into the EU in May 2004. But a government collapse is possible, as is an early election if negotiations on a new government were to fail.

The government is attempting to restart its privatisation programme, which stalled after a string of failed attempts to sell stakes in Cesky Telecom, the electricity producer CEZ and the petrochemicals company Unipetrol.

Inward direct investment $bn

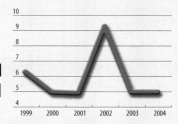

To watch
Václav Klaus. The Czech Republic's president insists on playing a role in foreign affairs. He opposed the war in Iraq—the government sent its highly regarded chemical-weapons team—and did not endorse the EU referendum. To the chagrin of both the prime minister and the foreign minister, Mr Klaus will continue to meddle.

DENMARK

GDP growth: 2.1%
GDP: $232bn
Inflation: 1.3%
Population: 5.4m
GDP per head: $43,080

Anders Fogh Rasmussen, the Liberal leader of Denmark's right-of-centre minority coalition government, is popular, and the opposition is weak. Mr Rasmussen will still need the help of the populist Danish People's Party to legislate, but he will cruise along safely—at least until the next election in the second half of 2005.

GDP % growth

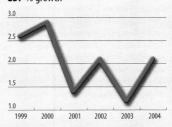

The government is introducing income-tax cuts as part of a programme of tax reform. Smokers and drinkers will applaud the reduction in excise duty on spirits and tobacco.

FINLAND

GDP growth: 2.5%
GDP: $177bn
Inflation: 1.5%
Population: 5.3m
GDP per head: $33,700

Finland's prime minister, Matti Vanhanen, will be wary of involvement in EU defence policy, preferring instead to focus on better crisis management. Labour-market reform is a priority. Wage costs are too high, skills too low and the population is ageing fast.

FRANCE

GDP growth: 1.7%
GDP: $1,911bn
Inflation: 1.5%
Population: 60.4m
GDP per head: $31,640

Jean-Pierre Raffarin, the prime minister, faced down the trade unions—and their nationwide protests—and successfully pushed through pension reforms. But his popularity is waning. Voters may have no stomach for the next item on his agenda: curbing rising health-care costs.

The state's direct role in the economy will be pared back as the tax burden is cut, the state's holdings in public enterprises are reduced and sectors still dominated by former state monopolies are slowly opened to competition. Expect the partial privatisations of Electricité de France and Gaz de France in 2004.

To watch
Two presidents. Jacques Chirac and George Bush are on speaking terms again, but only just. While an election year may make Mr Bush more conciliatory abroad, Mr Chirac should not expect an invitation to the ranch.

GERMANY

GDP growth: 1.8%
GDP: $2,543bn
Inflation: 0.5%
Population: 82.5m
GDP per head: $30,810

Gerhard Schröder is unpopular—most Germans do not trust him. But his coalition government looks secure for now, despite tensions between the Social Democrats and the Greens. The government will push urgent reforms to the labour, pension and health systems, but not hard enough: party mavericks will extract concessions, and the opposition controls the upper house.

Population % aged 65 and over

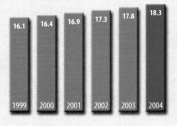

16.1 (1999) | 16.4 (2000) | 16.9 (2001) | 17.3 (2002) | 17.8 (2003) | 18.3 (2004)

The economy will begin to recover as demand for exports picks up. A tax cut scheduled for 2005 will be brought forward by a year—good news for consumers. But faster growth will owe much to the larger number of working and shopping days in 2004. There will be more budget blues: Germany will breach the 3% EU fiscal-deficit ceiling for a third year in a row.

GREECE

GDP growth: 4.1%
GDP: $184bn
Inflation: 2.7%
Population: 10.7m
GDP per head: $17,250

Time is running out for Costas Simitis, the prime minister. An election is due in the spring and his Pasok Party (in power for 19 of the past 22 years) is likely to lose, though by a narrow margin. Voters are fed up with high unemployment and the air of corruption. The New Democracy party, led by Costas Karamanlis, will lead the new government.

To watch
The Olympics. Back to where it all began. Coroebus won the first foot race in 776BC. The modern Greeks are in a race of their own to complete construction of Olympic venues before the games begin.

HUNGARY

GDP growth: 3.2%
GDP: $91bn
Inflation: 6.3%
Population: 10.0m
GDP per head: $9,130

Politics is polarised between left and right. Every attempt at budget cuts by the governing Socialists will be portrayed by the Fidesz opposition as an attempt to impoverish ordinary Hungarians. Ironically, the government is pursuing a classic tax-and-spend agenda: big spending increases are expected, and even bigger tax increases.

The embezzlement case at K&H Equities, the brokerage arm of Hungary's second-largest commercial financial institution, has the potential to derail some political careers. Convoluted even by Hungary's standards, it involves collusion by investors in a plastics company, alleged

misuse of state funds and the political connections of a K&H broker. Politicians are watching nervously.

IRELAND

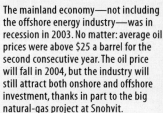

GDP growth: 3.7%
GDP: $173bn
Inflation: 2.9%
Population: 3.9m
GDP per head: $43,790

Bertie Ahern, the prime minister, may step down in 2004 if mid-year electoral losses cause a backbench revolt. But the ruling coalition will survive. A stronger American economy will help Ireland's exports and boost inward investment.

To watch
The air. A ban on smoking will be extended to all bars, pubs and restaurants from January 1st. Pub owners are predicting 65,000 lost jobs.

ITALY

GDP growth: 1.5%
GDP: $1,610bn
Inflation: 1.9%
Population: 58.2m
GDP per head: $27,640

Budget balance % of GDP

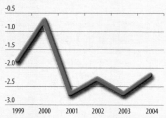

Silvio Berlusconi's shameless efforts to protect himself from prosecution over past business dealings will continue to dominate Italian politics. With a large parliamentary majority, the government is likely to survive 2004. But crises are brewing—federalist reforms are controversial and the economy will be a muddle.

Disagreement over how to reform pensions will divide the ruling coalition. Italians, especially those in the north, cherish the right to retire at 57. But the country cannot afford it. Mr Berlusconi is talking tough, but he will opt only for cosmetic changes.

NETHERLANDS

GDP growth: 0.9%
GDP: $538bn
Inflation: 1.2%
Population: 16.3m
GDP per head: $32,940

The government will go on the offensive against unemployment and the budget deficit. Severe spending cuts will hit

civil-service jobs and welfare benefits. Rising labour costs will hurt export-dependent Dutch firms, as will the rising value of the euro. The country will lead the EU as its president for six months from July; but in terms of economic growth, it will be the EU's laggard.

NORWAY

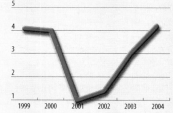

GDP growth: 2.1%
GDP: $220bn
Inflation: 1.4%
Population: 4.5m
GDP per head: $48,380

The mainland economy—not including the offshore energy industry—was in recession in 2003. No matter: average oil prices were above $25 a barrel for the second consecutive year. The oil price will fall in 2004, but the industry will still attract both onshore and offshore investment, thanks in part to the big natural-gas project at Snohvit.

The government will be in much worse shape. The Conservative-led coalition was dealt a severe blow in the 2003 mid-term local elections. With unemployment still high, the opposition is not eager to strike: it will let the government limp on until the 2005 election.

POLAND

GDP growth: 4.2%
GDP: $225bn
Inflation: 1.7%
Population: 38.2m
GDP per head: $5,870

GDP % change

The minority government, led by the Democratic Left Alliance, is weak and will not get any stronger in 2004. It will do little, therefore, to reform the public finances. An election, not due until 2005, could be brought forward if things get much worse.

The economy will do better, growing by around 4%. The financial condition of the Polish corporate sector is gradually improving. This should allow investment to build up again. A weak zloty will keep exports growing.

Poland will join the EU in May. Relations with America will remain strong: Poland is overseeing its own military zone in Iraq. Hurt feelings with France and Germany will ease.

PORTUGAL

GDP growth: 1.7%
GDP: $163bn
Inflation: 2.2%
Population: 10.1m
GDP per head: $16,090

With the opposition crippled by scandal, the coalition government led by the Social Democratic Party is looking more secure. The prime minister, José Manuel Durão Barroso, has been an effective economic reformer. If the economy picks up, as it should, an election victory is likely in 2005.

Portugal has been paying the price for the excesses of the late 1990s. Burdened with record levels of debt, companies and households have been shoring up their financial positions, and the economy sunk into recession in 2003. The outlook for 2004 is brighter as the imbalances begin to correct. EU-funded projects and hosting the European football championships will also help.

ROMANIA

GDP growth: 5.0%
GDP: $63bn
Inflation: 12.5%
Population: 21.6m
GDP per head: $2,910

A parliamentary election will be held in late 2004 or early 2005. The minority Social Democratic government has lost ground in opinion polls in the past year: living standards are not improving fast enough. But the opposition still does not look strong enough to win. The prime minister, Adrian Nastase, could emerge as the next president.

To watch

EU membership. If Romania is to join in 2007, it must complete negotiations by the end of 2004, an ambitious target. This assumes the EU declares Romania a "functioning market economy", a prerequisite for completing talks.

RUSSIA

GDP growth: 4.2%
GDP: $449bn
Inflation: 11.6%
Population: 144.4m
GDP per head: $3,110

With popularity ratings consistently above 70%, Vladimir Putin is on for another term as president in the March 2004 election. To many Russians, he is serious, sober-minded and effective. But his second term will be riskier than the first: economic reforms will be more difficult to pull off and Chechen-sponsored terrorism is a risk.

High energy prices have fuelled Russian growth. Much lower oil prices in 2004

and the continued erosion of export competitiveness from a strong rouble will hold back the Russian economy, despite a boost from planned tax cuts.

SLOVAKIA

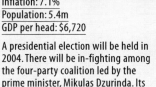

GDP growth: 5.0%
GDP: $37bn
Inflation: 7.1%
Population: 5.4m
GDP per head: $6,720

A presidential election will be held in 2004. There will be in-fighting among the four-party coalition led by the prime minister, Mikulas Dzurinda. Its conservative and neo-liberal wings cannot agree on much, and a wire-tapping scandal in 2003 did not help matters. The government should survive but two opposition figures, Robert Fico and Vladimir Meciar, are the country's most popular politicians.

The government will simplify the tax system by introducing a flat rate of 19% for personal and corporate income tax. Businesses will be happy and foreign investment should increase. The government will complete privatisation of the energy sector in 2004.

SLOVENIA

GDP growth: 3.4%
GDP: $30bn
Inflation: 4.7%
Population: 2.0m
GDP per head: $15,240

The ruling centre-left coalition should do well in the October parliamentary election, buoyed by euphoria over EU accession. But any missteps in the first few months of EU membership will be seized upon by the opposition.

To watch

Sea change. Croatia's proposal to establish an exclusive economic zone in the Adriatic would leave Slovenia 500km from the nearest international waters.

SPAIN

GDP growth: 3.0%
GDP: $931bn
Inflation: 2.2%
Population: 41.1m
GDP per head: $22,690

The governing People's Party is headed for victory in the March 2004 election. The economy has slowed, but is out-performing its big EU neighbours. Although the prime minister, José María Aznar, is stepping down, a smooth transition to new leadership is assured.

Mr Aznar's support for the war in Iraq made Spain America's strongest ally in continental Europe. With a change at the top, Spain's foreign policy will return to

its more traditional, lower-profile stance. France and Germany will be pleased.

SWEDEN

GDP growth: 2.3%
GDP: $349bn
Inflation: 2.2%
Population: 9.0m
GDP per head: $38,760

The minority Social Democratic Party government relies on the Greens and the Left Party for support in parliament. Tensions, mainly over budgetary issues, are straining co-operation. The three-way pact could break down in 2004. If it does, Goran Persson, the prime minister, will try to work with centre-right parties.

SWITZERLAND

GDP growth: 1.2%
GDP: $323bn
Inflation: 0.3%
Population: 7.3m
GDP per head: $43,930

The economy will recover slowly in 2004. Investment has been weak for years, the jobs market is still anaemic and the effects of a strong franc are only now wearing off. A stronger German economy will help. The government will try again to liberalise the electricity market after earlier setbacks. The gas and postal markets are next. Do not expect much progress.

The government will move closer to the EU, but only so far. Switzerland has already agreed to levy a withholding tax on interest earned by EU residents, but it will not relax its banking-secrecy legislation.

TURKEY

GDP growth: -4.5%
GDP: $212bn
Inflation: 39.4%
Population: 72.3m
GDP per head: $2,930

The inexperienced AKP government looks secure for now, but another economic crisis is looming. A sharp fall in the value of the lira and a rise in inflation is expected to trigger another recession: the economy will contract by more than 4%. Debt remains extremely high, but a default in 2004 is unlikely, thanks to help from the IMF.

To watch

EU-readiness. The political and social reforms required to keep EU membership in sight will divide Turkish society. Essential human-rights reforms and changes to the National Security Council will pose a direct challenge to the authority of the powerful Turkish military.

UKRAINE

GDP growth: 5.5%
GDP: $55bn
Inflation: 9.0%
Population: 47.7m
GDP per head: $1,160

Leonid Kuchma, Ukraine's scandal-plagued president, and his left-wing opponents are proposing constitutional changes that would turn the country into a parliamentary republic. While the two sides have sharply differing aims, both see the change as in their own interest. For Mr Kuchma, it offers the best prospect of retaining some degree of power once his term ends.

To watch

Viktor Yushchenko. A reform-minded opposition leader and former prime minister, he is Ukraine's most popular political figure and should be the leading candidate to win the presidential election, due by October. But don't count on it. Mr Kuchma is no fan of free and fair elections.

UNITED KINGDOM

GDP growth: 2.0%
GDP: $1,927bn
Inflation: 1.6%
Population: 60.5m
GDP per head: $31,860

Restive backbenchers could weaken Tony Blair's agenda for reforming the public services. There will be a gradual unravelling of the coalition of interests that has underpinned Labour's hegemony since the party came to office in 1997. But a leadership challenge to Mr Blair does not look imminent.

GDP % change

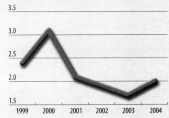

The government's priority is to deliver visible improvements to key public services. Taxes have risen to fund this. Mr Blair will hope that voters see this as a good investment. Adoption of the euro has all but disappeared from the agenda.

To watch

House prices. The British economy has done better than its continental neighbours, helped by the spending habits of consumers with ever more valuable homes. But this has pushed household debt sky-high. If house prices crash, the economy will crash with them.

ASIA

MAIN EVENT: India's elections. The world's biggest democracy in action.

WILD CARD: Exchange rates. Will China revalue, and will a strong yen choke Japan's recovery?

AUSTRALIA

GDP growth: 3.3%
GDP: $526bn
Inflation: 2.4%
Population: 19.9m
GDP per head: $26,400

Gross fixed investment % change

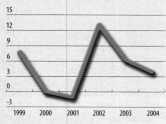

The government will focus more on domestic issues in 2004. Its health-care, education and labour reforms so far have been blocked in the upper house, but no matter. The opposition Labor leader, Simon Crean, is not popular, and John Howard, the prime minister, will win another term at the election likely in the second half of 2004.

After a long boom, the slowdown in the housing market will bite hard in 2004. This will mean less investment. But exports will pick up and the economy will do reasonably well.

To watch
The Solomon Islands. The South Pacific's failed state is now under Australia's care. Its peacekeeping forces will face risks, and the government may not have an exit strategy. With Aussie troops also in Iraq and Afghanistan, America's "sheriff" in the Pacific will keep busy.

CHINA

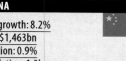

GDP growth: 8.2%
GDP: $1,463bn
Inflation: 0.9%
Population: 1.3bn
GDP per head: $1,120

The formal handover of power to the Fourth Generation of leaders is now complete, but backroom power struggles continue. President Hu Jintao will need to show more leadership if he is to eclipse his predecessor, Jiang Zemin. Mr Hu, who styles himself a man of the people, may call for greater internal democracy in the party.

GDP % change

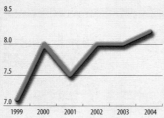

The economy is in danger of overheating as investment and trade soar. The government will rein in its six-year policy of public-works spending. But China's export growth will remain strong.

To watch
The yuan. How long can China keep its currency fixed to the dollar at such a low rate? The government will not give in to pressure from the United States for a big revaluation, but China is likely to widen the trading band in 2004.

HONG KONG

GDP growth: 5.4%
GDP: $174bn
Inflation: -0.9%
Population: 7.1m
GDP per head: $24,640

The anti-sedition proposal that provoked mass protests in July is off the agenda, at least until after the Legislative Council election in September. But while the chief executive, Tung Chee-hwa, has dodged a bullet, he remains unsteady and unpopular. If the pro-Tung party fares poorly, China may yet dump him. Almost like a real democracy.

Inflation % change

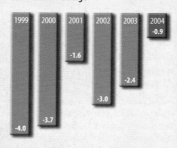

A stronger economy will raise spirits, provided SARS does not reappear. Hong Kong's exports will pick up. As deflation eases, real interest rates will fall and consumer and business investment will improve. After so much pump-priming, the budget will remain in deficit.

To watch
Mainland tourists. Surprisingly, the Chinese are the biggest spenders of all tourists to the territory. Visitors from the mainland will pour into Hong Kong in even greater numbers in 2004, as the government lowers travel barriers.

INDIA

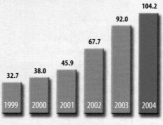

GDP growth: 6.6%
GDP: $639bn
Inflation: 5.4%
Population: 1.1bn
GDP per head: $593

International reserves $bn

A general election is due by October. The world's largest democracy could be in for a rough time. If the government campaigns on a Hindu nationalist platform, extremists will have an excuse to attack Muslims. The election will be close: the once-dominant Congress Party will make a strong showing.

Is an economic take-off finally in sight? No country has disappointed more than India but the outlook has brightened. Outsourcing has joined software as a mega-growth industry and the trade regime is becoming freer. The budget is still a mess and the election will prevent further reforms, but capital is flowing in.

To watch
Relations with Pakistan. Expect more confidence-building measures at a regional summit in January, but no resolution of the core Kashmir dispute.

INDONESIA

GDP growth: 4.6%
GDP: $248bn
Inflation: 6.8%
Population: 218.4m
GDP per head: $1,140

There will be a parliamentary election in April and the first direct presidential election, to be held in June. Megawati Sukarnoputri, the incumbent, is not popular, but there are few alternatives so she should win. A tougher line on terrorism would help her. But tolerance of endemic corruption will hold her back and her party will lose seats.

To watch
Jemaah Islamiyah. The Muslim terrorist group with links to al-Qaeda was blamed for a series of bombings, including the 2002 Bali attack. It will become a bigger threat in 2004. Indonesian courts have handed down death sentences against some of its leaders, but some are still at large and will be emboldened by their successes.

JAPAN

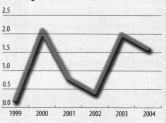

GDP growth: 1.6%
GDP: $4,366bn
Inflation: -0.5%
Population: 127.1m
GDP per head: $34,350

The Liberal Democrat-led government will remain firmly in command, thanks to the personal popularity of the prime minister, Junichiro Koizumi, and the party's strong grass-roots.

The economy will continue to recover. Years of corporate structuring will start to pay off, boosting investment. Consumers will be more willing to spend. But Japan's three Ds—debt, deflation and demographics—will hold back the economy.

GDP % growth

If Japan decides to co-operate with America on ballistic-missile defence, the impact on regional security would be profound. Japan's ban on collective self-defence would have to be scrapped. American power in the region would grow. China would be alarmed and North Korea's paranoia would be heightened.

To watch
Handy Wormy. This Japanese lifestyle product could become a global hit in 2004. A soft hunk of plastic, Handy Wormy hooks into the handles of plastic carrier bags so they don't dig into frail hands. Today's Japanese innovations are geared towards the fastest-growing part of its society—the elderly.

KAZAKHSTAN

GDP growth: 10.1%
GDP: $33bn
Inflation: 5.8%
Population: 14.8m
GDP per head: $2,260

President Nursultan Nazarbayev will tighten his authoritarian grip. But the core of his government is rotten: corruption is endemic, and a grand jury in the United States is investigating the payment of bribes to two high-ranking but unnamed Kazakh officials.

More than ever, oil will dominate the economy. Although the world price of crude will fall in 2004, the start of oil exports from new production facilities at the giant Karachaganak field will drive growth in coming years.

NEW ZEALAND

GDP growth: 2.4%
GDP: $81bn
Inflation: 2.0%
Population: 4.1m
GDP per head: $19,780

Helen Clark and her Labour government will continue to ride high in the polls. The opposition National Party will swing more to the right to counter Ms Clark and set itself apart.

Weaker export growth and less house building will cause the economy to slow, but the budget is firmly in surplus. A partial re-nationalisation of the troubled railway is likely.

To watch
Maori land claims. Courts have allowed the Maori, the indigenous people of New Zealand, to pursue ownership claims of the country's foreshores and seabeds. If the government goes soft on the issue, opposition parties will swiftly attack.

PAKISTAN

GDP growth: 5.5%
GDP: $83bn
Inflation: 4.5%
Population: 153.7m
GDP per head: $540

General Pervez Musharraf, the president, may replace the ineffective prime minister, Zafarullah Jamali. But the most pressing issue is General Musharraf and the powers he has given himself. The opposition wants to curb them. A deal is likely.

Several big sales of state assets are planned, including Pakistan State Oil and the government's 26% stake in Pakistan Telecommunications.

To watch
Afghanistan. The revival of the Taliban in neighbouring Afghanistan is being supported by sympathisers in Pakistan's tribal areas. If Osama bin Laden is still alive, he may be there. General Musharraf will come under increasing pressure from the United States to crack down.

SINGAPORE

GDP growth: 4.8%
GDP: $95bn
Inflation: 1.1%
Population: 4.3m
GDP per head: $22,330

Singapore's suffocating government is loosening up, a bit. More political debate will be allowed, but not on racial or religious issues. Anti-terrorism planning within the government will improve. Look for greater intelligence co-operation with its ASEAN neighbours.

Export volume % change

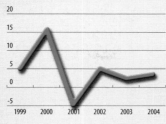

The economy will improve considerably in 2004. Demand for electronics is rising. Recovering from SARS, shops, hotels and restaurants will do much better.

SOUTH KOREA

GDP growth: 4.3%
GDP: $563bn
Inflation: 2.1%
Population : 48.4m
GDP per head: $11,630

The political scene will be tumultuous. The embattled president, Roh Moo-hyun, wants a referendum on his presidency. Without a strong new mandate, he may resign. The ruling party has already split, and parliamentary elections are due in April. Volatility everywhere.

After a recession in 2003, the economy will look stronger. Tax cuts and a government-spending plan will help.

To watch
North Korea's nuclear programme. North Korea will not give up its nukes without a security agreement with America, which is unlikely. Talks among the big powers will continue. George Bush will not attack in an election year.

TAIWAN

GDP growth: 5.4%
GDP: $300bn
Inflation: 0.5%
Population: 22.8m
GDP per head: $13,180

GDP % growth

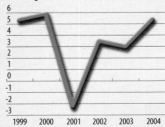

Farewell to Chen Shui-bian. He is likely to lose the March 2004 presidential election to the combined forces of the two main opposition parties. Lien Chan of the Kuomintang should become the new president with James Soong of the People First Party as vice-president.

A SARS-free 2004 and stronger growth in America will help Taiwan's economy. But reforming the banks and reducing the number of bad loans requires legislative funding. This will not happen until May at the earliest.

To watch
Beijing bluster? Before Taiwan's last election, China warned its neighbour not to elect a pro-independence president. Mr Chen won anyway. Beijing has learnt its lesson. Better to woo Taiwan's voters this time.

THAILAND

GDP growth: 5.7%
GDP: $143bn
Inflation: 1.1%
Population: 64.4m
GDP per head: $2,223

Thaksin Shinawatra, the prime minister, goes from strength to strength. His populist economic policies and moralising tone have been a big hit. His Thai Rak Thai party will probably absorb his coalition partners, giving Thailand a single-party government.

Thailand was one of East Asia's best-performing economies in 2003. It will continue to do well. Privatisation of state-owned companies is on the cards, and progress will be made in liberalising the telecoms sector.

To watch
Relations with Myanmar. Mr Thaksin is under mounting international pressure to abandon his policy of appeasement towards the Burmese junta. But he is worried about Thailand's large commercial interests in Myanmar, the need for Burmese co-operation on drugs control, border security and the many Burmese migrants in Thailand.

VIETNAM

GDP growth: 7.1%
GDP: $39bn
Inflation: 4.6%
Population: 82.6m
GDP per head: $476

Vietnamese companies will be in a good position in 2004 to exploit opportunities presented by the trade agreement with America. More state-owned companies will be closed, privatised or sold, but concerns over lost jobs and social unrest will prevent the government from moving too fast.

To watch
Fishy business. Relations with America had been improving, but they are coming undone over fish—mainly catfish, a big Vietnamese export on which America has imposed anti-dumping duties. American firms are now targeting another of Vietnam's growing exports: shrimp.

CANADA

GDP growth: 2.5%
GDP: $927bn
Inflation: 2.2%
Population: 32.0m
GDP per head: $28,950

The former finance minister, Paul Martin, will succeed Jean Chrétien as prime minister in February, and he is likely to call a general election in early 2004. Disunity among opposition parties will help the Liberals to a fourth consecutive election victory, maybe with an increased parliamentary majority.

Some 85% of Canada's exports go to the United States. As its economy improves in 2004, so will Canada's. Tax cuts will boost consumer spending, but higher interest rates in Canada later in the year will begin to bite.

To watch
Relations with the United States. With Mr Chrétien gone, the ice will thaw. Mr Martin will spend more on the military and be less dependent on the UN Security Council, pleasing America. But trade issues will still rankle.

MEXICO

GDP growth: 2.5%
GDP: $617bn
Inflation: 3.7%
Population: 105.2m
GDP per head: $5,870

Export volume % change

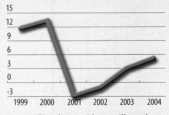

Vicente Fox, the president, will need to re-engage voters. His party took a pounding in congressional elections and 60% did not even bother to vote. All parties will make a show of greater co-operation. Major reforms that had languished during Mr Fox's first years, including electricity, tax and labour reforms, will be approved, though watered down.

Transport will improve. A number

of public-works projects are in the pipeline, such as expanding Mexico City airport and improving the national road network. Many of these projects will be carried out along the lines of the public-private partnerships in Britain and Spain.

To watch
A challenge from China. The number of *maquiladoras* (assembly plants) in northern Mexico is declining as companies relocate to China. Mexico has lost market share in 47 of the 152 main US import categories, while China has gained market share at Mexico's expense in 35 of those 47—including crucial areas such as TV and video manufacture.

UNITED STATES

GDP growth: 3.4%
GDP: $11,278bn
Inflation: 1.3%
Population: 292.0m
GDP per head: $38,620

Gross fixed investment % change

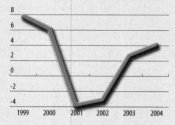

The race for the presidency will tighten considerably during the year but President George Bush will probably win the November election. The economy will not be booming, but it will be just strong enough to create a sense that the country is on the right track. Iraq will remain deeply troubling, but Democrats cannot beat a Republican on national defence. Mr Bush's political war-chest will be overflowing.

After a slow start, the economy will look livelier by springtime as business investment becomes more durable, factories add capacity and more workers are rehired. But the budget will be a mess: the costs of Iraq, Afghanistan, health-care programmes and recent tax cuts will be daunting. Mr Bush will need strong growth to keep control of the fiscal reins.

To watch
Foreign policy. America is perhaps more unpopular internationally than it has ever been. Mr Bush will try to mend fences in 2004, but with little success. Many Europeans will remain distant. Iran and North Korea are potential disasters. Mr Bush does not want another war in an election year and cannot afford one. But the hawks will not sit idly by if either becomes a threat.

SOUTH AMERICA

MAIN EVENT: Negotiations over a Free-Trade Area of the Americas.

WILD CARD: Venezuela's recall referendum on Hugo Chávez. Would he go without a fight?

ARGENTINA

GDP growth: 4.9%
GDP: $146bn
Inflation: 8.3%
Population: 38.7m
GDP per head: $3,786

The economy stabilised in 2003 and will grow by around 5% in 2004. A weak exchange rate will boost exports. But Argentina is not out of the woods. It must begin to repay its external debt, on which it has defaulted. This will require a budget overhaul. Frozen utility rates will have to be raised to fund investment.

Néstor Kirchner, the president, will face a difficult time in 2004. His popularity surged after a series of bold political reforms, but he must now focus more on the economy. His major opponents are within his own Peronist party.

To watch
GM crops. Around 90% of Argentina's soybean crop is genetically modified, and it also grows GM cotton and maize. Another international backlash against GM could hurt exports.

BRAZIL

GDP growth: 2.4%
GDP: $494bn
Inflation: 6.6%
Population: 179.0m
GDP per head: $2,760

President Luiz Inácio Lula da Silva surprised critics by pursuing investor-friendly policies. In 2004 he will lean towards his left-wing followers. Look for a greater focus on income redistribution, land reform and social welfare.

Inward direct investment $bn

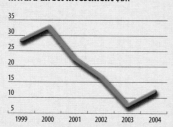

The economy will improve, helped by falling inflation and cuts in interest rates. The currency will depreciate moderately, which, along with rising overseas demand, will help exports.

CHILE

GDP growth: 4.7%
GDP: $76bn
Inflation: 3.0%
Population: 15.4m
GDP per head: $4,960

Following a wave of corruption scandals, the ruling Concertacion coalition and the Alianza opposition united on a series of modernising political reforms. For one, the civil service will gradually become less politicised. But with municipal elections scheduled for October, and presidential and congressional elections in 2005, expect a return to confrontation.

Export volume % change

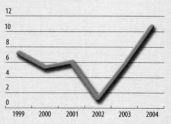

Industrial output will expand. Growth will be driven by the free-trade agreement with the EU, which took effect in 2003, and agreements signed and expected to come on stream in early 2004 with the United States, South Korea and the European Free-Trade Association. Exports will be the main growth engine.

COLOMBIA

GDP growth: 3.3%
GDP: $81bn
Inflation: 5.8%
Population: 45.3m
GDP per head: $1,780

Thanks to his determination to end the country's 39-year-old civil conflict, Alvaro Uribe will remain a popular president. Violent crime, though still rampant, has eased, and Colombians will feel safer travelling the country's roads.

However, with a persistent budget deficit, the government may have to take stern measures on the economy in 2004. Higher taxes and public-sector wage cuts are possible. Economic reforms could slow. President Uribe will have his hands full throughout the year. Expect plenty of grumbling.

To watch
The FARC. The main guerrilla group has retreated to its remote bases following the government's military offensive. The pause will not last. Surgical strikes by the guerrillas, possibly in wealthy urban areas in an attempt to undermine public support for the president, are likely. The prospect of any peace negotiations appears extremely remote.

MIDDLE EAST AND AFRICA

MAIN EVENT: Iraq's progress towards democracy.

WILD CARD: Yasser Arafat. Will the Palestinian leader survive the year?

ALGERIA

GDP growth: 5.7%
GDP: $61bn
Inflation: 2.6%
Population: 33.4m
GDP per head: $1,820

The political temperature is rising as the presidential election scheduled for April 2004 draws closer. The incumbent, Abdelaziz Bouteflika, has purged the cabinet of supporters of his likely rival, Ali Benflis, and has hinted that he might dissolve parliament as a means to assert his claim to a second term.

Crude-oil production was well over Algeria's OPEC quota in 2003. Expect more discipline in 2004, if only for a while. Growth will also be driven by reconstruction following the devastating earthquake of 2003. Exports will be helped by gas expansion as the In Salah development comes on stream.

To watch
Western Sahara. Movement on this vexed issue is possible as relations between Algeria and Morocco improve. Algeria is a long-standing supporter of Polisario, the rebel group fighting for independence from Morocco. A settlement, though, is not likely.

EGYPT

GDP growth: 3.0%
GDP: $69bn
Inflation: 3.5%
Population: 73.0m
GDP per head: $951

Exchange rate E£:$1, inverted scale

Hosni Mubarak's government will continue to take a security-first approach. Carefully controlled and heavily policed demonstrations over the Palestinian issue and the occupation of Iraq will be allowed. But the security forces will crack down hard if this anger is turned against the government.

If regional tensions remain contained, tourism will pick up. Exports should also accelerate because of the fall in the value of the currency. Strong government spending will also support faster economic growth.

IRAN

GDP growth: 3.6%
GDP: $134bn
Inflation: 15.0%
Population: 70.3m
GDP per head: $1,900

The government claims its nuclear programme is focused on peaceful energy supply, but suspicions about weapons development will persist. Iran will seek to defuse international concerns by allowing UN inspectors greater access to its facilities. Should suspicions persist, and if all other means of coercion appear to be failing, America or Israel may take military action against Iran's nuclear facilities.

The six-year struggle of the reformist president, Mohammed Khatami, to liberalise the country is on the brink of failure. Despite two election victories, Mr Khatami remains powerless in the face of an increasingly hostile hardline establishment. This could spell low voter turnout at the 2004 parliamentary elections.

IRAQ

GDP growth: 19.0%
GDP: $22bn
Inflation: 20.0%
Population: 25.8m
GDP per head: $836

A larger role for the UN in the wake of American floundering will lead to a more credible interim government. An expansion of coalition and Iraqi troop numbers, coupled with the faster transition to Iraqi self-rule as part of a deal for more international military involvement, should lead to better security. The military occupation should end around mid-2005.

A resumption of pre-war levels of oil output may not occur until the second quarter of 2004 at the earliest. Increased production from this period onwards, together with the slow recovery of the rest of the economy as reconstruction spending gathers pace, should lead to growth of close to 20% in 2004.

To watch
Iraqi banking. The selection of a 13-strong consortium of banks, led by J.P. Morgan Chase, to operate the country's new Trade Bank will give them a foothold in Iraq's trade credit market and a vital role in training a new generation of Iraqi bankers. The central bank will have to shed its image as the old regime's piggy bank and establish credibility.

ISRAEL

GDP growth: 2.3%
GDP: $120bn
Inflation: 1.2%
Population: 6.9m
GDP per head: $17,590

Budget balance % of GDP

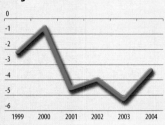

Even if there is a respite in the violence, progress on peace talks with the Palestinians on substantive issues will be difficult.

To ease its fiscal strains, the government will try to accelerate the privatisation programme. The national airline, El Al, has already been part-privatised. Other stockmarket sales of government stakes—in Bank Leumi, Discount Bank and the state-owned telecommunications firm, Bezeq—are likely. From late 2004, Israel Electric Corporation, the oil refineries and Zim Shipping could be sold off.

To watch
A government collapse. Ariel Sharon's government is likely to remain in place only until the close of 2004 or early 2005. Diplomatic developments will highlight ideological differences within the coalition, forcing fresh elections well before the deadline of October 2007.

JORDAN

GDP growth: 5.2%
GDP: $11bn
Inflation: 2.8%
Population: 5.6m
GDP per head: $1,946

The government will continue to face widespread anger over Israel's military incursions into Palestinian areas, and over the foreign occupation of Iraq. But King Abdullah will not be seriously threatened. He is generally popular—crucially, he has strong support from the army—and the country's security services are ruthlessly efficient.

Iraqi demand for foreign goods will accelerate in 2004, providing a powerful motor for the Jordanian economy. American purchases of Jordanian goods, principally textiles, will also increase. Demand in another leading export market, India, will slow as it develops its own gas resources, reducing the need for imported fertilisers.

KENYA

GDP growth: 3.1%
GDP: $13bn
Inflation: 3.0%
Population: 32.6m
GDP per head: $386

The euphoria of victory has faded for Kenya's president, Mwai Kibaki. His skills will be sorely tested in 2004 as he struggles to keep the fragile coalition together. Without major reforms—such as creating the position of prime minister—the government could blow apart.

A recovery in tourism, combined with increased activity in trade and finance, should boost growth. So too will the return of foreign assistance. But Kenya will still suffer from run-down infrastructure, weak institutions and a fragile economy. It also remains vulnerable to terrorist incidents, which damage tourism.

To watch
A crackdown on corruption. The clean-up is spreading through the entire civil service, including the judiciary. Many officials, high- and low-ranking, are likely to be implicated in ongoing investigations. Although the former president, Daniel arap Moi, has not yet been directly implicated, that may change in 2004.

LEBANON

GDP growth: 2.5%
GDP: $19bn
Inflation: 2.0%
Population: 3.7m
GDP per head: $5,120

Rivalry between the prime minister, Rafiq al-Hariri, and President Emile Lahoud may prove increasingly difficult to contain if the president steps up his campaign to have his term in office extended beyond its late-2004 end. At best, this could see increasingly frequent clashes between the two men; at worst, it could culminate in the prime minister being forced from office if his position continues to weaken.

To watch
Economic policy. Political in-fighting has slowed economic reforms, notably the sale of two mobile-phone operating licences. The sale will be delayed into 2004, a serious blow to Mr Hariri's credibility and a threat to prospects for more contentious privatisations.

NIGERIA

GDP growth: 3.7%
GDP: $52bn
Inflation: 10.4%
Population: 136.5m
GDP per head: $382

Olusegun Obasanjo, the president, will slowly turn his attention to the need for political and economic reform: he will want to establish some sort of legacy from his two terms in office. Vested political interests will stand in his way.

After the uncertainty of an election year, economic growth will pick up in 2004, as offshore oil production rises and investment in the gas sector increases.

SAUDI ARABIA

GDP growth: 1.4%
GDP: $184bn
Inflation: 0.5%
Population: 25.0m
GDP per head: $7,370

Oil price, Brent blend $/barrel

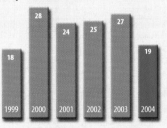

Saudi Arabia will hold elections for municipal councils in 2004. As Iraqi oil production increases, and Venezuelan and West African outputs rise, the market will be awash with crude. OPEC will enforce cuts, and Saudi Arabia may pump less, but average oil prices will fall.

SOUTH AFRICA

GDP growth: 3.5%
GDP: $154bn
Inflation: 4.9%
Population: 46.4m
GDP per head: $3,310

Thabo Mbeki will be re-elected president in 2004 and the ruling African National Congress will easily retain its majority in parliament and consolidate its position in the provincial assemblies.

Consumers will spend more, thanks to reduced taxes, less inflation, an improved jobs market and lower interest rates. Investment will pick up as privatisation draws in more foreign capital.

To watch
Black empowerment. The government will begin implementing its black economic empowerment strategy, which aims to increase black participation in all sectors of the economy.

The world in figures: Industries

GLOBAL TRENDS

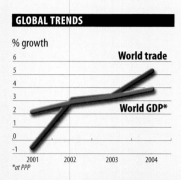

% growth

World trade

World GDP*

*at PPP

The Economist Intelligence Unit forecasts global growth of 3.9% (on a PPP basis) in 2004, with US growth at 3.4% and the euro zone up by 1.8%. But risks abound. Investors remain wary; exchange rates are wobbling; property could crash.

The failure of rich countries to make bold concessions on agriculture has left the World Trade Organisation's Doha round of talks in disarray. Chances of reaching a pact by the end of 2004, as planned, are slim. It would be worth the effort, though: the World Bank calculates that a well-drafted pact would add $520bn to the world economy by 2015. In its stead, taxpayers in rich countries will keep spending some $300bn a year supporting their farmers, at the expense of some of the world's poorest people.

M&A watchers insist that activity is set to pick up, spurred by globalisation and consolidation in many sectors.

Top five FDI recipients $bn

United States	153
China	65
Belgium	55
France	47
UK	46

Increased cross-border M&A activity should bolster foreign direct investment (FDI). A rebound is likely in 2004. Asia— in particular China and India—should continue to attract solid interest. So will the new entrants to the EU.

2004 forecasts unless otherwise indicated. World totals based on 51 countries accounting for over 95% of world GDP.

Economist Intelligence Unit

london@eiu.com

AGRICULTURE

The impact of the heatwave that wreaked havoc in Europe during the summer of 2003 will be felt well into 2004. Winter and spring plantings will be difficult in parts of the continent. The UN's Food and Agriculture Organisation warns of flash-flooding because the capacity of soil to absorb water has been reduced. Meanwhile, southern Africa, in particular Zimbabwe, will struggle to produce the food it needs.

Wheat and maize are not the only crops unlikely to meet global demand in 2004. Global rice production is expected to reach 391m tonnes, up 11m tonnes, but consumption will be 412m tonnes. A shortfall will be plugged by releasing stocks from storage.

Global demand for transgenic seeds (genetically modified organisms, or GMOs) will grow 13% to nearly $3bn in 2004, mainly in the United States, Canada and Argentina, according to Freedonia, a market research company. New entrants in the GMO market will include China and Brazil. Corn will remain the biggest crop, with cotton increasing fastest.

Europe fears GMOs and America's commercial dominance of the technology; the United States is sold on the potential benefits of disease and pest control. Will Europe start to relax in 2004? Research from the Washington-based National Centre for Food and Agricultural Policy estimates that crops such as insect-resistant corn, currently planted in Spain on a small scale, could increase yields in Europe by as much as 5%. In addition, crops such as biotech sugarbeets could significantly lower costs to growers, and a fungal-resistant potato could reduce pesticide use by over 7.5m kg.

To watch
Supercows. Scientists at Australia's Adelaide University have combined with the world's leading artificial-breeding organisation, Canada-based Semex Alliance, to create cows able to produce more than 14,000 litres of milk in a single lactation cycle—three times the norm.

AUTOMOTIVE

The world's carmakers have been on cruise control far too long: the American and west European markets are saturated. Global output is 30% greater than it needs to be and manufacturers are resorting to crippling consumer incentives to keep sales figures respectable. Tough decisions are in order.

World car registrations
m

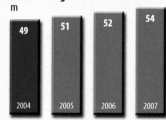

2004	2005	2006	2007
49	51	52	54

America's big three—General Motors, Ford and DaimlerChrysler—have the most soul-searching to do, not least because the productivity of Japanese firms like Toyota, Mitsubishi and Honda puts them to shame. But of the big names, none is more immediately imperilled than Italy's debt-ridden Fiat.

With the American and European operations of Japanese and Korean carmakers frequently outperforming their local rivals, western carmakers will look at their own overseas activities. BMW is setting up a regional information-technology centre in Malaysia and in 2004 will relocate a parts-distribution centre there from neighbouring Singapore, where it may open a pre-development and design centre.

The focus on emerging markets will intensify, with China as the prime candidate. Less flashy opportunities exist. Thailand will attract investment, especially from Japanese makers, as it can capitalise on low tariffs on exports within ASEAN, which has a population of 500m. South Korea's Hyundai will build a new plant in eastern Europe in 2004; Ford will try to build its Futura line in Mexico, at the expense of a plant in the southern state of Georgia. Unions will try to stop it.

After a lot of talk, the green car is finally becoming a reality, and preparations will accelerate in 2004. From 2005 major American carmakers will start selling a range of low-emission vehicles in earnest, such as electric/petrol hybrids and modified gas cars, following the lead of Toyota and Honda. In California, manufacturers are now required to aim for a sales goal of 10% low-emission vehicles by 2008. Manufacturers are splurging on R&D (for example hydrogen fuel-cell technology) and the Bush administration—driven by a desire to reduce dependence on foreign oil—has announced $1.2bn in hydrogen research funding. A European consortium, including oil giant Royal Dutch/Shell and France's Renault, will work to ensure the Americans do not speed ahead in the market.

Cost will be an issue: a hydrogen fuel-cell stack for a car costs as much as $25,000. Other stumbling blocks include hydrogen storage, refuelling infrastructure and efficient hydrogen extraction from sources such as water and gasoline.

To watch
China. The world's fastest-growing car market could go seriously off the boil due to massive over-investment. After a stunning growth of 35% in 2003, carmakers from around the world are now piling into the market, almost guaranteeing that prices— and profits—will plummet in 2004.

CONSUMER GOODS

Although economies are picking up, consumers are still hanging on to their wallets. Global retail sales will inch up by 1.8% in real terms (4.9% in nominal terms) to $9.65trn in 2004. The German government has tried to boost demand by extending weekend trading hours, but with little effect. A combination of high personal debt and low consumer confidence conspires to keep demand low in the mature markets of North America, Europe and Japan. And with ageing populations changing spending patterns, big retailers will pay attention to emerging markets to spur growth.

Income-tax cuts in the United States will prompt a slight rebound, but gains will not mirror the booming 1990s.

World retail sales
$trn

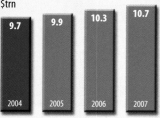

9.7 — 2004
9.9 — 2005
10.3 — 2006
10.7 — 2007

Americans seem intent on reducing debt rather than succumbing to conspicuous consumption. Major retailers such as Wal-Mart, Kroger and Costco will pursue opportunities overseas. M&A activity will start to pick up.

At the beginning of 2004, according to China's WTO entry agreement, foreign companies will be able to establish wholly owned subsidiaries. India, another market with a burgeoning middle class and degrees of deregulation creeping into various industries, also presents an opportunity, although controls on foreign investment remain tight. The popularity of the traditional retail sector will also dictate the terms on which foreigners enter the fray— they will have to adapt to Indian price and product preferences.

Other major global firms such as France's Carrefour, Germany's Metro and Tesco in Britain also plan expansion into new markets. Adopting the right sales strategy will be key, as Dutch company Ahold knows only too well. It was among the first to establish a foothold in Asia but is now paying the price for choosing the wrong shop format—supermarkets, instead of hypermarkets. It was forced to sell 22 supermarkets in Indonesia and will spend 2004 fighting for survival.

To watch
Price elasticity. Retailers will begin to charge different consumers different prices for the same product, depending on their shopping habits, based on loyalty cards and in-house credit cards.

DEFENCE

America's taxpayers will dig deep for defence in 2004. The Pentagon's budget will top $400bn, on its march to $1trn by the end of the decade. The R&D budget will rise by 17%, and spending on new hardware by 15%. The tab does not include the cost of occupying and rebuilding Iraq, running at roughly $4bn a month by the start of 2004.

All welcome news for military contractors, especially domestic

ones, which dominate the market. Many stood to lose from the Bush administration's early plans to axe some cold-war-era programmes to pay for "transformational" modernising technology such as unmanned drones. Both Britain and America have embarked on programmes to phase in more efficient aircraft carriers. Although costly, they come in handy when other countries will not grant permission for landing bases.

Some $10bn of American investment will go towards the "Star Wars" scheme. President Bush wants the first stage of the Ballistic Missile Defence System, for shooting down long-range ballistic missiles approaching American soil, to be in place by September.

Defence spending
$bn

United States	399
Allies*	219
Russia	65
China	47
Rogue states**	11

*(NATO, Australia, Japan, South Korea)
**(Cuba, Iran, Iraq, Libya, North Korea, Sudan and Syria)
Source: Centre for Defence Information

The United States alone represents half the global market for defence goods. However, the American Department of Defence reckons that on a comparable basis China spends significantly more than it claims: the true figure is said to be close to $70bn. The country now produces about 75 short-range ballistic missiles a year. The Americans believe that by 2005 China could have 30 intercontinental ballistic missiles capable of reaching American shores.

The first of Russia's new generation, diesel-fuelled submarines, which have been under construction since 1996, will take to the oceans. Signalling ever-closer relations with Israel based on shared perceptions of the threat from terrorism, India will install a Phalcon airborne early-warning and control system purchased from Israel. The deal, cleared by the United States, promises to give India an operational edge over neighbouring Pakistan and China.

To watch
NATO enlargement. Seven former communist countries—Bulgaria, Romania, Estonia, Latvia, Lithuania, Slovakia and Slovenia—will join the NATO alliance at its May summit. Under the accession terms, each will be required to maintain defence spending of at least 2% of GDP.

E-COMMERCE

Online ventures have proved they can be profitable; now they must prove their staying power. In their favour: the internet is still spreading. Europe's online population, for instance, will top 200m in 2004. Forrester Research forecasts the industry will grow by 19% a year. On the business-to-business side, California-based InfoTech Trends says efforts to reduce costs and streamline supply chains will push the global B2B market to $5.5trn in 2004.

Advertisers can be more creative, thanks to broadband uptake and the evolution of rich-media formats. Worldwide online ad spending will grow by 4.7% in 2004, predicts ZenithOptimedia, as top-draw companies join the likes of Procter & Gamble, Novartis and Mitsubishi in applying serious money to the medium. The Interactive Advertising Bureau claims the industry will hit its target of a 2% slice of the overall ad market in 2004. It may sound small, but it is progress.

Encouraged by dramatic revenue and stock improvements by eBay, Yahoo! and others in the past year, many expect an IPO by search engine Google in 2004. As the industry's first high-profile IPO in the new, sober regulatory environment of the Sarbanes-Oxley act—which, among other things, prevents analysts from functioning as cheerleaders—it would be a true test.

To watch
Your next PC. It may be worth waiting to buy a new computer. In the wake of SoBig, the fastest-spreading virus ever, Microsoft, whose software runs on 95% of all PCs, said it could not eliminate such threats without a complete redesign of the PC to remove security loopholes. That will take until 2005 or 2006.

ENERGY

Slow growth in global oil demand in 2004 and the more rapid expansion of global supply will push the market into surplus. The test will come in mid-2004, when Iraq, Venezuela and West Africa are expected to open up their supply taps.

Gas remains the fuel of the future as coal power plants lose favour. The key technological frontier may lie with liquefied natural gas, a process for cooling gas so it can be moved to market on tankers instead of through pipelines.

ChevronTexaco, the world's fourth-biggest oil company, is investing in LNG in Nigeria; BG, formerly British Gas, has Egypt in hand.

As Britain dims the lights on its nuclear dream, announcing that Sellafield's Thorp reprocessing plant will close by 2010, Iran is ramping up its own contentious programme. The country aims to develop nuclear power capacity of 6,000MW within the next 20 years. The first plant is due to commence operations in 2004.

Share of global oil consumption
%

Middle East 6.6
Latin America 5.9
Other Asia 10.1
China 6.9
Former Soviet Union 4.9
OECD-Pacific 10.7
Other 4.3
N. America 31.3
OECD-Europe 19.3
Total 72m b/d

As an initial step towards full deregulation of European energy (both electricity and gas) in 2007, from August 2004 non-domestic consumers will be able to buy electricity from anywhere in the EU. Some 60% of the EU's €250bn ($291bn) market for energy (of which electricity accounts for €150bn) will be open to competition.

To watch
Superconductivity. Hope for North America's old and blackout-prone transmission grid springs from a small project in upstate New York. State and federal funding is financing efforts by SuperPower to make superconductivity commercially viable. Superconductive cables can carry three to five times as much power as copper cables.

FINANCIAL SERVICES

The new framework of bank capital rules, called Basel 2, will influence bank behaviour as the 2007 compliance deadline draws near—provided it doesn't collapse because of its complexity. The new framework matches banks' regulatory capital requirements more closely to the credit risk-ratings of their borrowers. More capital will be required for lending to poorly rated companies, and for complex products such as securitised bank loans. Good companies in less successful countries will suffer.

Global investment banking and

corporate finance will be dominated by a shrinking number of players. Their everyday dealings are performed increasingly by the intermediation of exchanges, automated trading platforms and clearing houses. New frontiers are needed.

Like China. Market access is improving, as is the regulatory environment. Foreign companies must operate through joint ventures and good candidates are being found. Goldman Sachs will offer Chinese company shares to China's domestic market. An underwriting joint venture will enable Deutsche Bank to join the handful of foreign banks with access to the country's equity markets. Annual insurance premiums in China currently stand at around $25bn—just 1% of the world's insurance market. Prudential, AXA, Standard Life and AIG will all push expansion into the market in 2004. Leading domestic insurers, China Life and Ping An, plan stockmarket floats.

A single European market for financial services is still years away; the arrival of ten new EU member-states in May 2004 will complicate the drafting and enforcement of pan-European financial regulations. Among the large EU countries, only Britain and Spain are likely to maintain reasonable banking-sector profitability without substantial structural reform. The other big markets need to undergo more consolidation.

The Confederation of British Industry (CBI) says the nation's pensions black hole—the gap between current pension assets and expected future liabilities—could be as big as £160bn ($267bn). The list of companies lost in space includes British Airways, ICI and Rolls-Royce. The CBI estimates employers will be forced to double their pension contributions to about £43bn over the next four years, leaving them with less money to invest for the expected economic upturn.

Banking loans outstanding
$trn

2002	2003	2004	2005
22	24	26	28

To watch
Credit-card stress. The percentage of credit-card holders not paying their bills continues to soar. Factors range from increased unemployment to the high interest rates charged by the credit-card industry. The trend may lead to future write-offs for card-issuers and higher fees for consumers.

FOOD AND DRINK

The food industry stands out for its relative consistency. Annual growth rates simmer between 2% and 3%—and 2004 will be no exception. However, as a percentage of overall household spending food will fall slightly, to just under 17%.

We will eat more meat, fruit and vegetables—but less fish. We will indulge in more confectionery. We will consume more soft drinks and alcohol—beer companies will be buoyant while wine producers will struggle to cope with a market glut. Europe's burgeoning dairy-products sector will be worth $70bn by 2005.

Spending on food, drink and tobacco
% of total consumer spending

Economies in transition	40
Central & eastern Europe	32
Latin America	26
Middle East /North Africa	26
Asia /Australasia	22
Western Europe	17
N. America	10

Small food companies will find it hard to compete in an increasingly consolidated environment, with the balance of power shifting towards retailers. A "demand chain" is now replacing the "supply chain".

There are more single-person and dual-breadwinner households, and more men and children venturing into supermarkets. Convenience foods will grow in popularity. Manufacturers will employ "smart" packaging to give consumers greater control over the way they buy, such as more flexible portioning options. America's food-preservation and shelf-life-extension sector will grow especially fast.

Food safety—from bioterrorism to irradiation—will be big. Inspections of food imported into America quintupled between 2001 and 2003, and will keep rising with the help of an increased budget for the country's Food and Drug Administration (FDA). The EU will spend $20bn on food quality and safety research through to 2006. It also proposes regulations that would require food producers to start testing some 30,000 ingredients, such as salt, vinegar and methylated spirits. These would be registered and licensed in a similar way to pesticides and other chemical compounds. Compliance will cost a fortune.

To watch
Smoke-free drinking and dining. The list of countries with legal bans on smoking in cafés, pubs and bars, discos and restaurants will include Ireland, Norway, New Zealand and Malaysia. Sales of cigarettes will nevertheless grow marginally for the next couple of years, helped by emerging markets such as China.

HEALTH CARE

After decades of double-digit growth, global pharmaceutical sales will expand by less than 6% as drug companies juggle shareholder responsibilities and the demands of public-health systems. At least the WTO deal of September 2003, giving developing countries greater flexibility with regard to intellectual-property rights on drugs, clarifies matters. Poor countries that do not have their own drug manufacturing can import cheap copies if there is a compelling need. This is palatable to major producers such as America, Britain and Switzerland because "middle income" countries have agreed to opt out of the chance to over-rule patents.

India and Brazil stand to gain the most. Both have large generic-drug industries that have been banned from expanding globally until now. Brazilian companies, for example, are producing AIDS drugs for as little as $0.25 a dose while American drug-maker Abbott sells the same product for $1.48. India's Ranbaxy expects to hit $1bn in revenues in 2004, and aims for $5bn by 2012.

Health-care and pharmaceuticals sales
$ per head

North America	4,710
Western Europe	2,670
Central & eastern Europe	360
Middle East /North Africa	290
Latin America	220
Economies in transition	200
Asia/Australasia	170

The potential rewards are huge: drugs with estimated annual sales totalling $42bn will go off-patent before 2007. "First to file" status for a generic version of a drug brings the manufacturer a 180-day period of exclusivity, alongside the patent holder.

Not all companies will suffer equally under the new regime. The largest drug-maker, Pfizer, forecasts profits of $2.13 per share for 2004, compared with $1.73 for 2003. But if industry projections of R&D spending are accurate, there may

not be sufficient funds to finance all research efforts through a period of low growth that could last until 2010.

Biopharm may have lost some of its buzz, too, but the numbers are not to be sneezed at. Biotechnology is said to be behind two-thirds of new medicines in development. In 2004 the top ten biopharm drugs alone will be worth $16bn and the total market more than $40bn. The FDA has approved more than 155 biotechnology drugs and vaccines; around 400 are undergoing clinical trials.

To watch
Drugs online. Forrester Research says global online sales of prescription drugs will reach $15bn in 2004. Canada's 110 internet pharmacies are said to pull $1bn from the United States market, where an estimated 1m consumers buy their medication this way. Not surprisingly, doctors say self-diagnosis is a dangerous trend.

MEDIA AND ENTERTAINMENT

There are 4bn television sets in the world, and at least 3.7bn of them will tune in to the Olympic games in Athens in August. Having paid $3.5bn in 1995 for American broadcasting rights from Sydney 2000 to Beijing 2008 (representing 60% of global rights), American network NBC will provide 24/7 coverage across its channels—twice the time allocated to Sydney. Advertisers will spend much more than the $900m spent four years ago. In another first, the International Olympic Committee will grant accreditation to webcasters.

By the time of the Olympics, assuming regulators and shareholders are happy, NBC will be part of a new entity, NBC Universal. French conglomerate Vivendi, which owns Universal's movie studios, theme parks and TV group, sees a merger with NBC as part of its exit strategy from a disastrous foray into entertainment.

Vivendi will hang on to its Universal Music division, which slashed the wholesale cost of CDs by up to 25% in 2003 as a ploy against declining sales. Piracy is partly to blame: two in every five disks sold worldwide are illegal copies. The other scourge of the industry, online distribution through peer-to-peer network services such as Morpheus and Kazaa, will thrive in 2004. But the Yankee Group expects it will peak in 2005, when 7.4bn unlicensed audio files will be swapped. One reason: the big recording labels and independents will fine-tune their own pay services. Independent surveys indicate consumer interest in legitimate music-download services.

Advertising expenditure
% growth

United States	4.5
Spain	4.0
Germany	3.5
Italy	3.0
UK	2.9
France	2.8
Japan	1.5

Source: Zenith Optimedia

The march of the multiplex will push European cinema-ticket sales past the 1bn mark by 2005, according to *Screen Digest*. This signals a 20% rise over three years, with France the largest market. Box-office revenues will rise by 33% during the same period, mostly due to ticket price rises. Some of the takings will be invested in digital cinema—in Britain, up to 250 screens should be digital by the end of 2004.

Responding to criticism that Hollywood's film-awards season was too long and over the top, the Academy of Motion Picture Arts and Sciences will bring its Oscars ceremony forward a month, to late February. But, as if to demonstrate that excess is not dead in Tinseltown, audiences can gird their loincloths for no fewer than three swords-and-sandals epics inspired by the life of Alexander the Great.

Despite bullish predictions for the games and games-console market, Sony had a rough year in 2003, up against Nintendo's Game Cube and Microsoft's Xbox. Sony will accelerate the shift to internet-ready home appliances with the launch of PSX—a hard disk drive (HDD)-DVD recorder that will also run games, allow web browsing and hook into both conventional and flat-screen TVs.

To watch
A mobile miracle. Tipped as the "Walkman of the 21st century", Sony's PlayStation Portable should be in the shops by the autumn. The "PSP" will combine the functions of a mobile phone, camera and games console which can play films and music as well as games.

RAW MATERIALS

Global steel consumption should increase by a respectable 4% in 2004, despite uncertainty about world economic prospects. In March the United States will announce further exemptions to the three-year steel-tariff

scheme introduced in 2002 to give America's domestic steel industry space to modernise. The Bush administration's protectionist move sparked a trade row but already 1,022 foreign steel products, representing a quarter of the 13m tonnes initially covered by the tariffs, have won a reprieve. Trading partners have been placated, to a degree, but will be relieved when the programme ends in March 2005.

Rising steel consumption implies strong demand for iron ore. The balance between domestic and imported iron ore in China—which recently usurped Japan as the largest importer—will be crucial to the global market. The country will

World steel consumption
%

- North America
- Middle East/Africa
- Brazil
- CIS
- Asia
- Europe

Source: International Iron and Steel Institute

not have the time or money to develop capacity to cover all its needs, which is good news for the likes of BHP Billiton, the world's largest mining company. It plans to spend almost $3bn by 2006 on projects to boost output not just of iron ore but also of other minerals such as platinum and oil.

South Africa's mining industry will adjust to new legislation on royalties, after the bill was delayed in 2003. The law ends a decades-long virtual tax holiday for mining companies. Royalties are applied on a sliding scale up to 8% on different minerals and metals. Diamonds will be hit the hardest. Mine operators reckon the tax will push investors into the arms of foreign competitors and reduce much-needed investment, which has been on the slide for a decade.

Chile is considering a royalty tax of its own, on its copper industry. It is the world's largest copper producer. Lawmakers and the head of the state-owned copper company, Codelco, support the tax but opponents say it would make many new projects and explorations unprofitable.

To watch
Nickel supplies. Shortfalls in the global nickel market will continue until 2006, predicts Bloomsbury Minerals Economics. Demand has been growing faster than for any other major metal—at about 4%—driven by stainless steel, its major end-use.

TELECOMS AND IT

Mobile-phone sales will grow by 13.5% in 2004, to 505m. Much of that will come from replacement handsets: one in four old phones will be traded for a new one, according to research by US Bancorp Piper Jaffray. Consumers will be lured by colour handsets, embedded cameras, MP3 players and value-added features such as global positioning systems and gaming. The stronger original-design manufacturers, such as Finland's Nokia and South Korea's Samsung, will prosper over weaker companies.

The underlying platforms will continue to vex and vary by region, but by the end of 2004 there will be broad availability of 3G internet-enabled handsets and coverage. Delays to the rollout of UMTS, the European standard, has given GPRS an opening to become the network technology that will deliver a lot of data services, supplemented by the faster speeds of so-called EDGE technology. Investment in UMTS equipment is likely to remain lacklustre in 2004, as carriers seek greater evidence of demand for data services. But infrastructure spending should reverse its four-year decline and return to modest growth in 2005, boosted in part by solid investments in Russia, India and Brazil.

IT vendors expect pent-up demand to be unleashed by companies itching to jump on to the upgrade cycle. Consumers are more likely to spend, too, with laptop computers especially popular. Reckoning on a broad-based recovery spread across computer, consumer and communications applications, the Semiconductor Industry Association forecasts that the global chip market will grow by nearly 17% in 2004, to $181bn.

PC shipments are expected to rise by 10.3% in 2004, although price competition may mean the total value of PCs shipped actually falls. Even so,

Internet users worldwide
m

598	713	840	965
2002	2003	2004	2005

Source: Pyramid Research

this would represent the first year of positive spending growth for PCs since 2000. Corporate software sales will not scale the heights of the 1990s, but rises are predicted in key segments. AMR

Research expects customer-relationship-management software to grow by 9% to $11.8bn in 2004, while supply-chain-management software will become a $46bn niche.

TRAVEL AND TOURISM

For the first time, Airbus will sell more aircraft than Boeing. The European consortium has orders for 300 jets in 2004 and as many again in 2005. Its Seattle-based rival, by contrast, expects to sell 280 aircraft in 2004. London's Heathrow airport will start redevelopment of Terminal 3's Pier 6, creating four new stands to accommodate Airbus A380 supersized planes, which will fly from 2006.

Laws creating a "single sky" in Europe are due to come into effect, replacing the patchwork approach in place since the 1960s. Cross-border communication between air-traffic controllers should improve. The reforms will reduce air-traffic congestion and emissions, and

International tourism receipts
$bn

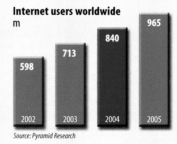

411	459	496	515
2002	2003	2004	2005

free pilots to fly by optimal routes. It will also accelerate restructuring of the traditional hub-based system. Other territories will follow the lead of a French court, which at the behest of Air France ruled that Dublin-based Ryanair's subsidy deal with the city of Strasbourg violated European competition law.

Bankrupt United Airlines faces make-or-break in 2004. Capacity is down 24% since September 11th, but observers say the airline must further cull low-yield destinations such as South America, where American Airlines is stronger.

After years of losses, Deutsche Bahn expects a return to operating profit in 2004, ahead of partial privatisation in 2005. The cruise industry also shows signs of rebirth. American-based Carnival, which merged with Britain's P&O Princess in 2003, will add 13 new vessels to its existing fleet of 70 by 2006.

To watch
Baghdad's runways. As the situation there settles, commercial flights to the Iraqi capital will resume.

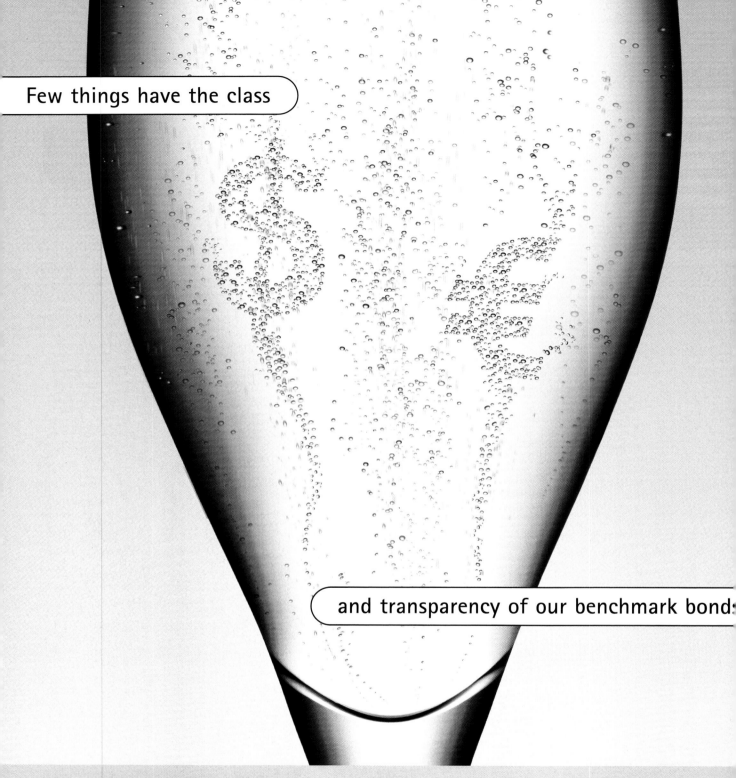

Few things have the class

and transparency of our benchmark bond:

The third age of globalisation

Tim Hindle

Enter the true multinationals

More and more multinationals will shift the operation and control of key business functions away from their head office. They will be following companies like IBM, which recently opened a regional head office in Singapore with 1,000 employees to watch over its growing activities in the area and said that it must accelerate the transfer of its white-collar professionals outside the United States. This diffusion of power will speed up in 2004 into what will become a third age in the global strategy of multinationals.

At first, when companies went global, they sold abroad, manufactured at home and controlled their operations from home. In the second phase, both sales and manufacturing moved around the globe, but control remained firmly in the hands of the parent's head office—invariably located in the "triad" of America, Japan and western Europe. Today we are seeing a significant shift in the location of this control. Almost for the first time, multinational companies are becoming truly global.

The first stage of global strategy was most famously expressed by Theodore Levitt in a 1983 article in the *Harvard Business Review*. In it, he foresaw "the emergence of global markets for standardised consumer products on a previously unimagined scale of magnitude". Mr Levitt's typical global firm was a big national producer which exploited its economies of scale to market and distribute products globally. He had in mind firms like the giant Japanese electronics companies. Based on home-grown R&D and domestic production facilities, they exported their uniform output around the world.

But already a second phase of globalisation was starting to take shape. Driven largely by a desire to cut costs, big western firms moved chunks of their production facilities to countries where wages were cheaper. In the 1990s this contributed to a rapid rise in foreign direct investment. By 2001, for example, foreign multinationals owned 39% of the 500 largest companies in Latin America, up from 27% ten years earlier.

This second age gave birth to a growing hostility among anti-globalist groups in the West (in contrast, governments around the world were keener than ever to attract foreign investors). In the first age, the main objection had been that multinationals reduced consumer choice by spreading blandly homogeneous products. In the second age, it was alleged, not only did multinationals destroy diversity, but they also exercised arrogant control over their far-flung empires, exploited the poor and imposed inappropriate practices on others.

Not for the first time, the multinationals were accused of being imperialists. In 1998 two business professors, C.K. Prahalad and Kenneth Lieberthal, published an article about the end of corporate imperialism. A few years ahead of its time, it argued that multinationals "will have to develop a new mindset and adopt new business ▶

2004
A new bull market in commodities could see Latin America back in favour with foreign investors, and the wealth of the Andes—notably Peru's mineral deposits and the Yanacocha gold mine in particular—more fully exploited.

Tim Hindle:
business features editor,
The Economist

models to achieve global competitiveness in the post-imperialist age."

Those models are only just beginning to appear. In July 2003 Rod Eddington, chief executive of British Airways, wrote a piece arguing that only the world's favourite empires will last. The British empire, he said, had faded because it "lost its early suppleness; the veins clogged and the mindset became crusty." Applying the lessons of empire to business, said Mr Eddington, means that companies like British Airways "need a centre that is strong without being crushing, and outposts that are true to themselves without losing our corporate identity."

More hints as to the shape of the post-imperial multinational will emerge in 2004. There will be:

● Further dispersion of headquarters. It is rare for big companies to move their main HQ from one country to another—although Ikea and BHP-Billiton have done it. But a growing number of companies are setting up regional headquarters or relocating specific HQ functions elsewhere. A recent UNCTAD survey found that 829 "HQ operations" of multinationals were relocated between January 2002 and March 2003, nearly a quarter of them in developing countries.

● More outsourcing of key business processes to the developing world (increasingly known as "offshoring"). This is happening at a rapid rate as IT skills and networks make the spread of digital information increasingly easy. A recent report by consultants Bain & Co estimated that the offshoring market in India will increase by 57% by 2006, and the market in Russia by 45% over the same period. Accenture, a firm of IT consultants, expects there to be particularly strong growth in offshoring finance and accounting functions, jobs that not long ago had to be within the purview of head office. The firm says companies are coming to realise that outsourcing involves a change of control, not a loss of it.

● More integration of managers of different nationalities. More chief executives of global companies will be of nationalities other than that of the company they work for. They are still surprisingly rare—a Welshman, Lindsay Owen-Jones, at L'Oréal, for example, and a Brazilian, Carlos Ghosn, at Nissan. At the level below, however, the pool from which future CEOs will come, managers are an increasingly polyglot bunch.

● Growing use of R&D from sources other than the firm's own laboratories. Examples of this are already not uncommon. In 2003, for instance, General Motors fitted some of its cars with an engine that can run on petrol, ethanol or any mixture of the two. The engine was developed at the Brazilian technological centre of Delphi, an American vehicle-parts manufacturer which (sign of the times) says that it has "headquarters in Troy, Michigan, Paris, Tokyo and Sao Paulo".

The new age of globalisation promises to be more harmonious than the previous two. In July 2003 Larry Ellison, the full-blooded American boss of software giant Oracle, said, "Isn't it remarkable that right now Oracle employs 3,200 Indian citizens, paying constantly increasing salaries, providing a very high standard of living and helping to create a new middle class?" It will be even more remarkable when one of those 3,200 is running the company from her office in Bangalore. Don't doubt it. That day is not far off. □

Matthew Bishop: business editor, *The Economist*

Return of the dotcom

Matthew Bishop

A few years later than advertised, the real internet boom

If you thought that the excitement went out of internet commerce for ever in the spring of 2000 when the Nasdaq bubble burst, think again. The phase of dotcoms turning into dotbombs is over. In 2004 e-commerce will finally come of age as a dynamic, global and, yes, highly profitable business. And firms that became famous as the pioneers of online commerce, such as Amazon.com, Yahoo! and, above all, eBay, will lead the way.

True, the evolution of e-commerce has not gone quite as was predicted back in those halcyon days around the turn of the century. Much of the money once thrown at hundreds of dotcoms is lost forever. Plenty of stupid ideas got funded, and were sold to investors by Wall Street firms that are now being punished for their sharp practice. Yet some excellent businesses also got funded during the bubble. Those that survived are stronger for having had to get their finances in shape during the post-bubble years when fresh money was almost impossible to come by, and any money in the bank had to be used as sparingly as water supplies during a drought. And the bubble had another invaluable side-effect: almost every imaginable idea for making money online was tried and tested, often to destruction—a period of unprecedented capitalist experimentation that quickly made clear what does not work and, crucially, what does.

The winners, it will become increasingly clear, are those firms that make the most of the internet's unique strengths by creating transparent, real-time places where people can interact with each other efficiently—especially in markets that have hitherto been fragmented, so that the cost of finding other people to interact with was often prohibitively high. No firm has done a better job of delivering efficient global interactivity than eBay, once an online flea market where collectors could auction Americana, now an increasingly important sales channel

2004

Shell will negotiate a $4 billion contract for the world's largest gas-to-liquids (GTL) plant in Qatar. The company says the GTL process is the most cost-effective way of reducing emissions.

for many of the world's leading branded companies. Sales of used cars on eBay in America exceed those of the nation's leading car dealer. And eBay is no longer merely a consumer-to-consumer or business-to-consumer firm. It is increasingly providing a place for business-to-business transactions, such as selling off inventory.

EBay takes a commission on every transaction that it facilitates and has been profitable practically from day one. Its profits in 2003 should exceed $400m on revenues of over $2 billion. In 2000 Meg Whitman, eBay's chief executive, set a goal for the firm's revenues to reach $3 billion a year by 2005. The firm may well achieve that goal in 2004. Amazon.com is now making an operating profit, which seems set to accelerate. InterActiveCorp, a firm run by Barry Diller, hitherto best known as an "old media" mogul, is also turning a tidy profit from online brands such as Expedia, a travel site, Match.com (online dating) and Ticketmaster, which it expects to grow fast.

So far online advertising has been a huge disappointment to websites, which have earned less revenue than expected; to advertisers, which have struggled to find ways to make online advertising work; and to site users, who hate slow-loading banner ads and distracting pop-ups. But here, too, things should improve in 2004. Advertisers are starting to learn what works and what does not. Online firms will also benefit as overall advertising spending starts to recover strongly from its recent recession, which could not have been timed worse for dotcoms. In particular, there will be spectacular growth in the combination of search engine and advertising pioneered by the likes of Google and Overture (now merging with Yahoo!), whereby advertisers pay to appear in a particular position in search results using specific keywords, and also according to whether they are clicked on. In 2004 Google is likely to revive memories of the dotcom bubble by selling shares in an extremely hot initial public offering.

Forrester, a research firm, extrapolating from recent trends much less optimistically than it once did, reckons that online retail sales in America will exceed $100 billion for the first time in 2004, on course for $230 billion, around 10% of total retail sales, in 2008. One reason for this is the growing comfort of consumers with online trading. According to Jeffrey Cole of the UCLA Internet Project, reporting surveys of internet users in 16 countries, the number of internet users surveyed who said that eventually they would make many more purchases online has risen to 71% from 55% two years ago. The convenience of e-commerce, and the ability to deliver much more information and interactivity, is also improving fast, as more users get broadband internet, and firms increase their data storage and processing capacity.

There will also be further consolidation, as the leading brands continue to buy up weaker rivals, and perhaps even merge with each other. Antitrust worries may emerge. Perhaps one of the well-known dotcoms—Amazon, say, or Yahoo!—will be bought by a traditional offline firm, such as Wal-Mart.

Should you buy the shares? Alas, it may already be too late. Shares of dotcoms have soared during 2003 and now boast some scarily high price-earnings ratios. Still, unlike during the bubble, it does at least seem a reasonable bet that these companies will actually deliver earnings. □

2004
Sales of camera phones in America are set to exceed the combined total sales of ordinary digital cameras and those quaintly old-fashioned contraptions that use film.

Crunch time for 3G

Tom Standage

Will Europe's mobile-phone gamble start to pay off?

Europe's troubled attempts to launch third-generation (3G) mobile-phone networks have reached a crucial stage. These high-speed networks are intended to provide extra capacity for voice calls and to allow data to be transferred quickly to and from mobile handsets, enabling new services such as internet browsing and video-telephony. But despite massive investment, demand for such services is still unclear, making 3G the biggest gamble any industry has ever taken on the introduction of a new technology. Whether this gamble will pay off will start to become clear during 2004.

The 3G project began during the frenzy of the internet bubble, when Europe's mobile-phone industry convinced itself that snazzy internet-powered mobile phones would be the next big thing. A report published in 2000 by the International Telecommunication Union is representative of the hype. Each 3G handset, it trumpeted, would function "as a phone, a computer, a television, a pager, a videoconferencing centre, a newspaper, a diary, and even a credit card...in short, the new mobile handset will become the single, indispensable 'life tool', carried everywhere by everyone, just like a wallet or purse is today."

European operators collectively paid over €100 billion ($116 billion) for licences to build and operate 3G networks. But then stockmarkets plunged, and operators fell back to earth with a bump. Burdened with debt, they were forced to scale back or delay their plans for 3G, and in some cases abandoned it altogether. To make matters worse, it became clear that it would take much longer than expected to get the technology chosen for Europe's 3G networks, known as UMTS, to work.

But 3G is far from dead. Networks have now been built in many European countries. Some networks in Britain, Italy, Austria and Sweden were even launched commercially during 2003, though they attracted few subscribers, largely because of continued teething problems. Despite all these difficulties, the terms of the 3G licences require ▶

Tom Standage: technology editor, *The Economist*

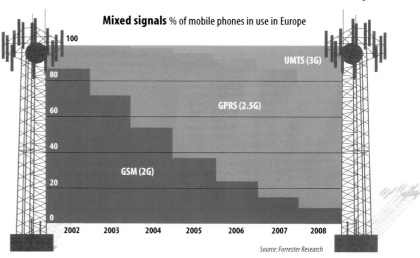

Mixed signals % of mobile phones in use in Europe

Source: Forrester Research

Why green is good.

Somebody once said that a principle isn't a principle until it costs you money.

So where does this leave those companies which have embraced a more responsible social and environmental attitude?

Does this make them a risky investment? Or an investment you can't risk ignoring?

Let's look at a few facts.

Over the last three years, we've out-performed the Morgan Stanley Capital World Index by several percentage points per year.

We have one of the strongest balance sheets of any company in any industry. Our dividends have grown each year.

We're investing $12 billion year on year in projects creating long-term value for shareholders.

We are one of the top performers in the energy sector of the Global Dow Jones Sustainability Index and included in the UK's FTSE4 Good Index from its inception in 2001.

And the highest quality talents continue to make their way towards us, as they look for a company whose corporate values match their own personal ones.

All of which tends to suggest two things.

A company which cares as much about *how* it makes money, as how much money it makes, will make money.

For its shareholders, its investors and its employees.

And whoever coined that phrase about principles was living in the past.

A past which grows dimmer and ever more distant by the day.

If you'd like to know more, a visit to **www.shell.com** could prove profitable.

Profits. Principles. Or both?

Meanwhile, here comes 4G

Tom Standage

And even 5G

With third-generation (3G) networks still stuck on the starting blocks in much of the world, it might seem premature to start thinking about what comes next. But some people are already looking beyond 3G to the next generation of wireless technology—known, inevitably, as 4G.

The term is being used in several different ways. WiFi, a popular short-range wireless technology used to link laptop computers to the internet, has generated much enthusiasm. But with its range limited to around 50 metres, WiFi lacks the blanket coverage provided by cellular networks. This has led to the development of hybrid wireless adaptors that switch automatically between WiFi and cellular networks, depending on availability. This patchwork approach is sometimes called 4G.

But it is not the only contender. Several companies are touting new high-speed wireless technologies, capable of transferring data as fast as the broadband internet connections used in an increasing number of homes and offices. This is much faster than the 3G networks being built in Europe and elsewhere, so it makes sense to refer to these improved technologies—from vendors such as IPwireless, Flarion, Navini and Arraycomm—as 4G. But since these

new technologies are already in use in some places, the curious result is that in some parts of the world, 4G has arrived before 3G.

Neither of these definitions of 4G is entirely satisfactory, however, because—unlike the term 3G—they do not have the endorsement of the International Telecommunication Union (ITU), the industry's standards body. Officially, 3G is referred to by the ITU as IMT-2000, and the next generation is known only as "Systems Beyond IMT-2000". Everyone is, of course, already calling it 4G.

The ITU expects 4G to be introduced around 2015. But Keiji Tachikawa, the boss of Japan's leading mobile operator, NTT DoCoMo, insists that it is not too soon to start work on it now, even though 3G has yet to prove itself. When you look back at the history of 3G, he says, the concept was first put forward in the 1980s and took over 15 years to reach the marketplace. DoCoMo's 4G research is focused on a technology called "orthogonal frequency-division multiplexing", which seems likely to form the basis of the eventual 4G standard.

And beyond that? Researchers in the field of "ad hoc" networking dream of building mobile handsets that work, walkie-talkie

Test module for the next generation

style, even where there is no network infrastructure. Instead, each handset acts as a relay for other nearby handsets. This kind of approach is already used in some military radios, using an exotic form of wireless technology known as "ultra-wideband" transmission. Some day it might find its way into mobile phones. Some engineers are already calling it—you've guessed it—5G. □

▶ most European operators to launch their networks by the end of 2004. So 3G is coming, ready or not.

Having originally hyped 3G as a revolutionary technology, the industry now plans to take a more evolutionary approach and introduce it gradually. The first stage is to promote the wider use of data services over existing enhanced 2G, or 2.5G networks, using new handsets with colour screens. The wild success of text-messaging suggests that Europeans are willing to use their handsets for more than just phone calls. But attempts to promote a cut-down form of web-browsing, called Wireless Access Protocol (WAP), fell flat. Having learnt from this mistake, operators are now promoting bundles of easy-to-use services, rather than endlessly going on about complicated technology. Colourful menus enable users to download games and ringtones, read news updates, and send and receive photographs and small video clips.

There are promising signs that, when packaged in this way, data services do indeed appeal to consumers in a way that WAP did not. Vodafone, the world's largest mobile operator, signed up 2m subscribers for its data-service bundle, called live!, within nine months. The company says that on average, live! subscribers' phone bills are 7-10% higher than those of non-subscribers.

The next step is to use these data services as the bridge to 3G. The capacity of 2G networks is limited, so as more subscribers sign up for data services, Vodafone and other operators plan to start switching users over to new handsets that work on both 2G and 3G networks. These users will, in other words, be using 3G without being aware of it, as operators emphasise their own brands rather than the underlying technology.

Switching stealthily over to 3G will be tricky, however, because existing 3G handsets are bulkier than 2G ones. Worse still, their batteries run out much more quickly because 3G is a more power-hungry technology. Operators are banking on smaller, lighter models emerging in 2004. Japan's leading mobile operator, NTT DoCoMo, found that adoption of its 3G service was sluggish until new handsets, comparable in size and battery life to 2G handsets, became available.

The success of 3G is therefore dependent on continued interest in data services, and the emergence of new 3G handsets. Operators are hoping that both of these conditions will be met during 2004. The irony is that, if all goes to plan, consumers should be unaware that anything has changed. After all the hype, the mark of 3G's success will be if nobody notices that they are using it. □

Larry Ellison, CEO of Oracle, identifies three ideas whose time has come

Changing the game

"Nothing is more important than distinguishing passing fads from genuinely disruptive technologies"

If you work in Silicon Valley long enough, you cannot help noticing what a close resemblance the technology industry bears to the women's clothing business. Both are fashion-driven. Fashionable ideas are hot while the others are not. Sometimes, as with internet computing, something comes along that really does change everything, but more often than not the hype fails to live up to the reality. Nothing is more important than distinguishing passing fads from those genuinely disruptive technologies that will fundamentally change the game.

If I were to identify three things which will matter not just in 2004, but for a long time to come, they would be: Linux; grid computing; and software as a service. Linux, the open-source movement's free operating system, has been around for several years, but it is only now that its full potential and significance is becoming widely understood. Grid computing, utility computing or computing-on-demand—whatever you want to call it—is also not new as an idea, but only now is the technology emerging to make it possible. The same is true of selling software as a service: it has been coming for some time, but in 2004 it will really start to take off.

When Linux first burst on the scene in the late 1990s, it was viewed by many as a potential challenger to Microsoft's Windows monopoly. It did not happen. It was not user-friendly enough for non-geeks and there was no Linux alternative to Microsoft's even more valuable monopoly—its suite of desktop applications, Office. But something else, potentially much more important, is going on. Microsoft's long-standing ambition to make Windows the dominant operating system for servers could be thwarted because of Linux. Intel, IBM, Hewlett-Packard and Dell have all seized the opportunity to escape from Microsoft's bullying and provide their customers with something that is both better—more stable, more secure—and much, much cheaper.

Microsoft is fighting back by tying its dominant desktop software to its server software, just as it did with its browser a few years ago. At Oracle, we fully support Linux. A couple of years ago we brought out a new version of our database, Oracle 9*i*, with a feature called Real Application Clusters (RACS). With RACS, any business application can run across multiple computing nodes as if it was just one big computer. The expensive multiprocessor machines that are the mainstay of the data-centre are no longer needed. By using lots of cheap, two-processor boxes you can now get faster performance and complete reliability. Ironically, we had just helped to make Windows unbreakable but, much more interesting, we had also done the same for Linux. And if Linux can successfully compete with Microsoft on servers it may, in time, get traction on the desktop.

Those low-cost Linux boxes can become foundation stones of true grid computing. Since the puncturing of the dotcom bubble, enterprise IT has become a constant challenge to do more with less. Typically, because of the unpredictability and immediacy of computing needs, companies are forced to spend heavily on server capacity and data-centre staffing levels that will deal with the most demanding contingencies. Most computer systems run at less than 50% of their capacity: a very inefficient model.

True grid

The idea of grid computing is that computing power should be on tap in the same way as electricity or gas. You use what you need when you want it. That means computing has to be as reliable and pervasive as any utility. Grid computing also has to lower costs through resource sharing, incremental scaling and reduced IT administration requirements (people frequently forget that the biggest expense in IT is always the labour).

New hardware and interconnect technologies, such as blade servers, storage-area networks and InfiniBand are playing their part. But the key to grid computing is the creation of a critical software infrastructure.

That is the reason we launched Oracle 10g (the "g" is for grid) at the end of 2003. Two ideas are central: implement one from many; manage many as one. The software has to create the illusion that clusters of machines are a single entity, such as a database or an application server, thus allowing users to add or remove capacity incrementally and on demand. The software also has to be able to manage groups of computers as if they were one, balancing loads and resources automatically throughout the "stack".

The spread of the computing grid will finally establish the idea of software as a service. The old way of buying software, in which buyers try to guess their needs for years ahead and vendors attempt to sell them more than they really want, has worked badly for both sides. Customers have too often been left with "shelfware", while software firms have suffered from chronically unstable earnings. I have long believed in a subscription model that can adapt to shifting customer requirements and which forces vendors to take responsibility for getting their software to work.

In recent years, a few pure software-as-service firms have emerged, offering applications designed for web-hosting. In 2004 some of these, such as Salesforce.com and NetSuite, a firm I have personally invested in, will come of age. Initially, they saw their market as small and medium-sized businesses that needed basic functionality and would be attracted to cheap and rapid implementation. That is changing. In 2004 these companies and Oracle's own outsourced E-Business Suite will offer an alternative to conventional ERP and CRM software that will be good enough for all but the biggest enterprises, and dramatically less expensive. Disruptive technology? I think so. □

Slow take-off

Iain Carson

And plenty of turbulence still ahead for the airline industry

2004

A merger between Air France and KLM, due to be completed in April, would create one of the world's largest airlines, up there with American, United and Delta.

The aviation world will realise that the climb back from the four afflictions it has suffered since 2001 will be tougher and more complicated than most in the industry had expected. The International Air Transport Association (IATA) may talk up the sector's chances chirpily, forecasting international traffic growth of 7% in 2004 and 2005. But the damage from the terrorist attacks of September 2001, the economic downturn in America and Europe, SARS and the Iraq war was severe. And as the obvious effects wear off, some of the airline industry's old demons, such as over-capacity and rising costs, will return to haunt the traffic recovery.

Estimates suggest that the world's carriers lost $10 billion in 2003. The recovery remains feeble. International traffic was still falling through July 2003, down 3.6% on July 2002 and 8% below pre-crisis 2000. Only in Europe is traffic up, by 2.4%, though the real figure is much higher since low-cost carriers (not counted by

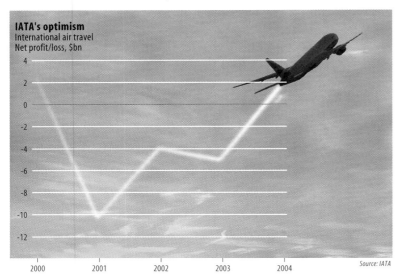

IATA's optimism
International air travel
Net profit/loss, $bn

Source: IATA

IATA) were growing by around 15%. The International Civil Aviation Organisation (the UN body that oversees safety and technical standards) counts domestic American flights in addition to the international traffic monitored by IATA. It sees total world traffic stable in 2003 for the second year running, with a 4-5% rise in 2004.

But recovering traffic volumes will mask the real headache for the airlines in 2004. The problem is that airlines are having to drop their fares to woo back travellers. The pain is particularly acute in Europe, where the ascent of low-cost airlines, led by easyJet and Ryanair, is squeezing them. Not even pressure from the French courts and the European Union antitrust authorities (which seem set to clamp down on inducements paid to Ryanair to fly into municipal airports) can stop them grabbing over a quarter of the intra-European market. If the authorities pursue a finding that these payments are

illegal state aid, they will make a small dent in Ryanair's business model. Michael O'Leary, its chief executive, can choose to take the impact on the bottom line (keep flying to destinations, without the inducements) or on the top line (cut the flights and forgo the revenue).

Half-year accounts filed by the big European carriers showed things getting much worse. According to an analysis by *Airline Business*, a trade publication, the European majors swung from a profit of $230m to a loss of $470m. As IATA talked up recovery and airline shares rose on both sides of the Atlantic, the chief executive of British Airways felt it necessary to point out that yields (the amount an airline gets per passenger) were still well down. Business travellers have moved to the back of the aircraft and do not take as many flights as they used to in the heady days of the dotcom and merger booms.

More pain lies ahead. In 2004 about a third of the 1,800 aircraft stored in the Arizona desert will come back into service. Every small sign of returning traffic will be greeted with airlines restoring routes and increasing frequencies, because they are each afraid of losing market share. The result will be over-capacity, further undermining the already weak yields.

Armed with instant information on the internet, passengers have a growing taste for cheap travel, even on full-service network carriers. Airlines such as British Airways and BMI (British Midland, as was) have led the way in showing how network carriers can use internet bookings and flexible pricing to fight back against low-fare, no-frills carriers. But there are limits to cost-cutting while maintaining the classic business model of a global network carrier, with heavy investment in people and resources at locations scattered across the globe. Employees in most airlines have had to endure pay cuts or freezes. Tolerance of such austerity tends to evaporate when business is seen to pick up.

But 2004 will not be all gloom. United Airlines will join US Airways in escaping from bankruptcy. Airlines in America will use codesharing deals to become more efficient, and as a substitute for the mergers that fierce antitrust watchdogs oppose. Such alliances at a global level will settle down around the Star, oneworld and SkyTeam groups, bringing marketing advantages to carriers and convenience to travellers seeking smooth connections. Also welcome, for passengers, is the growing development of low-fare carriers across continental Europe and within North America, where newcomers are springing up alongside Southwest Airlines and JetBlue.

The most important development of all will be the beginning of a real effort to jerk aviation out of its arcane bilateral air-service agreements. The lasting impact of the aviation crisis could be progress between America and the European Union in creating an "Open Aviation Area" across the Atlantic. This would sweep away ownership restrictions, and all government overseeing of routes and traffic rights. Talks will continue in the spring to see what goals can be reached.

If the ambition of abolishing bilateral restrictions is seen to be on the way, it could lead towards a global scrapping of restrictions on aviation trade. The term flag-carrier would be consigned to the dustbin and aviation, which has done so much to foster globalisation, would itself become a global industry. □

Iain Carson: industry editor, *The Economist*

EMIRATES | OMAN AIR | CATHAY PACIFIC | QATAR AIRWAYS | GULF AIR | AIR INDIA | MALAYSIA AIRLINES | SINGAPORE AIRLINES

BANGLADESH BIMAN | SAUDIA | ASSEMAN AIRLINES | ROYAL BRUNEI AIRLINES | KLM | PAKISTAN INTERNATIONAL AIRLINES | KISH AIR

AEROASIA | KUWAIT AIRWAYS | ROYAL JORDANIAN AIRLINES | BRITISH AIRWAYS | LUFTHANSA | SWISS AIRLINES | IRAN AIR

 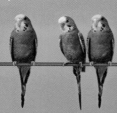   

SRILANKAN AIRLINES | ETHIOPIAN AIRLINES | AIR FRANCE | VIETNAM AIRLINES | EGYPT AIR | ALITALIA | KENYAN AIRWAYS | AEROFLOT

OPEN ALL HOURS
TO 105 AIRLINES AND COUNTING

With our open-skies and open-all-hours policies the sky is the limit. Not too long ago just 8 million passengers passed through our doors annually, in 2002 that number grew to 16 million passengers linking to 136 destinations worldwide. By 2010 we estimate that around 30 million passengers will pass comfortably through our doors. Now there's something to chirp about.

Dubai International Airport, the Middle East's most impressive hub. Email: airlinemarketing@dca.gov.ae

مطار دبي الدولي
DUBAI INTERNATIONAL AIRPORT
where the world connects

www.dubaiairport.com

The new LS430. Change the way you look at luxury.

Even greater levels of refinement have been combined with leading edge technology, such as Bluetooth™ connectivity to offer an effortless driving experience. But the LS430 is also a masterclass in power and control. The new sequential 6-speed automatic transmission delivers a smoother response from the 4.3 litre V8 engine. Add to this the latest generation air suspension, and you are guaranteed a superior drive. The new Lexus LS430, a whole new way to look at luxury. For more information, call 0845 601 9933 or visit www.lexus.co.uk/newls430

THE LS430

Lexus – 1st place, Gold Award J.D. Power and Associates 2003 UK Customer Satisfaction Study.SM

Model featured LS430 with metallic paint at £56,850 OTR. Prices correct at time of going to press. Fuel economy figures: extra-urban 8.5 L/100km (33.2 mpg), urban 16.3 L/100km (17.3 mpg), combined 11.4 L/100km (24.8 mpg). CO2 emissions 270g/km. J.D. Power and Associates 2003 United Kingdom Customer Satisfaction StudySM based on a total of 24,255 responses from owners of two-year old vehicles. www.jdpower.com

A rough road

Graeme Maxton

Carmakers will have to go back to basics

The world's car industry will begin a major redesign in 2004. This will take a few years to complete. Problems that have been building up over the past decade are now in need of urgent, and radical, repair.

In terms of sales, 2004 will be another bad year. Global volumes will fall again. During the 1990s the industry grew by a measly 1.3% a year, but since 1999 it has fared even worse. Although demand for cars has boomed in headline-grabbing places like China, for the world as a whole it has been flat.

Aggravating the impact of the sales stagnation is over-capacity, which each carmaker seems to think is an issue only for its rivals. There are between 25% and 30% too many vehicle-making factories (more than 100) in the world today, and with productivity gains of 3% a year and sales flat, the problem is getting steadily worse. More worrying still, Asian carmakers will add 1.2m units of capacity in North America between 2003 and the end of 2006, on top of the 708,000 units they added in the previous four years. This in a market for 16m-17m vehicles a year with a 25% over-capacity problem already. New capacity will also come on stream in Europe and, most notably, in China, where thanks to so many feverish investment plans the current shortage will quickly become a glut.

For the industry itself, there is a competitive stasis which inhibits a speedy response to these problems. Six companies now account for three-quarters of global sales and production, and few have the fleetness of foot or the stomach for a radical overhaul. All fear loss of influence or worry that downsizing is a slippery slope to decline. But any hopes that new growth markets might come to the rescue will be disappointed. Despite the WTO and the drive for more open trade, the rising demand in the fastest-growing market, China, will go increasingly to local firms and not the big global majors such as Ford, Toyota and Volkswagen. A draft government decree states that half of new-car sales in China have to be in the hands of local companies by 2010, not foreign joint-ventures.

There is one much more serious trouble blighting the industry, however, and it is the one which will be the catalyst of change. It is profitability, or rather the lack of it. Most carmakers have been making rotten returns recently. This brought Fiat to the brink of collapse. Speculation abounds about which of America's Big Three (Ford, General Motors and Chrysler) will be the first to enter Chapter 11. Although there are some stars, notably ▶

Graeme Maxton: director of Autopolis consultancy and co-author of "Model Change: The Future of the Global Automobile Industry", to be published in 2004 (Cambridge University Press)

Copycars

Graeme Maxton   *Hong Kong*

China's latest growth industry

Martin Poste just laughed. "Could they ever make counterfeit cars in China? No!" he said. "Cars are not like watches or CDs. A car is too complex. The engineering required to design and manufacture one is much too difficult to copy." This was back in 1996, when Mr Poste was the head of Volkswagen China, the dominant foreign carmaker in the country with a 65% market share.

Within four years he was proved wrong. Today there are copies of Volkswagens, Toyotas, Mercedes and General Motors (GM) cars, among others. In 2004 "copycar" production will soar, and spread to new models.

The first copy of VW's Jetta appeared in late 2001, rebadged, slightly altered in appearance and about 20% cheaper. The quality was high—close to VW's own levels. The reason was simple: the car was being made in a VW factory. SEAT, VW's Spanish subsidiary, had sold a car plant to a Mexican group, which sold it on to a company in China. Moreover, the company that bought the plant, Anhui Chery, was 20% owned by VW's main joint-venture partner in the country, Shanghai Auto Industry Corporation (SAIC). Despite protests from VW, Chery has continued in business and has produced over

The ultimate challenge for copiers

100,000 of these cars, nearly half VW's own output for the Jetta.

In mid-2003 Chery made a still bolder move. It introduced the QQ, a copy of a car that had not yet even been launched. The car was about to be introduced as the "Chevrolet Spark" by SAIC's other main foreign partner, GM.

Another company, Zhejiang Jili Geely, has produced three different models which look remarkably similar to cars made by Toyota's Daihatsu subsidiary and which are made under licence by another Chinese firm, Tianjin Auto. The Geely cars cost as little as half as much as Tianjin's, and has taken 14% of the subcompact car market.

These developments should not have taken the carmakers by surprise. This is, after all, the pattern of industrial development and cloning seen in many other sectors in China in the past decade. It is also what the Chinese government said it would do. Plans from as long ago as 1994 and subsequent decrees are designed to encourage complete technology transfer from joint-venture partners to local firms.

Although there have been a number of legal attempts to stop the cloning, most of them have been half-hearted. The foreign carmakers seem to fear that if they complain too loudly they might find themselves locked out of the world's fastest-growing market. And that would never do. □

▶ Toyota, the biggest firms in the industry have been unable to make a decent profit for years, despite absolute volumes being at record (if static) levels.

Moreover, carmakers have made most of their money from doing things other than building cars. Ford, GM and Chrysler are now in effect banks, and not very good ones at that. They make most of their profits by financing vehicle sales. However, as they have also been selling these cars at a heavy discount and offering extended payment periods and 0% interest, the loans have become increasingly risky. Plummeting second-hand values have made leasing returns highly volatile too.

GM now makes one-third of its profits by selling mortgages. Most of the Japanese firms cannot make a profit the conventional way either, certainly in their domestic market or in Europe. They make money only if the yen is weak, through sales to the United States. Most producers in Europe can make a return only through selling parts or restricting cross-border sales of vehicles to reap profits in one country at the expense of another.

Now even these sources of profit are under threat. The banks and ratings agencies have downgraded many carmakers' creditworthiness to near junk, limiting their

Bumpy to bumpy
World car production, annual growth rate, %

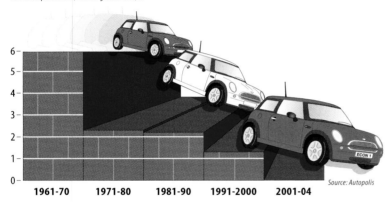

| 1961-70 | 1971-80 | 1981-90 | 1991-2000 | 2001-04 |

Source: Autopolis

ability to finance new loans on vehicle sales. Indeed, for the capital markets the car industry has simply lost its importance. A report by Deutsche Bank notes that "over the past 20 years, the car industry has continued to grow in terms of volumes, revenues and employment. Yet it accounts for just 0.6% of American market capitalisation today compared with 4% 20 years ago."

A weaker dollar has squeezed the earnings of the Japanese firms, while in the EU the European Commission has introduced legislation to ease cross-border car sales, harmonise prices and free up the market for parts. This will cut margins for carmakers in Europe too.

With all these pressures on profits, the industry urgently needs to shift gear. Carmakers will have to reformat their businesses to make money out of making cars again. They will have to cut capacity, reduce duplication, rationalise their range of models and, in some cases, sell off their subsidiaries and other assets to remain afloat until the benefits of these changes come through. The prices consumers pay for their cars are likely to rise gradually too. All this will be hard and it will take time. But the industry has run out of other options. □

Learning to grow again

Ian Davis

Three key questions as companies shift to expansion mode

If 2004 proves to be a year of recovery, then the challenges faced by management will be very different from those of the past few years. In recession, most companies know what they need to do: cut costs. But in recovery, corporate muscles that have gone unexercised must be flexed anew. In preparation, boards and top managers would do well to ask three basic questions.

■ What is success?
In earlier eras a company's success was judged by a mixture of measures, including fundamental economic performance, reputation with customers and employees, stock price and responsibility to society at large. That changed in the 1980s and 1990s. Academic theory, the takeover boom and shareholder activism led to a focus on shareholder value, all too often measured through the narrow prism of short-term movements in stock price. This raises troubling questions as companies look to manage the next era of growth while avoiding the pitfalls of the last.

First, are we rewarding and punishing management teams for something over which they have relatively little control? Research suggests that the relationship between a company's fundamental economic performance and share price over the near term is loose at best. Factors outside management's control, such as investor sentiment and overall market conditions, can have a major impact on share price. Did all those CEOs really deserve to get rich from the rising tide of the 1990s? Likewise, some strong management teams have doubtless been punished unfairly during the downturn.

Second, how do we reconcile the different timeframes of shareholders and management? The average stock is held for less than a year by institutional investors, and for even shorter periods by hedge funds. Yet the investments managers make, and the pay-offs from their decisions and strategies, occur over much longer periods. There needs to be closer alignment and understanding not just of objectives and expectations, but of timing too.

We should ask whether a more multi-dimensional definition of success is required. Management should be evaluated on what it can control—the fundamental economic performance of the business and the institutional strength of the organisation. It should set financial and non-financial goals and assess risks with an eye towards the long-term total value of the enterprise. A more balanced view of success, and the time over which it is measured, would ultimately serve shareholders (and society) better by encouraging more innovation and growth.

■ How can we nurture talent?
The world is not short of capital looking for opportunities. As recovery comes, the scarce resource for most companies will not be capital, but talent.

During the 1990s boom many management teams thought they could win the war for talent by throwing

Ian Davis: managing director, McKinsey

stock options and perks at their employees, and letting them wear jeans to work on Fridays. When the downturn came, there was an abrupt shift from "we value talent" to "you are a disposable cost". The options evaporated, the perks were withdrawn and the lay-offs came swiftly–in some cases, brutally. This tore the social fabric of many firms and left employees cynical. Trust will have to be earned again, and a new compact forged between companies and employees.

Employees recognise that it is unlikely they will have the "jobs for life" of their parents' generation, but managers also need to recognise that the needs of their most coveted employees are evolving. Money is important, as always. But people increasingly seek meaning, social connection and identity from their work.

The best companies will create jobs and roles where employees feel they have some control over what they do, where professional relationships are valued, where more than lip-service is paid to work-life balance and where

there is real belief in the social and ethical responsibility of the employer. The firms that translate these principles into concrete practices and build the social and knowledge capital of their organisations will establish a source of competitive advantage not easily displaced.

■ What is the role of business in society?

During the 1990s boom, business was viewed generally not just as a source of wealth creation but as the engine of growth and jobs around the world—a positive force. With the crash came scandal, backlash and a loss of faith. The pressures are coming not just from rock-throwing protesters but also from the mainstream media, politicians and well-organised NGOs.

Some of these criticisms are clearly valid. Market economies depend on integrity to function; companies should adhere to the values and norms of the communities in which they operate, as the great majority of businesses do. The drive for growth need not be at ▶

Hello, Columbus

Adam Raphael

New designer hotels will set the pace in 2004

The hotel industry likes to claim it has only 15 seconds to impress a guest. The explosion of new, stylish hotel groups shows that first impressions matter. Businessmen have become more demanding and their tastes more sophisticated. A lump-free mattress, multi-channel television, air-conditioning and a power shower are no longer enough. There is a revolt against the monotony of the big chains. Goodbye Hiltons and Holiday Inns; hello Columbus, Hotel du Vin and art'otel.

Ken McCulloch, a serial entrepreneur with a record as a developer of trend-setting hotels, is planning to launch a new "super-budget" hotel chain, called Dakota, in 2004. The first one is due to open in Nottingham in May. The basic price of a room complete with 32-inch plasma screen, broadband, sports channels and in-room work stations will start at £79 ($132). How can it be done at this price? The key, he says, is not to spend money on things that do not benefit the customer. That means no banqueting halls, no swimming pools and no big reception rooms. Mr McCulloch also says he is going to expand his upmarket international hotel chain, Columbus, in 2004. The first one is already operating successfully in Monaco; more are under way in Paris, Lisbon and other European capitals. Once again the emphasis is on design and value for money.

Many small hotel groups around the world are beating a similar path. Among the names to watch in 2004 are art'otels

Adam Raphael: Britain correspondent, *The Economist* and co-editor of "The Good Hotel Guide" (Ebury Press)

(Berlin, Potsdam, Budapest and Dresden) and Rocco Forte (Brussels, Rome and St Petersburg). Alias hotels, run by Nigel Chapman and Nicholas Dickinson, have successfully tapped the British luxury family market with Moonfleet Manor, Fowey Hall, Woolley Grange and Ickworth Manor. They have now branched out with stylish hotels in Exeter, Cheltenham and

Where's the service button?

Manchester. In London, Tim and Kit Kemp, owners of Firmdale, have set up a group of five classy town-house hotels. "Colourful décor, much technology": the description of their Covent Garden Hotel gives a flavour of the market they appeal to, though like most good central London hotels the price—a single room starts at £195—is not cheap.

The definition of a boutique hotel is elastic. In America, some hotels, such as W Hotels, owned by the Starwood group, have as many as 250 rooms. Targeted at business travellers, their establishments in Atlanta, Chicago, New York, San Diego and San Francisco offer good value (deals run as low as $59 per room). In Europe, the term "boutique" is applied only to hotels with fewer than 100 rooms. Robin Hutson, who with his partner, Gerard Basset, founded the Hotel du Vin group, says that guests will be looking for something different in 2004. What they do not want is a "bland corporate

offering". The goup's success in Birmingham, Bristol, Brighton and other cities shows that good service, good bed-linen (Egyptian cotton sheets) and, above all, obliging staff can reap big rewards.

But every new wave has its excesses. In the 2004 edition of "The Good Hotel Guide", we give warning that "a minimalist décor may excite, but visitors want somewhere to sit in a bedroom." Likewise, low-key lighting may be a lifestyle statement but it is worse than useless when you try to shave or put on make-up in the bathroom. It is not enough to dress young, attractive staff in black Armani suits. They have to be trained to serve visitors. Has a designer ever attempted to clear toothpaste stains from a black glass basin? Our special *bête noire*, second only to muzak, is the current vogue among hotels for spelling their names in lower case. Most of them would do better to concentrate on service with a capital S. □

odds with environmental and other societal concerns. Defensiveness, however, only provides ammunition to the rock-throwers. Business leaders should demonstrate more confidence in their moral position as creators of wealth, opportunity and rising living standards, and work proactively to build trust between their organisations and society at large.

These three questions ought to be high on managements' strategic agendas. By grappling with these issues more thoroughly than in the previous cycle of boom and bust, businesses can generate more durable growth. □

Spot the Asian brands

Charles Goddard

Hong Kong

More will embark on the journey to global status

Branding in Asia is coming of age. In 2004 the likes of Jollibee, A Bathing Ape, Legend and Lee Kum Kee will not suddenly become part of the global consumer vocabulary. But smart Asian companies are learning that brands can pay. Take companies such as Smartone (a Hong Kong telecoms company), BenQ (a Taiwan electronics-maker) and Haier (a Chinese white-goods manufacturer). Each of them to differing degrees has repositioned its strategic branding responsibilities, placing the branding proposition, as the consultants are fond of saying, at the centre of the business, with the CEO as the chief brand strategist and guardian.

With a little effort, a few Asian brands can trip off the tongue: airlines, hotels and beers, for the most part. Think of Cathay Pacific, Shangri-la, San Miguel. But Asia has few brands of global stature. Interbrand, a consultancy, rates just eight Asian brands among the world's top 100. Of these, seven are from the region's traditional branding stronghold, Japan, and one is from South Korea—Samsung, which ranks 25th.

Breaking the old "pile 'em high, sell 'em cheap" habits will be a slow process. Pragmatic Asian businesses will not easily be persuaded to place their faith, and their money, in something as abstract as a brand promise. Many, too, will continue to believe that superficial enhancements—like logos—will satisfy their branding needs. The typical Asian firm is a reluctant brand-builder; it spends less than 5%, often less than 2%, of revenues on branding, against up to 20% in some multinational companies.

Now, though, consultancies are seeing a surge in business from Asian companies that want to build their brands. More open markets, a burgeoning middle class and deepening consumer sophistication are all helping to drive up the competitiveness and service quality of Asian businesses. Asian economies—particularly South Korea, Taiwan and China—are migrating rapidly up the value chain, and brands must move with them.

Samsung, South Korea's leading *chaebol* (conglomerate), exemplifies this transition. It found itself dangerously overstretched in 1998, when Asia's financial crisis blew through. Although already a global company, it had failed to distance itself from its origins as a low-cost, low-quality badge. Indeed, it had failed even to register itself as a global brand at all. Five audacious years later, after pouring money into innovation and design—notably

The yellow apparel

China's uplift
Brassières, US market share, %

Mexico and Caribbean Basin

Source: American Textile Manufacturers Institute

Will women everywhere be wearing Chinese bras by the end of 2004? Not quite—though China, a bra-making powerhouse, does stand to gain more than anyone else from the expiry, in December 2004, of the Multifibre Arrangement (MFA), a quota system that has governed textile and clothing exports for the past 30 years. The arrangement helped small producers by protecting their access to the American and EU markets. When it expires, bigger and more efficient producers will make life harder for the little guys. The MFA has been phased out gradually since 1994; in that time China's share of the American clothing market has risen to 53%. A worried American Textiles Manufacturers Institute says it could hit 75% by the end of 2004. □

into mobile phones and flat-screen TVs—and hiring a Korean-American Silicon Valley veteran to head its global-marketing division, it is inching closer to that elusive emotional bond with the global consumer. Interbrand values its brand at $10.8 billion.

Samsung's fear, indeed the fear of most Korean *chaebol*, is of China, which they see moving inexorably up the same chain. Changhong (a television-maker), TCL (mobiles), Legend (computers), Huawei (IT equipment) and Bank of China are among a growing coterie of strong domestic brands with international pretensions. Many employ western consultants to devise their branding strategies. They are joined, too, by Taiwanese companies—Giant (bicycles), BenQ—seeking to make a rapid transition from equipment-maker to recognised brand and on to global brand, by way of China as a testing ground. Polls show that Chinese consumers, luxury goods aside, prefer to buy Chinese brands; "Made in China" is perceived as a sign of both quality and value. Up-and-coming domestic brands like Legend, which is cleverly outmanoeuvring IBM, have the advantage of being less risk-averse and culturally more attuned.

But there are no shortcuts for Chinese or other Asian companies on the way to becoming global brands. Samsung's swift rise has not simply been a trick of marketing; it also delivers a good product. For most businesses, building a strong domestic market, creating desirable products and nurturing a brand are unavoidable prerequisites. Asian global brands will have to follow that path—but more will be setting out in 2004. □

2004

Together with Boeing and Airbus, British Airways will look into adapting anti-missile technology for civilian planes in an attempt to thwart surface-to-air terrorist attacks.

Charles Goddard:
Asia bureau chief,
Economist Intelligence
Unit

Our high standards apply at only this site.

ASF is at home all over the world. So e think and act globally, based on alues and principles applied worldwide. hey cover sustainable development nd include safety, health, labour andards and environmental protection.

Valid codes of conduct ensure consistent compliance. That's how BASF lives up to its responsibilities and builds confidence.
e-mail: info.service@basf-plc.co.uk
Fax: 0161 488 4133, www.basf.co.uk

The Segments of BASF:
Chemicals, Plastics,
Performance Products,
Agricultural Products & Nutrition,
Oil & Gas

Thinking innovatively. Acting responsibly.

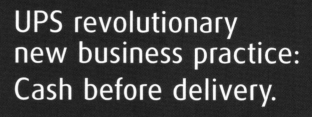

UPS revolutionary new business practice: Cash before delivery.

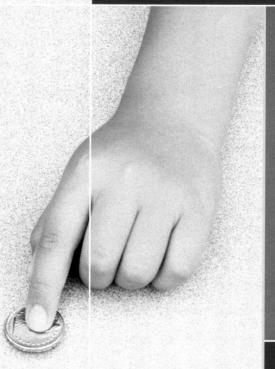

It couldn't be simpler.
UPS Exchange Collect℠ takes the risk out of doing business with unproven customers, especially if they're on the other side of the world. Your goods aren't delivered until your customer's payment has been received by UPS. You can view all your transactions online; which will help you manage and forecast your cash-flow. Your time management will also improve, because you'll spend less time organising credit terms and more time putting your money to work.
Simple.

www.ups.com

Giorgio Armani, founder of the Armani Group, forecasts a return to glamour and value for money in the luxury-goods industry

Luxuries are forever

"Luxury can be about something more than transient trends"

The past year has been hard for fashion and luxury-goods companies. In a climate of war, recession and SARS, people have been understandably reluctant to spend money except on necessities. Optimism is returning among consumers. But things will be different from the heady days before the bubble burst. The late 1990s were characterised by a desire for froth and instant gratification. Logos were dominant on clothing and accessories, brands fell over themselves to buy product placement in movies, and magazines were full of fast-moving trends.

When the recovery comes, the consumer will be more cautious and more selective, believing that luxury can be about something more than transient trends. In future, quality, craftsmanship and a real sense of value are going to be the key factors in determining a purchase. Buying fashion and luxury products will be more about a long-term investment than about getting a short-term kick from having the bag of the moment.

So I foresee a new emphasis on value: designers and manufacturers delivering products that will be perceived as really worth the money, even if they are expensive. Cars, clothes, accessories, watches—all will have to justify their price tag. It will become harder and harder to sell something just because it has a designer label.

The desire for long-lasting and well-made pieces will lead to a resurgence of small design companies offering products which are distinctive. The big corporations which have swallowed up many of the world's independent fashion houses will have to find ways of keeping their portfolios differentiated. Consumers suspect that globalisation leads to a homogenised product.

I am unusual in that I still own 100% of my business and can therefore make decisions quickly and independently. This means that my collections are driven more by a constant creative vision. I believe that my customers understand what my various collections stand for and it is important to stay true to my philosophy.

The consumer is now much more fashion- and design-literate than ever before. Fashion permeates everything. It's not just about what we wear, but also about where we choose to live, what car we drive, what food we eat. And the media plays a greater and greater role in subliminally reinforcing fashion messages.

Companies will dedicate ever more resources to trying to understand how to tap into the public's increased fashion-consciousness. Look out for fashionable advertising campaigns (for all sorts of products), in particular for overtly fashionable architectural concepts for restaurants, retail stores and other consumer destinations.

The Olympics will make 2004 the year that sportsmen and women become the new fashion icons, on a par with Hollywood in influence. David Beckham has done much to raise the profile of footballers as fashion and style beacons, but back in 1995 I put England's goalkeeper, David James, on the catwalk and on billboards, and now it is my pleasure to dress the England football team. Football has long been the global game, but its gladiators are proving that they can be stylish as well as supreme athletes. Get ready to see footballers, tennis players, athletes and others also competing as fashion ambassadors.

Another big cultural story will be the ongoing rise in the influence of the music industry, particularly hip hop. In 2004 this musical style from the margins will go further mainstream. Today, as hip hop and rap broadens its appeal to a wider audience, the leading artists are projecting a more sophisticated image with their own twist.

The hip-hop crowd is influencing not only musical style, but also promoting a love of the high life—of champagne and diamonds and fine clothing. They are making their fans aspirational. It is the opposite of early 1990s grunge and festival chic, of dour girls photographed in bedsits looking undernourished. Be prepared for a return of glamour: beautiful, bold glamour of the type Hollywood made famous in the 1930s and 1940s, but with a modern edge.

Femininity encapsulated

As I sense a return to the individuality of the sexes, I am moving away from the more androgynous style that characterised my work in the 1980s. I am known as a designer who promoted deconstructed suits for men and women, and thus levelled the sartorial playing field for professionals. This gave working women a wardrobe that allowed them to compete with their male colleagues on equal terms. I believe that this particular battle has been won—women can now dress in a more feminine way without compromising their professionalism.

However, if the sexes are ready to reassert their differences, then at the same time the barriers between daywear and eveningwear, and work wear and casual wear, will become more blurred. People are on the move as never before. They need a flexible wardrobe which can accommodate both office and home, day and night. The notion that one should be able to look equally comfortable in a board meeting, on a plane, in a bar or restaurant, or working from home is here to stay. So 2004 will be the year of the capsule wardrobe, made up of easy to co-ordinate items.

In 2004 fashion companies will once again head East. I hope significantly to expand our store network in China over the next five years. SARS delayed the push into China for many companies in my sector, but now we are ready to move again. Those aiming to grow there would do well to remember not to be too seduced by local culture. I opened a store in Beijing a few years back and decided to give it a red door. The customers hated it. They wanted Giorgio Armani of Milan. I won't make the same mistake again. □

Let's do lunch

Lucy Kellaway

Exuberance will return to the boardroom

After a year marked by corporate shame and stinginess, 2004 looks much brighter. There will be fewer redundancies, fewer cuts. There will be less emphasis on regulating companies, more on how to make them grow. The mood won't be the mad extravagant glee of 1999, but there will be a confidence that will seem like rain after drought.

The symbol of 2003 was the large dying pot-plant, bought in richer times, which companies could no longer afford to have watered. In 2004 office plants will be tended again. And all those service companies that employed people with watering cans will be back in business.

With budgets fatter, companies will start to worry about the damage to morale done by two years of cutting. Managers are not going to get any better at motivating people, but at least they will try. Some of the perks that were axed will be reinstated. Just as the plants will be watered, there will be biscuits for tea.

More important, companies will start to train again. Top managers and directors will rediscover the dubious pleasure of the offsite management conference. Away weekends in far-flung places will be entered into diaries and filofaxes (see below).

Companies will also spend more on training junior people, reassuring themselves that it is cheaper to train than to hire. However, the hiring freeze of the past couple of years will also start to thaw, and companies will fill the holes in their organisations.

The recovery in the job market will be mainly at the lower levels. This is going to be bad news for the slice of 40- and 50-something bankers, consultants and other professionals who lost their jobs in the past two years. Some of these may take lesser work, others will try to jump on to the non-executive bandwagon.

This sector will boom—indeed 2004 will be the best year yet for the non-executive, as companies eagerly demonstrate just how good their corporate governance is. Unfortunately, the new non-executive jobs will go to those who have jobs already. Companies will still prefer to hire non-executives who have too much to do than those who have not enough.

The corporate-governance debate will move into a new phase. In America there

Lucy Kellaway: columnist, *Financial Times*

will be a retreat from drawing up more rules; instead growth will be the top priority. And instead of looking at the behaviour of companies, it is the behaviour of big shareholders that will come under the policy spotlight. We are going to start worrying about how incompetent and lazy the big shareholders are when it comes to voting and to handling dividend payments and rights issues.

With balance sheets stronger, companies will start to make deals again. There will be little stomach for the hostile takeover. These deals will be mergers—lots of small ones rather than headline-grabbing record-breakers.

Prepare to bluesky

The style of leadership in 2004 is going to shift in line with the new, confident mood. The smart leader will be more domineering, more authoritative. The skills that will be valued will be discipline and execution. There will be a shift away from consensus, openness, coaching and naturalness. Replacing these will be a surreptitious return to command and control—though we are still not bold enough to call it that. The words we will use to describe our best new leaders will be inspirational, bold, focused. Leaders will be spirited rather than spiritual.

These big leaders will continue to pay themselves indecent sums of money. There will still be payment for failure (possibly a little better disguised than hitherto) and the pensions of retiring CEOs will defy all efforts to justify them. However, in 2004 we will be less outraged. Greed is winning the battle, and we will become so bored and battle-hardened by the stories that we will stop making such a fuss. Outrage fatigue will set in.

Companies will be shrewder in their approach to corporate social responsibility. This will remain important, though they will get better at working out which initiatives help their business and which do not. Intangible initiatives, which cannot be shown to give value for money, will be axed.

Communicating in 2004 will be different too. Everyone is roundly sick of spending hours deleting spam and reading e-mails needlessly copied. They are tired, too, of all those video conferences. In 2004 people will turn towards a long forgotten way of communicating—they will get off their backsides in greater numbers to meet people and talk to them.

The business lunch is going to make a big comeback. With expense accounts fatter than the previous year, and with the new craze for meeting people, in 2004 we will be lunching one another with a vengeance. The new business lunch will be different from the old one—the brandies and the cigars will be out—but the long convivial conversation will be back in.

Forward-looking companies may rediscover the charms of the human being in doing tasks that machines have been doing badly. They will start, gingerly at first, to experiment with having their telephones answered by people rather than by voicemail. In a similar retreat from less useful forms of new technology, the smartest managers will ditch their PDAs, realising that it is faster to put a lunch date into a filofax, or an old-fashioned diary. A fine leather pocket diary will be the new must-have accessory.

The English language will continue to be butchered by managers. New compound words will be very in. The *leadager* (the leader who can't stop managing) and *creovation* (a hybrid of creativity and innovation) are the sort of words we will have to get used to. Opinion formers will invent their own. The transformation of nouns into verbs will go on apace. In 2004 we will learn to conjugate I bluesky, you bluesky, he blueskies. □

Insight's UK Dynamic Fund.

Isn't it great when you find what you're looking for?

Finding funds that are performing well in today's market can be difficult to say the least, but Insight's UK Dynamic Fund is doing just that. Launched in January 2003, our fund is currently ranked in the top 2% of well over 300 funds in its sector*.

All thanks to its focused portfolio containing as few as 25 stocks, which are handpicked and constantly scrutinised by the fund's AA-rated manager and his team. The Insight Investment UK Dynamic Fund – one good opportunity you didn't have to search too hard for.

Talk to your financial adviser, call 0845 777 2233 quoting ECH or visit www.insightinvestment.com

This is a higher-risk fund aimed at experienced investors and won't suit everyone. Past performance is no guarantee of future performance. The value of investments and the income from them can fall as well as rise.

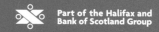

Part of the Halifax and Bank of Scotland Group

Laughter and tears
FTSE all-world index (1986=100)

Source: FTSE Group

Get ready for the readjustment

Hamish McRae

After their rough ride, three big tests for global markets

Phew! The markets have at last started to pick themselves up, dust themselves down, and think straight about the future. If 2003 was the year when financial markets began to recover their nerve, 2004 will be when they recognise that they have a crucial role in the adjustments that still lie ahead.

The markets will have to pass three great tests during 2004. The first will be to cope with rising interest rates, as governments borrow big and bigger. The second will be to help rebalance a world economy that is dangerously dependent on American demand. And the third will be to grasp the significance of the shift of economic power away from the present developed world and towards countries such as China, India, Russia and Brazil.

Test one: interest rates. The world's central banks will remain calm and cautious but they know they have to start pulling in the slack. They managed to pump in sufficient liquidity to engineer a decent recovery in the United States, Japan and Britain, and create conditions for recovery in the euro area. They did so without generating inflation, thanks in part to the surge of goods and services being generated by low-cost producers, in particular China and India. And they have managed to maintain a sufficiently benign environment that the markets can contemplate funding budget deficits in the developed world of, typically, some 4% of GDP.

But satisfying those borrowing needs comes at a price. Unless the central banks start to tighten, the bond markets will do the tightening for them. The cycle has turned: short-term rates will not be as low again until the next cycle (in, who knows, 2011?). Long-term rates will continue to nudge upwards too. The governments will fund their deficits, because governments do. But the price at which they do so will depend on the central banks, in particular the United States Federal Reserve, maintaining the confidence of the markets. So during the course of 2004 policy has to tighten.

The markets are prepared for this. They will accept that rises in rates are a necessary and inevitable aspect of the big adjustment towards a more balanced world economy. So the rise in bond yields will be quite modest and certainly not severe enough to unsettle the world's equity markets. Spreads between corporate bonds and government bonds will narrow further. Shares will nevertheless have to lean against a strong headwind. A year of modest progress is in store for the main developed-country markets—only modest, as much of the recovery is already priced in—with the markets reflecting real profitability rather than hoped-for triumphs in the future.

Test two: the adjustment. One element, the shading down of the dollar, was already under way towards the end of 2003. But the developed countries' currencies cannot alone fix imbalances. The other potential engines of growth in the rich world, Japan and the euro zone, have ▶

2004
The London Stock Exchange will decamp from Old Broad Street to new digs in Paternoster Square.

Hamish McRae:
associate editor,
The Independent

129

Wanna bet?

John Smutniak

Opinion markets will proliferate in 2004

New markets will spring up in unusual places in 2004. No, not stock-and-bond markets, of which there are now arguably too many. The growth will be in "opinion markets", which enable traders to profit on everything from the fate of starlets to the outcomes of elections and wars.

For the shape of things to come, try the Hollywood Stock Exchange (HSX), an internet-based exchange where you can take a punt on the performance of films and celebrities. (HSX bonds on Sharon Stone, for example, traded at nearly $1,000 in the late 1990s, but have since fallen to $8.) Having started as an online curiosity in the mid-1990s, to provide film buffs a place to forecast the Oscars, the HSX was bought by the high-finance brokers at Cantor Fitzgerald two years ago. Today the HSX boasts over 1m users, and lets you guess at such details as a film's opening-weekend box-office haul.

Companies will use opinion markets in their own sales forecasting, as HP (Hewlett-Packard) is doing. Sports bookies, too, will continue to move up from their previous digs in dark, airless betting shops and offer ever-increasing varieties of gambles. Tradesports, an Irish company, lets you do more than take a flutter on football matches. It also offers bets on the outcomes of celebrity trials.

An election year in America, 2004 will see other opinion markets put to the test. Iowa Electronic Markets is a university-based system that allows traders to bet on political contests. Iowa's markets have proved more

John Smutniak: finance correspondent, *The Economist*

What do you mean eight bucks?

accurate than opinion polls over the past two decades. People are never so honest, or diligent in their forecasts, as when they put their own money behind their opinions.

Markets in other types of political analysis are in the works. In 2003 the Pentagon cancelled a scheme to fund a market for the odds of instability in the Middle East (the Economist Intelligence Unit supplied the data), after politicians protested. In 2004 the private sector may take up the idea.

New computer programs make such markets work more efficiently than ever. One company, Longitude, makes software indebted to the pari-mutuel-style betting used at racecourses. This has enabled traders at big banks to wager their forecasts of

unemployment and other economic data. The internet has provided deeper and more liquid markets.

The hope is that such "gambling" serves a higher purpose, by aggregating opinions efficiently and translating them into prices. The odds can provide more reliable information than any single expert. A bigger hope is that this can be used to insure against a range of bad outcomes. Markets for forecasting the prices of houses in certain neighbourhoods, or lifetime earnings in a certain career, could prove quite useful. A contract to insure against the failure of a marriage cannot be far behind. But whether the HSX can help to improve the quality of American films is a more distant hope. □

> to play their part. They do not need to do very well to do better, and the markets will be satisfied with modest progress. Anything would be better than Japan's performance in 2002 or the euro zone's in 2003. In addition, the major new powers of the global economy—China, of course, but also the other East Asian nations, plus India, Brazil and Russia—have to recognise that a world dependent on the enthusiasm of the American consumer is a dangerous world for them too.

That leads to the third big test of 2004: understanding the significance of the shift of power. There are immediate practical issues here, such as the exchange rate of the yuan, but there are also longer-term philosophical ones. Investors still think in terms of a US-centric world and they are right to do so for the time being. "Emerging markets" have had their moments in the sun and their moments in the shade, but their very name suggests something peripheral, something that is not core to

investment strategy. Many of these countries have compounded this impression by piling their spare savings into American assets, without reckoning that it might be better to invest in their own fast-growing economies.

Short-term, such a policy may seem to make sense, though any shake-out of the dollar would undermine it. Medium-term, it is not sustainable. The rising economic power of the big non-OECD nations will increasingly be reflected in their financial power. People in the developed world will invest in emerging markets not because they are emerging, but because they are big.

And people in these new big markets will apply their own values to global investment. So far there have been only glimpses of their presence—a bit of "bottom fishing" in the high-tech world, for example, or some canny bargain-hunting for rich-country property—but that will change. Greater signs of active non-developed-country investment will start to shake things up in 2004. □

2004

Following several recent earthquakes and floods, Japan's Financial Services Agency, which regulates insurance companies, will tighten up its rules on how to set aside reserves for natural disasters.

RULE #8:
TO FIND THE RIGHT PARTNER
PLAY THE FIELD

Reuters offers the largest possible pool of potential
trading partners so you can secure the best deals.

REUTERS :D
KNOW. NOW.

This is not a glass of wine.
It's the taste of a
Tuscan summer earned
in the winter sales.

AMERICAN EXPRESS
3742 01001
99

LONG LIVE DREAMS

With **MEMBERSHIP REWARDS**® making everyday purchases earns you points that can
be turned into the things you've always dreamed of. Like stocking up your wine cellar
with some of the finest wines from top vineyards all over the world.
VISIT WWW.AMERICANEXPRESS.CO.UK TO FIND OUT HOW YOU COULD REWARD YOURSELF.

Something's got to give

Patrick Lane

In theory, the dollar should weaken further in 2004. In practice, will it?

Predicting the paths of foreign-exchange markets is a hit-and-miss business, even for those who do it for a living. In May 2001, for example, the economists from J.P. Morgan Chase—whose forecasts appear quarterly in *The Economist*—estimated that the euro would be worth $0.91 a year later. They were almost spot-on. They then forecast a virtually unchanged rate, $0.92, for May 2003. The actual outcome: $1.15, 25% more.

Guessing what will happen next is still a mug's game, yet one theme for 2004 can surely be inked in: America will continue to have a vast current-account deficit, possibly of more than 5% of its GDP. If its economy grows as strongly as optimistic commentators think, the deficit will be greater still. Because a country's current-account deficit is simply the amount by which its saving falls short of investment, this means America will once again have to borrow a huge sum, more than half a trillion dollars, from the rest of the world in 2004. How willing foreigners are to keep lending will go a long way to determining the fate of the dollar, and with it the shape of the currency markets.

The sheer scale of America's borrowing is bound to weigh on its currency: surely there is a limit to foreigners' appetite for dollars? Indeed, during 2003 the current account seemed finally to be taking its toll. In addition, American policymakers switched from lauding the "strong dollar" to making it plain that they wanted to see the greenback weaken, especially against Asian currencies. All set, then, for a further fall for the dollar in 2004? Maybe, but there are good reasons why the groggy greenback may stay on its feet.

One reason is that Asian countries—notably Japan and China—will not want to see their currencies strengthen. Japan's economy, despite showing welcome signs of recovery in 2003, needs all the oomph it can get. China's, by contrast, is racing and the yuan, pegged at around 8.28 to the dollar, is plainly undervalued. A revaluation of the yuan next year is a possibility, if the Chinese authorities thought it was in their interest: it might, for instance, stop the export-driven components of the economy from overheating. But

Patrick Lane: finance editor, *The Economist*

No rush to revalue

the Chinese think that the cheapness of their exports, an irritant not only to America but to many other countries, is other people's problem. So if there is a revaluation, it is unlikely to be dramatic. Floating the currency, letting it find its own level, is out of the question. It would mean full capital-account convertibility—a long-term aim of the Chinese but unthinkable now, with China's banking system in a chronic state.

On top of this, Asian central banks are among America's biggest creditors. The Bank of Japan holds perhaps one-eighth of outstanding Treasury notes; the Chinese authorities also hold a big slice. America's need to finance its current-account deficit is not going to disappear. So when American officials ask the Chinese to revalue the yuan or the Japanese to let the yen appreciate, they are, in effect, asking their creditors to accept depreciating IOUs.

A second possible prop for the dollar is the performance of the American economy. A prime reason for the decline of the euro in the first three years after its launch in 1999 was simply that the American economy looked in much better trim than the euro zone. Investors saw investment opportunities in America, and bought. In 2002 and the first half of 2003 that sentiment faded. America seemed to be sputtering. Private investors turned away, and Asian central banks took over as the chief lenders to the United States.

When investors think about where to put their money in 2004, there is a good chance that the answer will be America. The American economy made a better and earlier recovery from the post-bubble slowdown than the euro zone, where growth has been sluggish or even non-existent. American productivity is growing strongly; Europe's is not. European investors might therefore conclude that there are richer pickings on offer across the Atlantic than at home. In other words, if America looks strong, Europeans will be willing to lend to it, and that will support the dollar. Asian investors, too, have hitherto been far keener to send their money to America than to put it into assets in their own continent. Despite the prospect of decent returns at home, America can offer deeper, more liquid capital markets than Asian countries can. Until Asian tastes change, the dollar will continue to have friends abroad.

Quite possibly the dollar is due for another tumble. American growth could prove fragile. Investors might simply look at the current-account deficit and gulp. Asians might be browbeaten into letting their currencies rise. But the dollar has defied gravity before: why not again in 2004? □

William Donaldson,
chairman of the US
Securities and Exchange
Commission, describes
the reforms—and the
mindset—needed to
restore confidence in
corporate America

Not by rules alone

"I believe that America is now entering a new business era"

There are approximately 15,000 publicly held companies in the United States, and the vast majority of them are run by honest, dedicated people who consistently strive to make good decisions on behalf of their shareholders, employees and other stakeholders. But over the past decade, some of these companies—and some financiers who advised them—permitted a serious erosion of sound business principles. Earnings were manipulated. Equity research was compromised. And portions of the initial-public-offering market became a rigged, get-rich-quick game for insiders.

Restoring investor confidence is no small challenge. There has been progress, such as the passage and implementation of the Sarbanes-Oxley law on corporate reform. But restoring confidence will be a long-term undertaking, requiring companies in America—and abroad—to move beyond basic compliance and into the setting of new standards of integrity. Investors must be able to see that business is living up to the spirit underpinning all of our securities laws.

In 2004 companies listed in the United States will be required to create independent audit committees and to certify their internal controls over their financial reporting. These laws are important, but as business moves ahead what's really needed is not necessarily more laws, but rather the full engagement of business leaders in an effort to advance an underlying spirit of reform. These reforms must inculcate a company-wide mindset to do the right thing, and must become part of the DNA of the corporation, from top to bottom. Moreover, if companies treat Sarbanes-Oxley and other measures as opportunities—to improve internal controls, the performance of the board and public reporting—they will be better run, more transparent and more attractive to investors. There are real costs associated with stepped-up compliance, but these must be measured against the long-term benefits to each individual company and to the global economy.

Fundamental to spurring improved corporate governance will be the role of company directors. Directors have an opportunity to let their hair down and inject new candour into boardroom discussions. Boards should begin the audit process with serious discussions about their vision for the companies they are serving. They should seek to set the tone for company executives and other employees. A precursor to this effort must be an intense examination of the dynamics of the board meetings—a "getting down to basics" focused on the candour and openness that are needed if the tough questions are to be asked. Directors must find out what's really happening at the companies they are serving. And if management doesn't answer the questions adequately, directors need to look elsewhere for answers.

Corporate directors must also be prepared to devote more time to their duties. In the case of

WorldCom and other major-company failures, we have seen the high price of inattentive boards. Board members need to make an honest assessment of the number of boards and committees they can serve on in order to meet the heightened expectations of shareholders.

Measuring up

Every board must also give particular attention to its management committees. In 2004 and beyond I hope compensation committees will form a more profound definition of corporate performance: the criteria by which performance is measured and how it should be rewarded. The disturbing syndrome of forcing earnings into an artificial model of apparent uninterrupted quarter-to-quarter growth is all too common. This practice is frequently driven by Wall Street research analysts and influenced by the many temptations available to corporate management to "make the numbers work". The pattern is one that pays no regard to the cost of postponed investment or bending of accounting standards.

As companies seek a new definition of performance, beyond the straitjacket of earnings per share, they also need to examine the methods used by outside consultants to assist compensation committees in determining the scale of performance rewards. Like the children of Lake Wobegon—where all are above average—too many companies want to be in the top quarter in all areas (compensation, in particular), which leads to the ratcheting up of executive compensation unrelated to measures of true performance.

Similarly, nominating committees need to expand their thinking about who is qualified to serve on company boards. Current or past service as a CEO need not be a prerequisite. Just as we strive for diversity in our workforce, we should also strive for diversity of thought and experience on our boards. Monolithic backgrounds are destined to foster monolithic thinking.

As reforms proceed, there are two caveats to keep in mind. First, the board's role—to provide strategic guidance and effective oversight—must not be compromised or misinterpreted. Allowing boards to devolve into operating committees will not benefit shareholders or employees.

Second, there are no one-size-fits-all solutions. A chairman who also serves as CEO, versus a separate chairman and CEO, or a lead director structure, may work for Company x, for example, but not for Company y. The key is for companies and their boards to understand the need for greater transparency and accountability.

While there is still much work ahead, I believe that America is now entering a new business era, one that will be marked by greater responsibility and more realism. The spread of these values is essential to restoring confidence—and will help our markets resume their rightful place as the engine of prosperity in America and the world. □

Economist Conferences

The Economist

The Leadership Forum:
The World in 2004

December 5th 2003
The Millennium Mayfair
London

Taking its inspiration from The Economist Group's highly successful "World in ..." annual publication, which combines articles from *The Economist* writers and contributions from outside experts, the Forum will offer insights into the future of world commerce from those who help to shape it.

The discussions and debates will be held at the very highest level among participants and speakers, creating a unique "off the record" atmosphere in the renowned challenging style of *The Economist* newspaper.

Over 120 delegates attended last year.

94% of those who responded to our conference evaluation said they would attend this year.

Confirmed speakers to date:

Daniel Franklin
Economist Intelligence Unit
Forum Chairman

Accenture	Michael May	Global Managing Partner, Strategy and Business Architecture
Deutsche Bank Group	Professor Norbert Walter	Chief Economist
Economist Intelligence Unit	Robin Bew	Chief Economist
Economist Intelligence Unit and Editor of *The World in 2004*	Daniel Franklin	Editorial Director
General Motors Corporation	Mustafa Mohatarem	Chief Economist
Mitsubishi Motors Europe	Stefan Jacoby	President and CEO
Sony Europe	Miles Flint	Executive Vice-president
T-Mobile	Nikesh Arora	Chief Marketing Officer
The Economist	Clive Crook	Deputy Editor
The Economist	Tom Standage	Technology Editor

A FREE copy of World in 2004 will be given to all delegates at the Forum.

Special and early booking discounts apply. See website for further details.

Conference format. We have developed a highly interactive format, with a carefully designed mixture of plenary sessions and panel discussions allowing for greater discussion of the main themes.

PR Partner:  **Edelman**

Some comments from last year's event...

Excellent venue and facilities. Appropriate breaks enabling useful networking. Good set of topics – great start in the morning on global economy.

Excellent 'chat show' formats.

Good calibre of speakers.

Online: Register at **www.economistconferences.com**
E-mail: **weurope_customerservice@economist.com**
Telephone: **+44 (0) 20 7830 1020** to reserve your place

Lead Sponsor:

Innovation delivered.

Fore! Elderly dependency ratio: people 65 and over as a percentage of those between 15 and 64

United States   Germany   Japan

Source: UN Population Database

The end of pensions pretensions

Paul Wallace

Reality bites for both state and private schemes

The era of illusion about pensions is over. In 2004 governments, companies and individuals will have to grapple with the harsh realities of pensions in an ageing world. Politicians will strive to restore financial sustainability to state "pay-as-you-go" (PAYG) schemes, in which worker contributions finance pensioner benefits. Companies will intensify their efforts to move away from risky defined-benefit (DB) schemes, which offer pensions linked to final salary and years of service. Individuals will have to shoulder more of the pension burden through defined-contribution (DC) plans, in which they build up their own pot of retirement savings.

For reform of PAYG schemes in 2004, look to Europe and Japan: there will be no changes to America's Social Security in an election year. The need for reform is in any case even more urgent outside America. State-pension outlays already represent 10% of GDP in the EU, about double the burden in America. Yet the future demographics of Europe are more forbidding. Rising life expectancy and low fertility since the post-war baby boom mean that the elderly dependency ratio—the number of people of pensionable age as a proportion of the working-age

population—will rise in the EU from one-in-four today to one-in-two by 2050, much higher than in America. Ageing will be even more intense in Japan.

There are only four ways to escape the unforgiving arithmetic of PAYG schemes when the elderly dependency ratio rises. The first is to raise worker contribution rates. The second is to cut pension benefits. The third is to raise employment rates among the working-age population. The fourth is to raise retirement ages.

The first door is virtually closed. Politicians now recognise that contribution rates are too high and should if anything fall in order to make work pay. In Japan rates are still rising but will be capped at 20% of eligible pay. Japanese reform in 2004 will be directed towards the second exit route. Future pension benefits will be cut through an automatic mechanism that takes account of the falling number of employees as the population declines.

Europe will try to escape the pension trap mainly through the third and fourth exits. Only 64% of the working-age population is employed, compared with 72% in America and 68% in Japan. The gap is still wider for the 55-64 age group, with employment rates of 41% in the EU contrasting with 60% in America and 62% in Japan. Even with further labour-market reform, the EU will be hard-pressed to reach its targets of a 70% working-age rate and a 50% older-worker rate by 2010.

This explains why European politicians will be resorting to the fourth strategy of raising the retirement age. This is doubly effective because it acts on both sides of the elderly dependency ratio, both reducing the number of pensioners through shorter retirement and increasing the number of workers through longer working lives. The French pension reform in 2003 was designed to bring about later retirement by lengthening contribution periods. The Italian government is following suit. And in Germany, a government-backed commission has advocated raising the retirement age from 65 to 67.

The political obstacles to such reforms mean that state PAYG pension systems are invariably behind the curve of rising life expectancy. So expect governments in 2004 to revisit Sweden's pioneering pension reform. The system mimics the operation of a funded DC plan: individuals build up notional accounts from their contributions. Rises in life expectancy are taken into account when these accounts are turned into annuities, forcing individuals to work longer if they want to enjoy a prosperous retirement.

A further switch towards DC is also the way forward for battered company pension schemes in America and Britain. The three-year bear market from 2000 tore a hole in pension funds which will take years to repair. The crisis exposed the risk of offering final-salary schemes, since no investment offers an exact match to pension liabilities.

DC pension plans create clear incentives to save for retirement when working and to carry on working if the nest-egg is insufficient. But not enough workers join them and savings rates are inadequate. In 2004 automatic enrolment will spread, so that workers have to opt out of—rather than in to—DC plans. This can raise participation rates substantially. And there will be greater efforts to encourage higher contribution levels through financial education. If these methods fail, there will be mounting pressure for compulsion. □

2004
The American $50 bill, following its poorer relation, the $20 bill, will undergo a makeover. The familiar likeness of Ulysses S. Grant will be set against a subtly jazzed-up background.

Paul Wallace:
finance and economy correspondent,
The Economist

Basel faulty

David Shirreff   *Frankfurt*

Simpler rules for bank regulation, please

The intense scrutiny undergone by the financial sector will reach a hiatus in 2004. Regulators will have learnt that they cannot, by prescribing ever more complex or draconian rules, prevent financial companies from taking disastrous risks, or from exploiting privileged information and diddling their customers. Those two dangers, which have preoccupied bank supervisors since the collapses of Long-Term Capital Management in 1998 and Enron in 2001, are inherent in the financial business and cannot be magicked away.

With luck, 2004 will see regulators take a different tack and begin to simplify the complex rules on bank capital, known as Basel 2. It should also see the witch-hunters, such as Eliot Spitzer, the New York State attorney-general, accept that digging ever deeper into the way financial firms do business will not reach clear blue water—there is none. Financial dealings are nearly always at root unfair for someone.

The real challenge for banks is the change being forced on their behaviour. Technical advances are concentrating more and more of bank dealings in exchanges and electronic clearing houses. Banks are dealing less with each other as correspondent or agent banks, and treating fellow banks more as they would any other customer. In the interbank lending market, once a club in which institutions took each other's integrity on trust, banks demand collateral and other pledges, just as they do from their corporate customers. Credit is being repriced by banks—under pressure from regulators and rating agencies—with wide-reaching consequences for companies that borrow, and perhaps for economies as a whole. Generally, borrowing is becoming more expensive for all but the most creditworthy entities.

All this was triggered at the end of the 1990s by a tussle between regulators and banks. Banks insisted that their methods of calculating their risks were far better than anything regulators had so far devised. The regulators called their bluff and agreed to accept their methodology, insisting only that their workings should be transparent. The Basel Committee on Banking Supervision, a forum of leading bank regulators, together with the world's major banks and their various trade associations, set about hammering out rules on prudential capital for banks that would reward good and transparent risk management. But the rules became ever more

Coming unstuck

David Shirreff: finance correspondent, *The Economist*

> **2004**
> A five-year pact which limited the amount of gold to be sold by 15 European central banks expires in September.

complex and compromise-prone under pressure from lobbying groups as well as time.

Rules made by the Basel committee have no legal force. But the European Union has pledged to convert the Basel principles into law. There was a rush to get an EU version of Basel 2 into final shape by the end of 2003. If it missed that deadline the project would become embroiled in European parliamentary elections in June 2004, and might possibly founder altogether.

American regulators refused to be rushed by this tight European timetable, which raised the possibility that the Basel 2 project might be derailed. That would be frustrating for those who had worked at it so long, but it might be the best outcome. Banks, regulators and investors have learnt a huge amount in the past few years about financial risks because of their work on Basel 2. Whereas five years ago there were serious concerns about the vulnerability of the financial system to contagious shocks, now the system seems robust. The threat of imposing new complex capital rules on banks has caused them to be more prudent already.

Since Enron, the anxiety of regulators has focused more on the financial sector's ethics and indecent pay cheques. Most financial institutions, which in 2002 had been reeling from over-exposure to bad loans and to plunging equity prices, were able to recover somewhat in 2003. The most severe cost-cutting and retrenching of businesses had been done. In 2004 the prospects are for further recovery and more consolidation of banks, insurance companies, exchanges and clearing houses to produce ever greater economies of scale.

But consolidation brings its own headaches. The handful of global banks find that their biggest exposure by far is to each other. With so much dealing between a few banks, there are dangers that they have too much control over pricing and liquidity. Newcomers are being discouraged by the expense of operating as a bank or investment institution. The cost of buying and running sophisticated information systems, and of staying in compliance with complex regulations, means that financial services are shifting towards ever greater economies of scale.

The upshot is the development of a few very strong financial institutions but within a financial sector that may be growing less efficient at pushing capital through the economy. The ascendancy of rating agencies does not bode well for creativity and entrepreneurial flair. The heavily regulated financial institutions must either break out of this straitjacket or see their business migrate to more lightly regulated competitors, such as hedge funds, leasing companies and private-equity partnerships. If so, it won't be long before the regulators switch their attention from banks to non-banks. □

Baden-Württemberg's top ratings are not the result of chance. But of hard work.

With kind assistance from

L-BANK
Staatsbank für Baden-Württemberg

An AAA rating is an international sign of safety, strength and solidity. Businesses coming to Baden-Württemberg can benefit from one of the world's most solid and progressive economies. Take advantage of these qualities – invest in Baden-Württemberg and in the bond issues of L-Bank. For more information visit www.l-bank.de

JUNG v.MATT/Neckar

Claude Bébéar, founder of AXA Group and chairman of its supervisory board, sees a revolution ahead for health insurance

The new economy? It's health

"Health should be viewed as an item of household consumption"

What activity is set to grow faster than GDP in most developed countries, integrating on a massive scale the advances of biotechnology, information technology and nanotechnology? Health care, of course. In the 1990s spending on health grew by an annual average of 3.4% across the OECD countries, compared with 2.1% for GDP. In developing countries, health spending will only gain in significance as living standards improve.

The drivers of this growth are familiar; they include the ageing of the population in many developed countries, increasing availability of basic health care in emerging markets and the advances of medical science. Consumers in developed countries are also better informed. They know how to gain direct access to medical information over the internet, and they are increasingly aware of medical malpractice, which in many countries claims more victims than road accidents. They will constantly be demanding better health care and seeking guidance to navigate the medical labyrinth.

In this new context, both public and private health insurance will move from offering traditional products to broader services. Such services will include health information and advice; help in choosing the best hospital services; the choice of a second opinion ahead of risky operations; the chance to benefit anywhere in the world from consultation with one of the world's top specialists; plus the advantages of telemedicine, telesurgery, home care and sensor devices. Ideally, all these services will be managed in conjunction with a medical network providing expert guidance and a high level of professionalism.

The conditions are currently right to make these developments possible. Health information systems, electronic medical records, electronic prescribing and e-health are all evolving. These advances open the way to a personalised service to patients, one that can keep track of their case histories, follow their paths through the health system and reliably assess the quality of care they receive. Information technology should help bring about a re-engineering of traditional health systems, with productivity gains comparable to those seen in other service industries.

As things are, however, neither public nor private health insurance is up to the challenge of these changes. In countries whose health financing is mostly public, with the practice of medicine in private hands, governments face serious difficulties in controlling growth in public-health spending. This is the case in France, which nonetheless ranks at the top of the World Health Organisation's league tables, and in Germany. Countries with national health services keep a tight rein on tax-funded public-health spending at the price of long waiting lists for specialists as well as for hospital and surgical care. This is the case not only in Britain, but also in Spain, Italy and Canada; in these countries, a small fraction of the population takes out private insurance to benefit from quality hospital care when needed. Conversely, in countries where health insurance is not compulsory and is mainly provided by private insurers, as America, whole segments of the population are cut off from health insurance, either by choice or against their will.

To complicate matters further, in some European countries and in America health insurance is closely tied to one's employer. In countries whose public insurance systems are built on a Bismarckian model (France, Germany, Belgium and the Netherlands), a big share of public financing comes directly from corporate payrolls. American corporations, particularly the largest, bear the brunt of health spending for a different reason: the total absence of public cover for most working people. The big three carmakers are sometimes referred to as "HMOs [health maintenance organisations] with wheels" or "a social insurance system selling cars to finance itself".

Health goes global

How to evolve towards a comprehensive health service? The answer can be quite simple.

Health should be viewed as an item of household consumption on a par with food, housing or transport. Personalised family health insurance would cover a household's health risks and provide the services the family deems necessary according to its needs and lifestyle. But, as a matter of national solidarity, any democracy must see to it that no one is excluded from essential health care. The financing of this universal health cover should be fully transparent. It must be based on clearly defined public-health priorities and guarantee an adequate level of quality.

To achieve this, although the financing of universal health cover remains public, it should be managed by private operators. These operators could group together both universal and family cover to offer a comprehensive health service, through contracts with partners who would play a much wider role than the existing managed-care organisations. Family health cover could be highly diversified, offering households a broad choice. For example, "medical savings" could enable individuals to deposit tax-free funds in an account usable only for medical expenses, provided they have an insurance policy that limits the maximum out-of-pocket expense. South Africa and Singapore have experimented with medical savings accounts.

As a comprehensive health service takes shape, it will offer a wealth of opportunities for health insurance at the world level. With global health insurance, competition will be based on the services provided, no longer on prices alone, as with today's managed-care organisations. It will finally create a community of interests among insurers, doctors and patients. □

Science and technology

The smart-dust revolution

Alun Anderson

Sensors of the world, unite!

For almost 40 years we have all been subscribing to a simple dogma about the growth of the information age: progress means making more and more computing power available at lower and lower prices. Back in 1965 Gordon Moore laid out his famous law that the number of components that could be squeezed on to a silicon chip would double every year or two. Now everybody can buy a laptop computer with the computing power that entire nations were aspiring to in the 1970s.

Moore's law still has a long future. But in 2004 the belief that progress means packing in ever more computing power will be seen as far too narrow. Just arriving is another kind of information revolution, driven by the ability to manufacture billions of tiny, intelligent communicating sensors. Capable of organising themselves into networks, intelligent sensors will make up for their small brains by their immense numbers.

The intelligent-sensor revolution has its origins in a simple shift in viewpoint. Rather than trying to cram ever more computing power into the same space, imagine putting the same computing power into an ever smaller space. Big boxy computers that were state-of-the-art 20 years ago can now be made about the size of an aspirin. Very soon they will be the size of a grain of rice and, before long, a grain of sand.

Enter "smart dust": computers so small that you would not notice if one floated in through your window on the breeze (and, of course, the CIA has already spotted what that might do for them). They lie at one extreme end of the sensor revolution that sees a glorious future in combining sensors, limited intelligence and communication abilities in vast numbers of tiny computers. Smart-dust advocates have visions of sending billions of these machines into the atmosphere so that the entire planet could be wired. Stupendous networks of communicating sensors would give the earth a digital nervous system accessible to the web and giant search engines, from which we could instantly access anything about the state of the planet, from changing weather to the state of forests.

At the other end of the sensor revolution are entirely practical applications that are just coming on the market. Already, new American start-up companies (among them Dust Inc, Ember Corporation, Millennial Net, Crossbow Technology and Intel Research) are creating highly practical devices that can sense, compute and communicate—and make businesses more efficient.

The American military is enormously interested. In

2001 they tested small (match-box rather than dust-sized) sensors called "motes", which had been designed to act as intelligent surveillance devices. The motes were dropped from a drone plane alongside a road, set up a communication network among themselves and activated magnetic sensors to detect passing vehicles. By comparing readings among themselves, the mote network calculated the speed and direction of passing ▶

> **2004**
>
> NASA's robot *Genesis* will return to earth bearing samples of the solar wind, which may contain clues about the composition of the original solar nebula that formed the planets.

Alun Anderson: editor-in-chief, *New Scientist*

Now you see it...
Microprocessor size, mm

350
300
250
200
150
100
50
0

1974   1999

...now you don't
Microprocessor size, mm

5
0

2002   2004

Sources: Intel; The World in 2004

military vehicles and then beamed the information back up to the drone plane when it passed overhead an hour later. The test was a complete success.

Supermarket chains are interested too. For they have realised that sensors do not even have to be smart to revolutionise daily life. Radio-frequency ID tags (RFID) are the dumbest kind of sensor and do no more than bounce back a unique signal when they are hit by radio waves of the right frequency. But they are so small that they can be built into product packaging, just like a bar code.

Long waits at supermarket checkouts could disappear. Just shop and head for the exit, where a reader will send a message to everything in your trolley, instantly read all the responses they send back and print out the bill, without your having to take a single item out to be scanned. The tags are already being used to trace the movement of goods. If the cost of manufacturing the tags by the billion gets just a little lower, they will be cheap enough to attach to individual items. Then supermarket chains will find it hard to resist automated stores that need no more staff than a few security guards.

Make sensors more intelligent and the number of jobs they can do grows exponentially. Already the first buildings are being plastered with intelligent temperature sensors that communicate with one another to ensure that cooling and heating systems function optimally. Cosmetics companies are using them to sense humidity levels in their warehouses. Industrial machinery can be fitted with vibration sensors that pick up developing faults long before they turn into a breakdown. Sensors can be scattered on fields to measure moisture and temperature and to tell farmers when is the best time to plant crops. Attached to gas and electricity meters, sensors can make meter readers redundant, as all the information can be picked up from a passing vehicle.

What is so clever about all this? In these new sensor networks, there are no wires, so installing sensors costs very little. Messages pass from one sensor to another using radio waves (or even laser beams), choosing whatever route is most efficient until messages reach the point where the information is to be picked up. By passing on messages via multiple, changeable routes, the network is self-organising, fault-tolerant and scalable—it can easily be made to grow, shrink and change configuration.

Just as important, because the network operates through short-range hops, very little power is used. Unlike a mobile phone, which runs its batteries flat in hours while communicating with distant base stations, smart sensors can keep going for years. Not far off are sensors which will scavenge power from light or just from the faint vibrations in building walls caused by distant machinery. Like a self-winding watch, they will keep going forever. Standard protocols are being written for how smart sensors operate and communicate. That means that new sensors which are added to a network can automatically inform the system what they do and then get on with their job.

With the ability to expand systems with sensors of every kind, the sensors web begins to look more like our own nervous system, where vast arrays of sensors for heat, touch, pressure and so on are embedded in our skin. Giving the earth a digital skin is just a vision now, but in 2004 it will start to seem less fanciful. □

Geoffrey Carr: science editor, *The Economist*

Meet industrial biotech

Geoffrey Carr

A new form of biotechnology will enter into the public consciousness in 2004. Even greens should welcome it

At the moment, biotech has a Manichean image. The medical sort (new drugs) is broadly approved of. The agricultural sort (genetically modified crops) is, in many places, anathema. And when biotechnologists dare to trespass into areas such as cloning people, the fur really begins to fly. In the end, though, a rather different sort of biotechnology may turn out to be more important than those producing drugs, crops or even clones. Industrial biotechnology, which aims to replace things made from oil with things made by modified bacteria and plants, could turn into a trillion-dollar business.

Industrial biotech is just getting going in the plastics industry. Two American firms, DuPont and Cargill-Dow, make biotech fibres that can be woven into fabrics. Chemically, the fibres are polymers, chains of small molecules called monomers. In these fibres some or all of the monomers are produced not by modifying molecules from oil using traditional chemistry, but by modifying glucose using genetically engineered bacteria.

Doing this has involved scouring the bacterial world for suitable bits of biochemical pathways. There may be no natural organism that turns A (the raw material, glucose) into D (the finished product); but find a bug that can make A into B, another that can make B into C, and a third that can make C into D and you are in business. The genes for these pathways can be extracted from their original hosts and stitched together in a new bug where, with a bit of tweaking, they will do what you want.

DuPont and Cargill-Dow still use traditional chemistry to link up their biotech monomers. But a third American firm, Metabolix, whose products will come to market in 2004, has bugs that not only make the monomers but also link them up into polymers. These, without question, are real bioplastics. The next step (already working in the laboratory) is to

A beautiful crop of plastic

Not so lonely planet

Oliver Morton

A bumper year for Martian research

The first humans to land on Mars will be farther flung than any explorers in history. But their destination will already be familiar to them, thanks to a long line of robots. Earth's first unmanned mission zipped past in 1965, snapping 22 blurred and grainy pictures as it went. NASA's *Mars Global Sur-*

veyor has sent back about 130,000 high-resolution pictures since 1997, as well as all sorts of other data, and is still going strong. Its younger sibling, *Mars Odyssey*, arrived in 2001. And now more are on the way.

By early 2004 seven spacecraft will be on or around Mars. These include two orbiters, *Mars Express*—Europe's first mission to another planet—and Japan's *Nozomi*, also a

first. *Nozomi* ("Hope") has had its problems, and may not quite make it to Mars. If it does, it will study the thin plasmas swirling around the planet. *Mars Express* carries instruments for probing the planet itself, including the first radar capable of returning data from below the Martian surface, where vast layers of ice are expected.

Cadging a lift on the back of *Mars Express* is *Beagle 2*, a lander developed by British scientists. *Beagle 2* is a cheap mission, said to have cost little more than $50m, but it is also a very ambitious one, aimed at finding evidence of life.

The two American landers, *Spirit* and *Opportunity* (pictured), are the first missions designed to land, look around for the most promising parts of the landscape to study, and then trundle off and study them. Given two interesting landing sites—one that seems to have been an ancient hydro-thermal system, and one that might have been the bottom of a lake—the chances are good that the rovers' masters will learn something new about the planet's geological history.

If the masters could go there themselves, they would undoubtedly do a better job of it. But in a world where the odds of a Mars mission succeeding vary between one-in-three and three-in-five, sending humans seems a little premature. When they do set off, though, the data sent back by decades of robot scouts will make them the best informed explorers ever. □

Oliver Morton: author of "Mapping Mars: Science, Imagination and the Birth of a World" (Fourth Estate and Picador USA)

---

put the new biochemical pathways into fast-growing plants, such as switch grass, and farm these. Then there is no need to start with glucose, which costs money. Photosynthesis will do the job for nothing.

Biotechnologists also have their eyes on the motor-fuel market. Replacing petrol with ethanol is an easy switch (many cars in Brazil, and some in America, run on a mixture of the two). At the moment, though, ethanol, like plastics, is made from glucose. And that is too expensive for the process to be truly economic.

Biotechnology will change this too. Using the ruthless logic of Darwinian evolution, biotech firms are improving natural catalysts (enzymes) by shuffling their DNA blueprints, testing the new enzymes produced, selecting the best and shuffling again. The result is enzymes that work far faster and in tougher conditions than natural ones. This means that it is becoming possible to make glucose from cellulose—the tough, fibrous material that acts as part of a plant's "skeleton". Cellulose is a polymer whose monomers are glucose molecules. A lot of cellulose in the form of plant stalks left over from harvesting is thrown away. Soon those stalks will be thrown instead into "bioreactors". There, the souped-up enzymes will chop the cellulose into glucose.

All this will put environmentalists in a quandary. On the one hand, it involves genetic modification, of which

many of them disapprove. On the other, it means that plastics and fuels currently made from non-renewable petroleum will instead be made from renewable living things. And renewability is not the only environmental advantage. Plants get their carbon from the atmosphere, so biotech plastics and fuels will be part of the natural carbon cycle. Carbon dioxide produced by their combustion or decay will not result in a net increase in greenhouse gases, so cannot contribute to global warming.

Bioplastics should appeal to greens for another reason too. These plastics will be genuinely biodegradable, since they are made from chemicals that bacterial enzymes can recognise and chew up. Throw them into a landfill and they will be gone in weeks. Indeed, their biodegradability is one of the features being used to market them. Their manufacturers hope that charging a "green premium" will make them more profitable.

Industrial biotech may also help farmers in rich countries who now depend on subsidies. A new generation of genetically modified plants could become high-value crops that genuinely pay their own way. Their bulk means that initial processing is likely to be done locally, which would bring industry to the countryside. The countryside might thus once again become economically viable. How green will be my valley? Green enough, perhaps, for all but the most hardline environmentalist. □

> **2004**
>
> Linguagen, a biotechnology firm in New Jersey, plans to license the first molecular compounds that block bitter tastes in foods, drinks and medicines.

James Dyson, re-inventor of domestic appliances, sees domestic architecture returning to the medieval great hall

Back to the future

"Separate rooms and wasteful corridors are on the way out"

Within a few years, the average home could be a much more pleasant place to live, better suited to modern demographics and lifestyles, easier to manage and making more efficient use of resources. Domestic appliances would monitor their own performance, forewarning of possible breakdowns and helping manufacturers to design better products. Boilers, washing machines, dishwashers, ovens, fridges and central-heating systems would be networked, constantly communicating with each other to make the most efficient use of energy. And domestic robots would be genuinely autonomous devices, able to perform those tasks more efficiently and just as judiciously as a human, without running out of power.

Certainly there are plenty of reasons to consider such technologies seriously. We need to solve the domestic challenge of an increasing number of single-person households and an ageing population, a need for low-cost, energy-efficient homes to house vital workers and, in many countries, the political desire for smaller, more densely built housing. This could be solved today by using good design, intelligent engineering and appropriate technology, but too often domestic-appliance manufacturers adopt new technologies without thinking through their true purpose or benefits to the consumer, society or themselves.

A classic example is the networked fridge. This is supposed to keep you informed of your shopping needs and make relevant recipe suggestions. Dialling up your fridge to ask about its contents might sound appealing, but really it is rather stupid. Even I know what is in my fridge and I don't do the shopping. A fridge connected to the internet has few real benefits for the consumer and just about none for the manufacturer.

Connectivity to the manufacturer makes much more sense. At Dyson we are developing a motor, codenamed x020, which will be the basis of our power and communications in the future. An x020-powered machine could communicate directly with our service centre. Currently, customers who call our helpline have to tell us their name, postcode and the serial number of their machine—a real bore if you have to put the phone down, delve behind a product and call back again.

x020 transmits a binary code, like a fax machine. The customer could call the service centre, hold the receiver to the machine's communication port and press a button. A series of pips—essentially the machine's DNA—would tell us everything we need to know: serial number, diagnostics and usage data. So x020 offers a tangible benefit to our customers (less of a nuisance if the machine has a fault) and several benefits to us, including learning more about usage patterns to improve our product design, which again will ultimately benefit the customer.

This is only the first stage of appliance connectivity. If the device was permanently connected to its manufacturer, or at least able to connect at will, the benefits would be even greater. We could update control software remotely, downloading gentler wool programmes and faster cotton washes to our washing machines as soon as we developed them, for instance.

But the biggest benefit would be advance diagnostics—anticipating faults before they happen. We have looked at this already, but I am not sure customers want a phone line in their washrooms, even though we would pay for the cost of the calls. Cellphone technology is an alternative, but a more cost-effective and flexible option would be a radio link, such as Bluetooth, to a central domestic server, possibly the home computer.

If all the appliances were supplied either by a single manufacturer or several makers tied in a consortium with uniform standards, then we would be able to manage our customers' entire domestic-appliance needs. The management company could anticipate faults before they happen and service or replace the appliance. By using 3G phones and their cameras, consumers could grant repairmen access to their property for servicing. It would take away all the hassle and ensure the central heating does not break down, or the oven turn off when you are cooking the Christmas turkey.

The company could also minimise energy consumption, for example by using heat from the oven or the cooling apparatus of the refrigerator to heat water. This need not be expensive. Already many appliances are assembled from common parts. All it needs is for manufacturers to work together to make it happen. In Britain, the Department of Trade and Industry is backing the Application Home Initiative, in which domestic-appliance manufacturers, university research laboratories, telecoms and computer companies are working together to develop common standards.

A pad with a pod

I believe appliance systems management is just around the corner; if it isn't, it ought to be. How else are we going to cope with the demand for more energy and space-efficient housing? I am building a flat in London in which all the appliances will be contained in a central machine pod, saving power and space. It is illogical to have the washing machine in a room that you have to trudge down a corridor to reach.

Domestic architecture is changing in a fundamental way. Separate rooms and wasteful corridors are on the way out. Loft-living is just the first manifestation of this return to a way of living more akin to the medieval great hall. It means you can talk to your spouse while he or she is having a bath and you are cooking the dinner—something particularly useful to busy people who do not see that much of each other. □

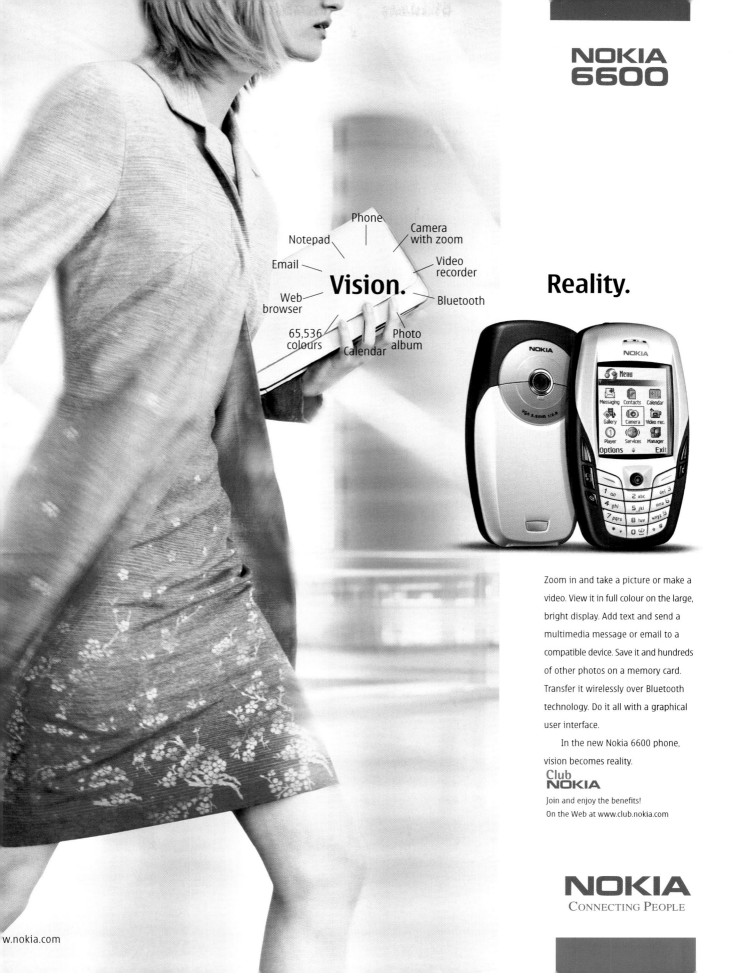

Getting a grippe

Shereen El Feki

The battle between man and microbe goes on

When China sneezes, the old saying goes, the rest of the world catches a cold. In 2003 the world was not so lucky: China's main epidemiological export turned out to be a rather more serious condition called Severe Acute Respiratory Syndrome (SARS). From its suspected origins in Guangdong province, the SARS virus spread quickly through Asia and on to North America. More than 8,000 people developed the high fever and hacking cough which characterises SARS and over 700 died. The Asian Development Bank reckons that SARS cost the region more than $18 billion in trade, travel and other losses.

What infectious delights might lie in store for 2004? SARS for one, says David Heymann, who led the World Health Organisation's response to the outbreak. The virus has merely been contained by the controls introduced to fight it. In the absence of a vaccine, or a specific drug targeted to it, new outbreaks are possible.

As for other microbial menaces, there are some 5,000 kinds of virus, 100 species of fungus, more than 300,000 species of bacteria and countless other parasites which could launch an assault. There are the old familiars, such as tuberculosis and malarial parasites, which will continue to afflict vast swathes of the world's population. A relative newcomer, HIV, which causes AIDS, is set to infect more than 5m people, and kill at least 3m, in 2004. Human papillomavirus, which is linked to cervical cancer, kills roughly 200,000 women a year, mainly in developing countries. There are also exotic novelties, such as West Nile virus, which is making its way across North America, or the peculiar prion molecules which cause "mad cow" disease and its associated human affliction, variant Creutzfeldt-Jakob disease. All in all, infectious diseases kill more than 14m people a year, over a quarter of all deaths worldwide and more than half the deaths in developing countries.

Thirty years ago public-health experts, armed with a new arsenal of anti-infective drugs and spurred on by success against smallpox, confidently predicted the eventual demise of infectious disease. Today they are not so sure. On average, a new infectious disease has been identified almost every year since 1973.

Why are infectious diseases still so strong? Changes in human activity are largely to blame. Urbanisation is facilitating the spread of disease. Intensive agriculture is putting pressure on livestock, leading to the outbreak of nasty microbes such as Nipah virus, which appeared in Malaysian pigs in the late 1990s and killed more than 100 people. Risky behaviour, such as intravenous drug use, is bringing new viruses, such as Hepatitis C, into wider circulation. Organ transplants provide new routes and victims. Easy air travel and efficient shipping mean the ancient routes of trade and travel can now spread disease farther and faster than ever before, as SARS clearly shows. As Dr Heymann points out, infectious diseases have a way of finding the weak points in human behaviour, whether it be unsafe sex (AIDS) or poor hospital hygiene (Ebola), and then moving in for the kill.

Humanity at least has science on its side. Thanks to modern molecular biology, researchers have unprecedented understanding of microbial life. But translating this into new drugs, vaccines and tests is far from easy, for commercial as much as scientific reasons.

Pharmaceutical firms are wary of devoting money to new antibiotics whose sales can be sharply limited by the development of resistance in the target microbes. There is more corporate enthusiasm for medicines to tackle viral assailants such as HIV and hepatitis, where there are large and lucrative markets in the rich world, but relatively little interest in tackling less prominent infectious agents which hit the developing world hardest.

That said, there are encouraging signs in the battle against the bug. New scientific tools, such as the growing array of microbial genomes, should boost development of anti-infective products. A range of public-private partnerships—between biotechnology firms, philanthropic bodies and governments—will breathe new life into the development of vaccines, diagnostics and drugs to combat infectious diseases in poor countries. New methods of disease surveillance, including the internet, which proved so effective in monitoring the spread of SARS, will help track infections. And new global rules on reporting disease outbreaks should help to contain their spread, if countries comply.

Complacency, however, is no longer an option. After all, bacteria first appeared on earth more than 3 billion years ago, whereas modern man is just over 100,000 years old. In evolutionary terms, microbes are to the manor born; mankind, by comparison, is merely parvenu. □

Battle of the bugs
Major outbreaks of infectious diseases over the past ten years

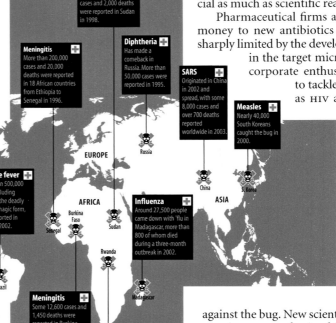

Relapsing fever
More than 400,000 cases and 2,000 deaths were reported in Sudan in 1998.

Meningitis
More than 200,000 cases and 20,000 deaths were reported in 18 African countries from Ethiopia to Senegal in 1996.

Diphtheria
Has made a comeback in Russia. More than 50,000 cases were reported in 1995.

SARS
Originated in China in 2002 and spread, with some 8,000 cases and over 700 deaths reported worldwide in 2003.

Measles
Nearly 40,000 South Koreans caught the bug in 2000.

West Nile virus
Came to America in 2002, where 4,200 cases were reported that year, nearly 300 of them fatal.

Dengue fever
More than 500,000 cases, including 2,000 of the deadly haemorrhagic form, were reported in Brazil in 2002.

Influenza
Around 27,500 people came down with 'flu in Madagascar, more than 800 of whom died during a three-month outbreak in 2002.

Meningitis
Some 12,600 cases and 1,450 deaths were reported in Burkina Faso in 2002.

Cholera
Some 23,800 Rwandans died in a single month in 1994.

EUROPE

AFRICA

ASIA

AMERICAS

US

Burkina Faso

Senegal

Sudan

Rwanda

Brazil

Russia

China

S. Korea

Madagascar

Source: World Health Organisation

Shereen El Feki: health-care correspondent, *The Economist*